Praise for Dr. Sells' *Parenting Your*

"For all parents who want good, immediately applicable ideas that are effective with acting-out teenagers, this is the book for you!"
—John Gray, Ph.D., author of *Men Are from Mars, Women Are from Venus* and *Children Are from Heaven*

"A brave, right-on, to-the-point, extremely helpful, invaluable book for teaching parents where they've lost it, where their kids have lost it, and how they can all get it back together."
—Dr. Laura Schlessinger

"An excellent combination of research and practice—with a difficult population! Good practical ideas that help parents answer hard questions."
—Thomas W. Phelan, Ph.D., author of *1-2-3 Magic* and *Surviving Your Adolescents*

"Parents of problematic teens will find *Parenting Your Out-of-Control Teenager* to be an easy-to-read book filled with practical solutions for difficult problems."
—Rex Forehand, Ph.D., author of *Parenting the Strong-Willed Child*

"A standout among the multitude of parenting books. Dr. Sells has a rare combination of practical experience coupled with an academician's need for researched and effective answers for responding to very difficult teens. For all those parents who want good, immediately applicable ideas that are effective with a severely acting-out adolescent, I can say, without reservations, this is the book for you!"
—Foster W. Cline, M.D., author of *Parenting with Love and Logic*

"Sells' approach is all 'how-to': he provides seven basic steps, backed up with lists of strategies in the 'What do I do if . . .' mode. These steps will empower parents to regain authority, bring families out of deep trouble, and begin to restore the love parents and teens once held for each other."
—*Library Journal*

"I found Scott Sells' new book to be amazingly helpful. He really does go to exactly those most difficult places where teenagers step over the line, and where there seem to be few effective answers. Dr. Sells gives answers for real parents and real teenagers."
—Anthony E. Wolf, Ph.D., author of *Get Out of My Life, but First Could You Drive Me and Cheryl to the Mall?*

Also by
Scott P. Sells, Ph.D.

Treating the Tough Adolescent:
A Family-Based, Step-by-Step Guide

Parenting Your Out-of-Control Teenager

7 Steps
to Reestablish Authority and Reclaim Love

Scott P. Sells, Ph.D.

 St. Martin's Griffin ✺ New York

*To the parents of tough teenagers,
your love and refusal to give up
is the reason this book was written.*

*And to God, who worked through me
to write the words in this book
and help ease the suffering
of our parents and teens*

PARENTING YOUR OUT-OF-CONTROL TEENAGER: 7 STEPS TO REESTABLISH AUTHORITY AND RECLAIM LOVE. Copyright © 2001 by Scott P. Sells, Ph.D. All rights reserved. Printed in the United States of America. No part of this book may be used or reproduced in any manner whatsoever without written permission except in the case of brief quotations embodied in critical articles or reviews. For information, address St. Martin's Press, 175 Fifth Avenue, New York, N.Y. 10010.

www.stmartins.com

Library of Congress Cataloging-in-Publication Data

Sells, Scott P.
    Parenting your out-of-control teenager : 7 steps to reestablish authority and reclaim love / Scott P. Sells, Ph.D.
        p. cm.
    ISBN 0-312-26629-4 (hc)
    ISBN 0-312-30301-7 (pbk)
    1. Parent and teenager. 2. Interpersonal conflict. 3. Adolescent psychology. I. Title
HQ99.15 .S45 2001
649'.125—dc21   2001041963

10   9   8   7   6   5   4   3   2

Contents

CONTENTS vii

Acknowledgments

I wish to thank the many people who supported me throughout the three years it took to write this book. Special thanks go out to my editor, Hope Dellon, her assistant Tanya Laplante, and my agent, Brian DeFiore. Hope and Brian, you believed in me when others did not. Your passion for this project and its importance to parents inspired me. Thank you all from the bottom of my heart.

Special thanks to my family and friends. Mom, you have stuck by me through thick and thin. You even gave up your retirement to work for me because you believed in what I am doing. Mom, you will never know how much that meant to me. Thank you. Dad, the values you instilled taught me never to give up. You are the best dad ever. Thanks to my sister Nancy, my brother-in-law Chris, and their three children for all their support. To my grandmother, Mary, and my grandfather, Treb, who taught me compassion and to believe in myself. To Stacey, your courage and friendship helped me become a better man. Thank you.

To the Rough River Gang (Tom Smith, John Walker, Mark Parrish, Tom Robbins, and John Robbins). Once a year we meet at a remote cabin in Rough River, Kentucky, to rejuvenate one another and find better ways to help difficult teens and their families. Your guidance and unselfish support was incredible. Thank you so much. To Dr. Neil Schiff and Jay Haley, without your support and knowledge this book would not have been possible. To Sally, who refused to give up on me and whose friendship I will always treasure. To Jane, thank you for your caring and most of all your unconditional friendship.

I am grateful to the social work faculty at Savannah State University, my director, Dr. Beverly Watkins, president Dr. Carlton Brown, and vice president Dr. Joseph Silver. All of you gave me the encouragement and support I needed to finish this project. I also wish to thank my editorial board (Patricia Bischoff, Shelia Affonso, Robert and Barbara Raju, Laverne Ricks-Brown, Ann Stout, Lorraine Farrall, Janet Tomasscheski, and Steve and Sonja Shrewsbury), who edited each chapter and provided suggestions. Because of your expertise, this book is much improved.

Finally, I wish to thank Ms. Yolanda Negron, who taught me that the name of our poor and emotionally hurt children is "Today." Today they need our help and prayers and Today they need food, clothing, shelter, and unconditional love. Thank you to all of Today's children and families who touched my life over the years and whose stories, trials, and courage are contained within these pages. I wrote this book for you through God's help.

DO YOU KNOW THIS TEENAGER?

Michael is not your typical teenager. As early as age four, there were signs of troubled waters ahead. Michael's parents, Jim and Sharon, had to threaten or plead to get Michael to do anything. He had a difficult time getting along with other children; he refused to share toys and had temper tantrums at the drop of a hat. Time-out was a joke, and bedtime was an ordeal.

By ages six and seven, things got so bad that Jim and Sharon took Michael to their pediatrician. The pediatrician suggested that Jim and Sharon spend more quality time with Michael and let him negotiate all rules and punishments. Michael would then feel heard and start obeying.

Since their pediatrician was a highly regarded "expert," Jim and Sharon thought their problems were solved. Michael, however, did not get better. The pediatrician's advice only seemed to make matters worse. The more Jim and Sharon tried to negotiate the rules, the more skillful Michael became at manipulation.

By the ages of eight and nine, Michael was drunk with power. His problems controlled the mood of everyone in the household. A stubborn refusal or an angry outburst could instantly change the way everyone felt.

1

Jim and Sharon began to argue over "the right way" to discipline. It was as if they had two different parenting philosophies. Jim thought Michael needed more structure and firmer limits, while Sharon thought they needed to follow the pediatrician's advice.

When Michael was ten and eleven, Jim and Sharon began to get calls that he was failing and ditching school. Every time they confronted Michael directly, he lied. He began to skip school regularly. The teachers declared him "a handful in the classroom" and sent him to the principal's office at least three times a week.

By the time he was thirteen and puberty kicked in, Michael started spending more and more time with his friends. These friends, who seemed to feed off each other's bad behavior, became like his "second family," one he greatly preferred to his own family.

On the advice of a friend, Jim and Sharon took Michael to another expert, a mental health counselor. The counselor diagnosed Michael as having a conduct disorder with attention deficit disorder (ADHD) features. She recommended a ninety-day wilderness boot camp and medication. Convinced that Michael had a chemical imbalance in the brain, Jim and Sharon believed they could do nothing personally to stop Michael's problems. They were so persuaded that outside experts were their son's only chance that they used their life savings to send Michael to a boot camp.

At first, there were positive changes, signs of hope. Michael was softer and actually told Jim and Sharon that he loved them. It looked as if turning Michael over to the experts was a stroke of genius.

Unfortunately, these changes were short-lived. When Michael returned home, there was a short honeymoon period of calm. But after only three weeks, the same old behaviors started to recur. Jim and Sharon did not understand the key principle that it was the outside "experts" who had caused the change in Michael, *not* them. Michael had no more respect for his parents when he came home than he did when he left. Jim and Sharon were still using the same old parenting styles, and Michael was still getting away with the same old tricks. Four crucial things happened in Michael's family:

1. Traditional punishments failed.

Traditional punishments had little or no effect on Michael. If his parents tried to ground Michael, he would simply laugh and walk out the door. Whereas before he might throw a temper tantrum, now Michael would ditch school or threaten to punch a hole in the wall. These acts of "teen terrorism" made Jim and Sharon scared and they backed down. This only gave Michael more power.

2. Nurturance turned to bitterness.

Over time, all the softness between Michael and his parents had disappeared from the relationship. While Jim and Sharon still loved their son, they no longer liked him. When he was a baby, Jim and Sharon spent 90 percent of their time with Michael giving him hugs and loving attention. As Michael grew older and more rebellious, however, the percentage of soft communication decreased dramatically. Now, 90 to 98 percent of the time was devoted to telling Michael what he did wrong and getting into bitter arguments. There was no time left over for special outings, hugs, or affectionate interactions. This lack of softness made matters worse, forcing Michael to seek nurturance elsewhere. This often came in the form of friends with corrupt values and morals. This in turn made Michael even more out of control.

3. Button-Pushing

Michael was extremely skillful at the art of pushing his parents' buttons. Buttons are words or actions ("I hate you"; "You never let me do anything"; a whiny voice; a disgusted look) that Michael would intentionally use to make his parents angry or frustrated. To Michael, arguments became a game. The object of the game was to win by controlling the opponent's mood in any argument through button pushing. The longer Michael could make his parents argue and explain themselves, the quicker their chronological age dropped. Soon his parents acted the same age as Michael.

4. Every "expert" had a different answer.
Every expert had a different opinion or philosophy on how to stop Michael's problems. One expert said to take a hands-off approach, while another said to get tougher and send him to a wilderness camp. Jim and Sharon also read dozens of parenting books, but none of them had concrete answers for extreme behaviors that went beyond normal teenage problems. As a result, the parents were confused. They no longer trusted their instincts. At this point, they did not need "therapy"; they needed concrete steps and answers.

If your teen's story has similarities to Michael's, you are not alone. According to the U.S. Census Bureau, an estimated 11 million households contain teenagers who have exhibited serious problem behaviors such as violence at home or school, threats of suicide, chronic running away, truancy, teen pregnancy, and alcohol or drug abuse.

Is Your Teen Out of Control?

This book is written for every parent, teacher, or counselor who knows a teenager like Michael who goes beyond normal everyday problems and enters into an "extreme," or out-of-control, state. Your teenager is out of control if he or she is between the ages of twelve and eighteen and has exhibited at least one of the following behaviors in the last six months and three or more in the last twelve months:

☐ Persistent and serious lying	☐ Ditching school repeatedly
☐ Physical cruelty to people or animals	☐ Stealing
☐ Running away repeatedly	☐ Bullying or threatening others
☐ Destruction of property	☐ Setting fires
☐ Threats of suicide	☐ Defying adult requests/rules
☐ Using or possessing weapons	☐ Sexual misconduct like rape

Other characteristics commonly found in out-of-control teenagers include

- Blaming others for their mistakes and refusing to take responsibility for any wrongdoing.

- Quickly losing their tempers and acting impulsively.

- Poor academic grades and problems in the classroom on a consistent basis.

- Alcohol or drug abuse that goes beyond simple experimentation and other illegal activities, such as joyriding, damaging property, or shoplifting.

- Difficulty maintaining a job and getting along with coworkers.

- Projecting an image of "toughness" when deep down they feel insecure.

- A high risk of developing what is called an antisocial personality disorder as they move into adulthood at the age of eighteen. This means that the teenagers will show little remorse or guilt for causing pain or harm to others. They become cold, unfeeling, and have difficulty maintaining any long-term relationships.

Within the mental health system, these teenagers are often given the diagnosis of *conduct disorder* or *oppositional defiant disorder,* according to the fourth edition of the *Diagnostic and Statistical Manual of Mental Disorders* (Washington, D.C.: American Psychiatric Association, 1994). I will purposely avoid using these labels throughout the book. These labels imply that your out-of-control teen is mentally ill and therefore not responsible for his or her misbehavior. For example, Marcus, age sixteen, used to tell me, "My shrink said that I have this disease called 'conduct disorder' and I need pills to calm down. So everyone needs to get off my back. I have a disease and can't help it when I get mad or run away."

There may be times when it is appropriate to label your teen and some teens may experience a true mental illness like schizophrenia.

Labeling is also necessary for insurance coverage and to receive special education services in schools. However, throughout the book, I will demonstrate how labeling can have a negative effect on your ability to parent and hold your teen accountable for their misbehaviors.

My Teenager Has *Some* of These Problems— Am I Overreacting?

It is normal for all children and teenagers to experience some of the behavior problems just listed. For example, many five- and six-year-old children are disrespectful or disobedient to some degree, and almost all teenagers commit at least one delinquent act like drinking or ditching school. But these problems tend to be relatively minor or isolated incidents. Teenage problems go from normal to out of control when these same behaviors are *persistent* and *repetitive* over a period of six months or more.

Why Was This Book Written?

This book was written because current parenting books and counseling programs do not offer enough specific and practical advice regarding the teenager who is not merely rebellious but out of control. Their principles and strategies fail to show you how to stop really serious behavior problems on a long-term basis.

The result is a defeated parent and a teenager who grows even more powerful with the realization that he or she defeated not only you but also the so-called expert professional. Mike, the parent of fifteen-year-old Jason, put it this way: "Yesterday, out of desperation, I went to the store to find a book on difficult teens. This book told me that I did not have the right to control my son and to use 'I' messages to promote better communication. I didn't understand what they were saying or agree with it, but the guy had a Ph.D., so I thought he must know his stuff. The next day I asked Jason to clean his room and he told me to 'f**k off.' I then tried to use this 'I' message stuff by saying 'I am angry when you talk to me this way.' Jason then laughed in my face and said, '*I* think you are full of s**t.' I said to myself, 'So much for the expert advice. Jason got the best of me, and I just wasted a good fifteen bucks.'"

If you are reading this book, chances are that you have had experiences like Mike's with other books. More than a few of you have paid thousands of dollars to hospital-based programs or counseling, only to find that the behavior changes didn't last.

You may also have gone to parenting seminars or been told by professionals that your teen will "grow out of it" or that you should give him or her "the freedom to fail." Some professionals regularly label teenagers as mentally ill and in need of heavy medication. With all this conflicting advice, it is no wonder that you stop listening to your own instincts and question your skill and self-worth as parents.

How Is This Book Unique?

The strategies in this book did not emerge from the comfort of my office, based on what I thought would work. Instead, they came directly from the *real* experts, parents just like you with teenagers who are out of control, who told me their stories and tested the solutions I had to offer.

I worked with parents in three ways to gather information and fine-tune the strategies that could help overcome their teens' problems. First, I conducted an intensive four-year research study with eighty-two out-of-control teenagers and their families. This study resulted in the creation of a step-by-step treatment model to help counselors, teachers, police, and probation officers treat these teenagers and led to the writing of my professional book, entitled *Treating the Tough Adolescent: A Family-Based, Step-by-Step Guide* (New York: Guilford Press, 1998).

Second, I conducted face-to-face interviews with you, the parents of out-of-control teenagers. Before sitting down to write this book, I spent three years traveling the country doing workshops and seeking out your expertise. When I asked you to tell me what you needed to regain control of your household and stop your teen from further destruction, here is what you said:

- **We Are Not Bad Parents.** Many of the books we read and the counselors we talk to do not come right out and say it, but you can tell that they judge us and blame us for our kid's problems. These people do not walk in our shoes. Show us that you're there to help rather than to judge us and look down on us.

- **We Are Tired and Burnt Out.** Please give us good reasons as to why we should take charge when our teenagers do not seem to care if we live or die. How do we get motivated, and what is in it for us? Other parenting books tell us either to back off or get more involved. Which point of view is the right one, and why should we keep trying?

- **Get to the Point.** Give us a clear and concrete step-by-step road map for each problem we might encounter, using language that makes sense to us. Forget the psychobabble. We are tired of watered-down concepts that do not give us the specifics of when and how to use specific steps and strategies.

- **Tell Us What to Do When Plan A Fails.** If your first suggestion fails, we need a backup Plan B and sometimes a Plan C and even a Plan D. Other books and counselors never tell us what to do if Plan A fails.

- **Buttons, Buttons, Buttons.** Our teenager always seems to know how to push our "hot" buttons (swearing, vicious looks, guilt trips, etc.) and make us so mad that he (or she) wins the argument. Our rules and punishments seem to go nowhere. How do we avoid getting our buttons pushed and losing our cool?

- **The Big Guns.** Please give us a menu of consequences that truly work to stop our teenager's big guns of running away, ditching school, threats or acts of violence, extreme disrespect, alcohol and drug use, teen pregnancy, and threats of suicide. These big guns get us so scared or frustrated that it is easier just to give up or back down. Give us something that works quickly to stop these big guns. We are in too much pain to wait much longer.

■ **Show Us How to Balance "Tough Love" with Softness.** We have all heard about "tough love" and the use of boot camps to regain control, but how do we restore lost softness and nurturance with our child? "I often feel that although I love my teen, I no longer like him. How do I start liking my son or daughter again?" Provide us with the concrete steps necessary to achieve the right balance.

■ **I Am a Single Parent or Stepparent.** The strategies we read about seem to work only if you have two parents in the house or families without a stepparent. We either have to work all day and have to do all the discipline ourselves, or our teenagers hate us simply because we are the stepparent. We need strategies that are custom-fit to handle these special circumstances.

■ **What If It Doesn't Work?** After we buy and read your book, what do we do if something doesn't work exactly as you wrote? Is there a Web site we can go to for help or a way to locate other parents with the same problems for advice and moral support? If you don't have these resources, can we call you at home?

This book is designed to address each of these concerns and show you how to proceed step by step. You *can* make a difference in both your teen's life and your own. The last step will provide you with a Web site for support and a way to connect with other parents nationwide.

An Editorial Board of Parents Just Like You

Finally, I gathered an editorial board of parents with out-of-control teenagers, who agreed to review the drafts of each step and offer recommendations.

The parent review board represented a wide spectrum of family composition, income level, and race. The board was made up of two single parents, one stepparent, and two parents living in a two-parent household as well as two teen counselors. The income levels of the parents ranged from the very wealthy to the very poor.

Throughout this process, it was clear that it did not matter if you were rich or poor or black or white. Each family had an out-of-control teenager or direct experience in working with one. Each parent lacked a clear road map to stop the teenager's destructive behaviors and repair the damaged parent-teen relationship.

The editorial board's input helped make the principles of this book clearer and the step-by-step guidelines more concrete and more responsive to your needs. I thank them from my heart for their suggestions.

Using all of this research and resources, this book will show you, the parent, how to be your own expert—how to reestablish authority and reclaim love with your out-of-control teenager. The many real-life examples in this book may make you laugh or even cry. These stories are primarily from my personal experiences or those of my colleagues. All names have been changed. These stories will guide you and help you see that you are not alone.

Step 1

UNDERSTANDING WHY YOUR TEEN IS OUT OF CONTROL

Parents ask me all the time: "Why does my teenager act this way?" It's an important question: Like an auto mechanic who needs to first figure out why your car makes those funny noises, you also need to first understand why your teenager misbehaves before you can solve the problem.

The confusing part is that there are so many experts with so many different theories. You have probably already read other parenting books and tried the suggestions of other experts; they may have sounded good at the time but haven't helped in the long run. You may be so burnt out that you are asking yourself, "Why should I believe that Dr. Sells's book will be any more useful than all those other 'experts'?" Good question.

Please read my top seven reasons for why your teen misbehaves, and then ask yourself one question: Do these reasons make sense and speak to my heart? If they do, please keep reading and try my suggestions. If not, I hope you will read on anyway with an open mind and consult other parenting books as well. If what you are doing right now is not working, what do you have to lose by trying something different?

TOP 7 REASONS FOR TEEN MISBEHAVIOR

Reason #1: Unclear Rules

One of the biggest reasons your teen may be out of control is that you don't have a clear, written contract with him or her. Your rules and consequences are verbal, open to interpretation, or made up as you go along. For example, you may declare a rule of "no disrespect" but fail to specify what your teen does or says that is considered disrespectful. Your teen, who is not only literal-minded but very concrete, now has the perfect loophole and can argue, "You never said that swearing was disrespectful." (I call this "literal disease.") As Nick's story illustrates, your teen can quickly turn into a shark who smells blood in the water.

"But you never said mumbling to myself was disrespectful."

Fifteen-year-old Nick understood all too well the power of literal disease. One day Nick's mother told him that the new rule was "no disrespect." Nick liked the fact that his mom never wrote anything down on paper. Sometimes she forgot about the rule or asked: "Nick, now what did we agree to?" All of this meant one thing: so many loopholes that he could drive a Mack truck through them.

Nick's theory was put to the test the next day. Nick started to roll his eyes and talk under his breath after his mom asked him to take out the trash while he was watching TV. Here is the conversation that followed:

MOTHER: Nick, that was disrespectful. Now turn off the TV and go to your room! *(Mom identifies "rolling of the eyes" and "talking under his breath" as disrespectful behavior.)*

NICK: Mom, you never said that mumbling to myself was disrespectful. I'm not going to my room. *(Nick suddenly comes down with a case of literal disease and points out the loopholes like an expert lawyer.)*

MOTHER: *(Mom starts to get angry and lose control.)* You knew what I meant! Don't play dumb with me. Now get your butt up those stairs and into your room. *(Mom now is busy spending her valuable time and energy trying to explain and justify her actions. This could have been avoided if the rule was clearly defined ahead of time.)*

NICK: I'm not going to my room. You never told me that was being disrespectful. I'll take out the garbage but I'm going back to watch my TV show. *(Nick senses that he has his mother on the ropes. Her buttons are pushed, she is losing control of her emotions, and she is wavering in her stance.)*

MOTHER *(Exhausted and defeated):* Well, as long as you take out the garbage, I guess I will let it go this time. But from now on, if you roll your eyes or mumble under your breath, you are grounded. *(Mom just wants the argument to end. Besides, Nick is taking the garbage out.)*

NICK: Sure, Mom, whatever. . . . *(Nick has won and feels more powerful than ever. The next time he is asked to do something, he will launch into the same tirade. It worked once so it will work again. Besides, unclear rules are always optional anyway, right?)*

Step 2 will show you how to make sure your rules are crystal clear, with no loopholes.

Reason #2: Not Keeping Up with Your Teen's Thinking

Out-of-control teens can defeat you and make you back down through a special gift called *enhanced social perception.* Just like Tonya in the next example, your teen can run through as many different scenarios in their mind as necessary to find a loophole in your rule or consequence.

"I'm Two Steps Ahead"

When fifteen-year-old Tonya received her punishment of "no phone use" for swearing at her mom, she went to her room to find a loophole. After diagramming out several different plans on a sheet of paper, she finally decided on the best one. Tonya told her friends that she would call them at 1:00 A.M. when everyone in the house would be sleeping. She instructed her friends on how to use a pillow to muffle the sound when the phone rang. Her plan worked beautifully. Tonya had no reason to stop swearing. Thinking two steps ahead of her mom, Tonya had found a loophole in the no-phone-use consequence.

In Step 3 on troubleshooting, beginning on page 67, you will find an expanded discussion on this topic. You will learn to create a backup plan for every what-if situation you may encounter with your teenager. For example, "What will you do if you sell your teen's CD collection at a pawn shop as a punishment and your son countermoves by trying to sell your stuff?" If you don't ask and answer such questions ahead of time, your teen will be more than happy to do this job for you later.

Reason #3: Button-Pushing

Another major factor in teen misbehavior is "button-pushing." If your teen doesn't want to do something you ask, he or she often will start pushing your "hot buttons" to make you angry or frustrated. For some of you, these hot buttons are swearing or rolling the eyes. For others, it is statements like "I hate you," "You're not my real father," or "I don't have to listen to you." Your teenager has an uncanny ability to know exactly what your buttons are and how to push them.

Teens know that if they succeed in pushing your buttons, your judgment will be clouded. And there is a better than average chance that you will back down or fail to follow through on a consistent basis. This is often why your consequences don't work. The consequence itself isn't the problem: It's the way you're unable to deliver that consequence calmly and firmly because your teen pushes your buttons, or you push your teen's buttons through lectures, criticisms, or attacks on his or her character.

| **"I was suddenly no older than my son."**

At the beginning of the argument, I was forty-five years old, but after only five minutes of constant bickering, I felt that I was thirty years old. As we continued to argue, my age continued to drop. Before long, I felt like I was suddenly my son's age [sixteen years old] and that we were two kids in the sandbox scrapping for power and control.

—A frustrated parent

When you are the same age as your teen in button-pushing years, it is difficult to play the role of parent. No matter how good your consequences look on paper, you won't be able to enforce them successfully. Step 4 on Button Pushing, beginning on page 85, will detail exactly how button-pushing works with you and your teen—and what to do about it.

Reprinted with special permission of King Feature Syndicate.

Reason #4: Teenager Drunk with Power

When your teenager is able to control the mood of your household and your life through extreme behavior, he or she takes on the power of an adult without being developmentally ready. At ages twelve through eighteen, your teen's time and energy should go toward being a kid, going to school, playing sports, dating, getting a job, and preparing to leave home. Instead, your out-of-control teen uses that same energy to figure out how to stay in control of your household and get one over on you or other adults.

The real tragedy in all this is that these kids don't have a childhood. What's ironic is that part of each teenager does not want all this power. Subconsciously, every teen wants structure and discipline.

The danger is that a teen who stays drunk with power for too long gets addicted to the feelings. Such teens can't rationally see how much better their lives would be if they were no longer in charge. This is why your lectures and negotiations don't work. Sometimes you have to take the power away forcibly before your teen can recognize that life can be happier without it. Your child will test you every step of the way: You will have passed the test when your teen stops having behavior problems for longer periods of time and looks more at peace.

© Lynn Johnston Productions, Inc./Dist. by United Feature Syndicate, Inc.

In Step 5, Stopping Your Teenager's Seven Aces, beginning on page 115, you will be given a menu of nontraditional and creative consequences to stop a teen who is drunk with power. These consequences should be attempted only after you have laid down a solid foundation for success through Steps 1 to 4.

Reason #5: The Pleasure Principle

Why do so many of us eat junk food, smoke, or never exercise, even though we know that doing so may eventually lead to obesity, lung cancer, or a heart attack? Because of what's called the "pleasure principle," living for the moment or for what gives us immediate gratification rather than thinking about our future.

This is the same way your out-of-control teenager thinks nearly all of the time. He or she cannot see past tomorrow, let alone next week. Advances in technology often make the problem even worse. Today's teens have instant everything—instant food, instant messages, instant calls on their cell phones. Remember when we actually had to get up out of our chairs to change the television channel or wait for the mail? All of these small things exercised our "patience muscles." Many teens have come to expect instant gratification.

This is why guilt trips, logical reasoning, and traditional punishments often fail. Your punishments or lectures are not strong enough to compete with the immediate pleasures that come with bad behavior. For example, the pleasure of staying out all night outweighs the punishment of a grounding they may receive the next day. The pleasure of smoking pot outweighs the lecture that you will give them if caught. In Step 2, Writing an Ironclad Contract, beginning on page 29, you will be given the top ten consequences you need to conquer the pleasure principle.

"I Do What I Want When I Want"

Fifteen-year-old Darren skipped school more days than he attended. His father constantly lectured him about how he was throwing his life away and would end up flipping burgers at McDonald's for the rest of his life. These lectures went in one ear and out the other. Darren could care less about his future. He lived for the moment.

When Darren's father tried to ground him for ditching school, the boy simply walked out of the house. When his father took the phone away, Darren would borrow a friend's cell phone or leave the house without permission to use a pay phone. When Darren's father asked him why he was doing these things, Darren said: "I may die tomorrow, right? Why should I go to school? I get to see my friends and do what I want when I want. I don't want to wait a whole weekend to get off grounding or wait until school is over to see my friends. Who cares what happens next week? I'll deal with that when it happens."

Reason #6: Peer Power

Today's peer groups have a tremendous hold on your teen's heart, mind, and soul. If it is a positive peer group with good morals and values, your teen can thrive. But if the group has poor values and exhibits negative behavior, your teen is likely to get more and more out of control.

Developmentally, the teen years are difficult for almost everyone. When teens' hormones kick in around the ages of eleven to thirteen, they get caught between childhood and adulthood. Part of your teen wants to be a child and find safety in your arms, while the other part wants to explore and experiment with being grown-up and having adult freedoms. This can be a very confusing and lonely time—a time that brings about an increased sensitivity to being accepted. Naturally, teens turn to their friends—those who look, think, and act the way they do—rather than to their parents for acceptance.

This acceptance may come at a high price, however. To avoid getting "kicked out of the club," everyone must follow the club's rules, both spoken and unspoken. These rules might include shoplifting, piercing body parts, drinking, doing drugs, or dressing "goth"; often teens follow such rules rather than risk rejection. In Step 6, How to Mobilize Outside Helpers, beginning on page 252, you will be shown how to recruit your teen's friends to help your teen or stop them if they continue to be a destructive influence. In Step 7, Reclaiming Love, beginning on page 285, you will understand the direct connection between the softness between you and your teen and the amount of influence peers have on their heart.

"But He Tells Me That He Loves Me"

Sixteen-year-old Alana did not get along with her parents. There was little, if any, warmth and nurturance. Alana met a twenty-one-year-old guy named Randy who gave her something her parents hadn't given her for a long time—hugs. He also listened to her and took her out. After about two weeks, Alana thought she was in love. Randy was so important to her that Alana managed to overlook it when he became possessive and made her give up all her friends. She even made excuses for Randy when he started pulling her hair and punching her in the stomach if he had a tough day at work. It was OK, she told herself: "Randy still tells me that he loves me."

These excuses continued until Alana got pregnant. Randy abandoned her, and Alana's parents forced her to move out of the house. Alana is now with another guy just like Randy, and it's all too easy to imagine the kind of life her child will have.

Reason #7: Misuse of Outside Forces

The misuse of outside forces is a final reason for your teen's misbehavior. In today's world, more and more of us are handing over our teenagers to outsiders like counselors, psychiatrists, hospitals, boot camps, or medication to "fix" them. What may initially look like the answer, however, can quickly become a double-edged sword. Even though your teen may change miraculously in a boot camp, detention center, group home, or counselor's office, often the same problems start up again soon after he or she returns home, comes off probation, or stops seeing the counselor. The reason is simple. Outside experts did all the work to turn your teen around, not you. Therefore, as Patricia's story illustrates, there is no reason for the teen to respect or obey you back home.

"The Honeymoon Is Over"

Fourteen-year-old Patricia ran away all the time. Her mother was unable to stop her. Out of desperation, Patricia's mother sent her to a six-month residential program. After the first few days, Patricia was calling and begging to come home. The mother held firm and did not remove her.

When Patricia finally returned home after six months, her mother could not believe the positive changes. Patricia did not run away, she did not swear, and she was a pleasure to be around. The honeymoon didn't last, however. After a couple of months, Patricia was once again running away and swearing up a storm.

The mother immediately started to threaten another residential stay. She felt helpless to stop her daughter all by herself. Patricia laughed in her face. She knew that her mom had no more insurance money left. When asked why she did so well in the residential program and not at home, Patricia had this to say: *"My mom just doesn't get it. At residential, I couldn't pull the same crap. If staff said no they meant it. When my mom says no, she doesn't mean it. She is so afraid that I will run away that she always backs down. When I got back, she was as wimpy as ever. Nothing had changed. I had her wrapped around my little finger. I started doing whatever I wanted again."*

In Step 6, How to Mobilize Outside Helpers, beginning on page 252, you will find seven key strategies to help recruit friends, neighbors, and even ministers to back you up and help you regain control of your household. Remember that there is strength in numbers. It is very difficult to change an out-of-control teenager all by yourself. It takes a village.

A Road Map of Defeat and a New Highway to Success

The road map that follows will show you how the seven reasons for extreme teen misbehavior merge to create a teenager who's out of control—and how to turn your teen around. If you find you've gone down the wrong path in the past, please don't waste time blaming yourself or analyzing how you got lost. You can't change the past, but you can use this map as a personal compass to point you and your teen in a more positive direction.

Defining Your Teen's Problem

As the map illustrates, your teen's misbehavior can be either solved or exacerbated by the way *you* define the problem. On one hand, you may see the cause as a chemical imbalance, a mental illness, or the "fact" that your child is frail and incapable. If this is your

A Road Map of Your Teen's Misbehavior
and the Path to Success

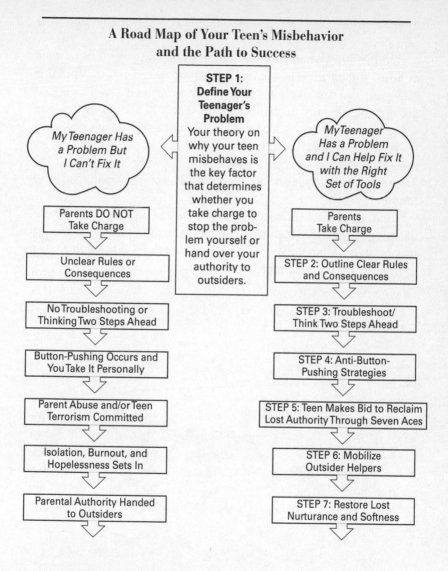

theory, you are likely to seek out outside experts like hospitals, medication, or boot camps to fix the problem. After all, you reason, a chemical imbalance or a mental illness needs an expert's intervention.

There's no need for you to take charge and personally stop your teen's misbehavior.

On the other hand, your theory might be that your teen is stuck in a rut, stubborn, or in need of more parental structure. With this mind-set, you are likely to believe that your teen should be held accountable for any misbehavior and that you should be the one doing the accounting. A teen who is stuck in a rut doesn't necessarily need an outside specialist; if a specialist *is* needed, his or her role changes from someone who does all the work to fix your kid to someone who provides backup so that you can personally stop the problem.

Finding the cause of your teen's problem can be compared to looking at a glass of water as either half empty or half full. Both viewpoints may have merit, but the way Rodney's parents defined his problem led to two entirely different approaches to solve his problem.

The Glass Is Half Empty

Rodney's father viewed Rodney's temper tantrums as being caused by a chemical imbalance in his brain (although there was no medical evidence to support this idea). As a result, he did not hold Rodney responsible for beating up his younger brother or throwing his food against the wall. Instead of punishing Rodney, the father said, "It's OK, son. Just let your anger out. We all know that you are doing the best you can."

Without any accountability, Rodney only got angrier and more violent as he grew older, bigger, and stronger. Unknowingly, the father had hurt, rather than helped, Rodney by defining his problem as a chemical imbalance. Because his father communicated that he was not responsible for his angry outbursts, there was no reason for Rodney to change. He always had a "Get Out of Jail Free" card.

The Glass Is Half Full

Rodney's mother disagreed completely with her husband. She saw Rodney's temper tantrums as a clear sign that he was spoiled and manipulative. Whenever Rodney became angry, everyone in the house got scared and backed down. If Rodney had chores to do and threw a temper tantrum, he did not have to do them. If Rodney threw his plate against the wall because he did not like the food, he got pizza for dinner. Rodney's mother begged her husband to see the problem from her eyes—a spoiled teen who needed limits and had to be held accountable.

The father would not hear of it. Instead the family consulted an outside expert who tried to solve Rodney's problems with one medication after another. Nothing worked.

One day the father woke up to find a small note from his wife on the bathroom mirror. It read, "I can't take it anymore. I'm leaving you and taking Rodney with me. Maybe now he and I will have a fighting chance."

These differences in opinion are far too common in households today. As in Rodney's case, how you define your teen's problem will bring you to a different fork in the road. Based on your theory, you will either (a) choose to take charge of fixing your teen's problem by going directly to Step 2 and establishing clear rules and consequences; or (b) choose not to take charge.

There is a third road that you can choose, though it isn't marked on the map. It is the "Fake It Till You Make It" Road. This is an ideal road to take if you are unsure about what to do or have a spouse or significant other who is firmly entrenched in the belief that "My teen has a problem, but I can't personally do anything to fix it." I will talk about this option a bit later on.

The Left Fork in the Road: "I Will Not Take Charge"

If you or another caregiver, such as a grandparent, aunt, or foster parent, refuse to take charge, one or more of these five things will happen:

1. Your teenager will be glad to take charge and may hold your entire household hostage with out-of-control behavior.
2. You will formally or informally transfer your parental authority to outside forces like hospitals, group homes, or boot camps and rely on whatever they decide.
3. You will quarrel with your significant other, spouse, or ex-spouse over the "best way" to parent your teen, thus ensuring that no one takes charge or presents a united front.
4. The button-pushing and constant conflict will drain all of the nurturance and softness from your relationship with your teen.
5. Your teen's second family of peers will take over the job of raising your teen with their own morals and values.

When these things occur, you will go down a path that will begin with unclear rules and consequences and end with your teen getting worse or pulling out of it as he or she moves into adulthood.

Parents have told me that it's helpful to use my Road Map to show them the future. Part of the problem has always been the unknown—waiting for the other shoe to drop and not knowing what your teen will do next. Here is also what's in store for you if you continue down the left fork in the road.

- *You Won't Set Up Clear Rules and Consequences.*
  As mentioned earlier, your teen has a case of "literal disease." Therefore, if you do not take charge and list both rules and consequences in the form of a written, ironclad contract, you will constantly have to explain and justify your rules. Your teen will find the loopholes and defeat you.

- *You Won't Troubleshoot, or Think Two Steps Ahead of Your Teen.*
  Unclear rules and consequences then will lead to your inability to think two steps ahead of your teen and troubleshoot all the things that could go wrong ahead of time. Your teenager will always be one step ahead of you.

- *Your Teen Will Push Your Buttons, and You Will Take It Personally.*
  Unclear rules and a lack of troubleshooting provides fertile ground for button-pushing. You are already thrown off balance when you don't have an ironclad contract to guide you through rough waters. Teens know this and will go in for the kill by using buttons like swearing or talking under their breath to make you mad. They know that if they control your mood and direction of the argument, they will win.

- *You Will Become a Victim of Parent Abuse or Teen Terrorism.*
  Parent abuse, or teen terrorism, is a teen's skillful ability to use one of seven aces—running away, disrespect, ditching school, teen pregnancy, threats or acts of violence, threats of suicide, alcohol or drug abuse—to intimidate you into backing down and handing over your authority. We will talk about how this works in

Step 5. Without a clear contract, anti-button-pushing strategies, and creative consequences in place, your teen will use these "aces" to defeat you.

■ *Isolation, Burnout, and Hopelessness Will Set In.*
After several years of chronic parent abuse, burnout and hopelessness begin to set in. It will seem as if the problem is only getting worse as your teen gets older. You will begin to feel isolated as you sense that friends do not want to hear about it any more. You may become a virtual prisoner in your own home, afraid to leave for fear of what your teen may do. Deep resentment and bitterness will then build toward your teen.

■ *You Hand Over Your Authority to Outsiders to "Fix" Your Teenager.*
The hopelessness and isolation may lead you to blame yourself. You may come to believe that your teen will only be helped by an outside counselor, removal from the home, or placement in a group home. You become hopeful, relieved, and excited when you find a counselor or a temporary placement outside the home. For the first time in a long while, there is often peace and quiet. Then, after a short honeymoon period, your teen begins to return to the same old behaviors and hang out with the same old friends. You become bitter toward your teen for letting you down again. You may then go back to the system again with more doctors, more medication, or more hospitals. It becomes a revolving door with your teen still ending up back at the same place as you started.

■ *Nurturance and Softness Will Get Sucked Out of the Relationship.*
By this time, you are so angry at your teen that you stop liking him or her on any level. You may feel guilty, but the years of pain and parent abuse have taken their toll. Part of you wants to open up and hug your teen, but another part is too afraid to risk more rejection. Deep down your parental instincts tell you that your teenager needs unconditional love to thrive emotionally. You also

may realize that part of the misbehavior is connected to a lack of softness. However, showing softness when you feel nothing but hurt is easier said than done. After all, you are only human.

■ *Your Teen Pulls Even Further Away from You.*
Teenagers feel your tension and bitterness. They are also hesitant to make the first move or open up. They desperately need your softness, but they either don't know that they need it or put up a front. As a result, they will seek out this softness through gangs, peers, or even drugs. Receiving acceptance and nurturance from these groups may come with the price tag of immoral or illegal acts in the forms of muggings, rape, or violence. In addition, teenagers may turn their anger inward and become depressed and isolated. If this continues, suicide attempts are often the next step.

■ *Your Teenager Will Either Get Worse or Eventually Pull Out of It.*
Your teen may continue to get worse or get better. Signs of getting worse include: (1) a lack of remorse for any hurtful acts on others; (2) blaming others for their problems; (3) persistent lying; (4) repeated acts of drunkenness or use of drugs; (5) repeated fighting; (6) repeated suspension from school; or (7) inability to hold a job. If this continues, your teen may develop, in adulthood, what is called an antisocial personality disorder and may pass these same traits along to his or her own children.

Other teens will pull out of it when they reach adulthood. Many of us were difficult teens, but we got through adolescence somehow. Something happened to us. Perhaps when we were on our own and had to pay bills and rent, we finally began to see how the real world worked and that we had to be responsible to survive.

After reading about this path, you may agree with where it is leading, but you may still be too tired or burned out to choose the other way. You may need a breather or a rest. One parent sent her son to a six-month wilderness program so that she could regroup and regain strength; it also made her teen appreciate what he had at home. If you are in similar circumstances, I ask only that you try to use the Steps in this book when you are ready.

Things may also need to get worse before you can commit to change. If this is the case, place this book in your cedar chest or in the back of your bookshelf. It may collect some dust, but the ideas can be put into practice later if you need them.

The Right Fork in the Road: "I Will Take Charge"

Once you make up your mind to take charge, proceed to Step 2 in this book on the next page to write an ironclad contract, and continue with Steps 3 through 7. While not every teen will progress in such an orderly fashion as my map indicates, your teen *will* likely improve if you follow this path.

The Third Fork in the Road: Fake It Until You Make It

If you or someone you know is firmly entrenched in the viewpoint that the teen has a problem, but you cannot personally fix it, ask yourself or that person these questions: *Is what I'm doing with my teenager currently working? Is my teenager getting better or is the teen pretty much staying the same or getting worse?*

If the present approach is not helping, then history will repeat itself. If you do more of the same, more of the same will happen. I urge you to perform an experiment to see for yourself if the right fork is the better road. Take the next three months to try each of the steps in this book. If you are not satisfied, you can always go back to the other path.

When you turn this page your journey will begin. This is the last chance you have to act as a parent to your child. They need you now more than ever. Through hard work, this road map, and the set of step-by-step tools contained in this book may change your teen's destiny.

Step 2

WRITING AN IRONCLAD CONTRACT WITH CLEAR RULES AND CONSEQUENCES

A ny good builder will tell you that your house will crumble unless it is built on a rock-solid foundation. In this case, that foundation is an ironclad, written contract with clear rules and effective consequences.

Here's why. Once again, your out-of-control teen has a case of "literal disease." If everything in the contract is not concretely spelled out and written down on paper, your teen will skillfully find a loophole and defeat you. Most parents tell me that their rules and consequences are administered verbally and with little to no preplanning. I learned my lesson the hard way with fifteen-year-old Jill.

"But You Never Said that Tardiness Was Part of the Rule"

Marcia came to my office with the complaint that her fifteen-year-old daughter, Jill, ditched school all the time. In fact, since the beginning of school two months ago, Jill had attended only fourteen days. In private, I asked Marcia if they had a rule for "ditching school" and if there were consequences for not attending. Marcia told me that it depended on which day of the week I asked. Most of the time, Marcia was so exhausted from work that she had little energy left over to argue. It was easier in the short term to just "let it go." Marcia went on to tell me that the ditching problem was only getting worse. Jill was now using her home as the designated party house during school hours. Marcia was desperate for answers.

I assured Marcia that I had the answer to her problem: a contract containing clear rules and consequences. When Jill came back into the room, Marcia told her that the new rule was no "ditching school" and the consequence was one day of grounding for each day of missed school. Jill stated that "she would try to do better."

Two days later I received a call from the family. Marcia was on one phone and Jill on the other. Marcia began by saying that "the contract was a complete and utter failure." Jill had been tardy the first day and missed the second.

Jill then started to yell over the phone about the fact that "tardiness" was not part of the contract. The girl also did not remember that "grounding" was ever part of the agreement. Jill stated, "Since it [the consequence] wasn't written down, it's my word against Mom's."

Marcia and Jill then started to get into a yelling match about who was right and who was wrong, and did not show up for the next three scheduled meetings with me.

As you'll see later on in the step, this story eventually had a happy ending, but my work with Marcia and Jill was not without its failures. In the beginning, I blamed the family for being resistant and unmotivated. I realize now that I was the one who failed. Looking back, I can see that I made the following four mistakes:

1. **I did not put the contract in writing.**

   Rock singer Richard Marx sang a 1980s hit song entitled "It Ain't Worth Nothing Until It's Signed on the Dotted Line." Without a signature, a verbal contract in the music business is worthless. It is the same in the business of parenting an out-of-control teenager. Since the rules and consequences were not written down, Jill was able to claim that tardiness and grounding were not included in the rule. Parents often come to my office and cannot quite remember what they agreed to the week before. I learned another valuable lesson. All contracts must be in writing. Otherwise, you are set up for failure.

2. **I left loopholes.**

   Jill was right: "Tardiness" was not part of the original contract. Marcia and I had both assumed that Jill understood that tardiness was part of "ditching school," and deep down, she probably did. Yet Jill was as skilled as a lawyer at finding a loophole and using it to her advantage. Jill was not mean-spirited, just crafty and more skillful than her mother and me put together. I learned a valuable lesson: It must be absolutely clear to whom the rule applies (you or your teenager), what the terms are (in this case, "no ditching" means attending of all classes without any tardiness), how it will be monitored (checking daily attendance records, calling the teacher, etc.), and when and where the consequences will be enforced ("grounding" will mean staying home on a weekend night).

3. **I neglected to troubleshoot "what-if?" details.**

   Before the rule of "no ditching" was initiated, I should have tried to troubleshoot with Marcia everything that could go wrong. For example: "What will you do if Jill claims that she is sick the next morning and cannot go to school?" "What will you do if Jill lies about attending school?" "What will you do if Jill refuses to accept the consequence of being grounded and simply walks out the door?" By not addressing these potential problems beforehand, Jill found and exploited loopholes in the contract. I learned another valuable lesson: If you do not think of what could go wrong with the contract beforehand, your teenager will be glad to do it for you.

4. **I did not recognize how the contract affects other parenting strategies.**
   Without a good contract, other strategies in this book will not work. For example, Step 4 will demonstrate how your teenager uses buttons to make you angry and win any argument. Without a well-written contract, Marcia was vulnerable to having her buttons pushed. The more loopholes Jill discovered, the angrier Marcia got. Bitter arguments and harsh words quickly followed. In this environment, it was easy for Jill to push her mom's buttons.

Why Your Current Contracts Fail

Perhaps you have already tried using contracts with your out-of-control teen, but they have failed. A better understanding of what does not work will help you to appreciate what does. While some of the pitfalls were described in Jill's case, the full list appears below.

What Happens Without an Ironclad Contract

- **"Literal disease" sets in.**
  Your out-of-control teenager is extremely literal and will continue to get into bitter arguments about the interpretation of rules or consequences. Therefore, rules and consequences must be clearly written down in contract format beforehand.

- **Rules become optional, not mandatory.**
  A mandatory rule is one that your teenager must obey. However, if the rule is not clearly stated in written and concrete terms, your teenager will think the rule is optional and refuse to obey. For example, in Jill's case, she concluded that coming home after school to serve out her punishment was optional. Jill was able to interpret the rule to suit her own wants and needs.

- **You try to enforce too many rules at one time.**
Without an ironclad contract, the risk is high that you will try to correct every negative thing that your teen does. This will lead to burnout and failure. An ironclad contract will give you the focus and energy necessary to solve one problem at a time.

- **Off-the-cuff decision making.**
Like everyone else, you have your good days and your bad ones. Without a contract, you will have a tendency to make up the rules and consequences as you go along, depending on how tired or angry you are. Seeing this inconsistency as a sign of weakness, your teen will test the limits still further and become even more uncooperative.

- **Rules are not predetermined.**
Without a written contract, rules are not predetermined ahead of time. As a result, both you and your teen become confused as to what was said and to how the rule was supposed to be enforced. This one problem can lead to most of your bitter arguments. You will find yourself getting into he said/she said arguments over what the rule was.

How to Write a Contract That Works

Now that you understand why your contracts may not have worked in the past, it is time to come up with one that does. Please follow the strategies in the order they are presented. Each one is a building block for the one that comes next.

When you follow these strategies, your teen will not know what hit them. Your teen will think that someone has messed with the wiring in your brain. I remember when Marcia, a sixteen-year-old teen, demanded furiously to see me alone in my office. There she exclaimed:

"Dr. Sells, what are you up to? I saw your book lying on my parents' night stand and I started reading the part about rules and consequences. I hate this written ironclad whatever deal. Since my parents started reading your book, I can't get away with anything! They seem to know what I am about to do before I do. Last night I got home fifteen minutes late and I tried to argue that it was only fifteen minutes. But before I could say another word, they brought out the stupid contract I signed. It said that if I was only one minute past curfew, I would lose my next weekend night. I had no more room to yell or a leg to stand on."

Please make sure that you complete Strategies #1 through #5 without your teenager present. This is because your teen will throw you off track by disagreeing with anything you suggest. Your teen has no reason to cooperate until after you have a working draft contract without loopholes. Once you have produced your first written contract, get your teens input and suggestions in Strategy #6 and include their ideas whenever possible.

Strategy #1: Tackle Only One or Two Problems at a Time

Before you write the contract, decide on the exact behaviors that you want to change. One of the biggest mistakes we make is to turn every single problem into a battleground or a win/lose situation. You may win the battle but lose the war by using up all your energy to stop the small stuff, leaving you too exhausted to tackle the more important problems.

"I Only Have One Gallon of Gas Per Day"

Lisa felt that she would lose all authority if she let her thirteen-year-old son Justin get away with anything. From the time she got up until the time she went to bed, it was a battle. Justin was disrespectful and cursed. He also refused to clean his room or go to bed on time, and left the house without permission. Lisa tried to stop every one of these problems all at once.

Halfway through the day, Lisa was so burned out that she had no energy left over to stop the bigger problem of running away. Lisa put it to me this way:

"Dr. Sells, I feel like I am constantly playing catch-up with Justin. It is like I wake up each day with only one gallon of gas. By three in the afternoon, I am running on fumes. I am constantly putting out Justin's fires. I have no gas left over to argue curfew times or punish him when I am being cussed out. Please help!"

Create a List of the Most Important Problems

It's probably all too easy to come up with a list of all the problems that you want to see your teen change. Write them down on a sheet of paper, asking yourself the following five questions about each:

1. Is the problem I am about to write down really important to me?
2. Could I let this problem go?
3. What would happen if I just waited?
4. Could I lose by doing nothing?
5. Is the problem a safety concern?

These questions will help you decide whether you really want to use your one gallon of gas to address every problem on your list. For example, one problem might be that your teen is moody and not talkative while another is stealing from other family members. Moodiness is often a normal by-product of adolescence and will likely stop if you wait and do nothing. However, stealing is something that may not get better without your input.

If you have a spouse or significant other, ask that person to make a separate list. (The blank worksheets to complete the exercises throughout this book can be ordered through my Web site, *www.difficult.net*.)

Remember, Safety First!

Your answer to question 5 is critically important. If your teenager is currently engaging in the following behaviors, you must include them at the top of your list:

- Threats or acts of suicide
- Running away or leaving the house without permission

- Threats or acts of violence to other people or animals
- Setting fires
- Drug or alcohol abuse that goes beyond simple experimentation

Any one of these problems could cause death or serious harm to your teenager or those around him or her. Therefore, other problems (such as not cleaning the room, ditching school, disrespect) have to take a backseat until these more serious issues are addressed.

If these problems are on your list, you need to see a competent counselor who specializes in children and teenagers. Why? The reason is that these problems are potentially dangerous and can cause harm to both you and your teenager. Please consult the Web site at (*www.difficult.net*) or the Appendix at the end of the book for guidelines and questions to help you select the right counselor for you.

Rank your teen's problems from most to least important, listing any safety issues as number 1. If your teenager is willing, ask him or her to make a list as well. It will be interesting to see if any of your teen's answers matches yours.

Combine the Lists into One

Single parents will skip this step and go directly to Strategy #2: Convert Problems into Concrete Rules. You would not need to exchange the list with anyone but I would recommend showing your list to a good friend or significant other. They can offer support and give their opinions on your list. In turn, this might help you generate new ideas or modify your list for the better.

After completing separate lists, exchange them with your partner and compare your answers. If your list is significantly different from your partner's, you must reach a consensus on at least one problem.

Reaching consensus can be difficult if you have different parenting styles or marital problems. However, if you are going to be successful in helping your teen, you *must* reach a consensus. Otherwise, your teenager will "divide and conquer."

You can agree to disagree on some of your teenager's problems but not on those that involve safety issues. When it comes to the other problems, try compromise: Promise to help solve a problem on your significant other's list if he or she in turn will help you solve one on yours. Flip a coin to see who will go first.

If your teen thinks that a particular problem is important and it seems reasonable, you may want to include it on your list. Teenagers' cooperation is likely to increase any time you can use their ideas.

When you're finished considering everyone's answers, write down the top two problems that you're going to address first.

Strategy #2: Convert Problems into Concrete Rules

One of the main reasons your contracts fail is because your teen has an uncanny ability to find loopholes in your rules if they are not concretely defined. For example, you might argue over the correct interpretation of what constitutes "a clean room." Such arguments can lead to bitter conflict and possibly even violence.

You can avoid this by writing concrete definitions of the problem behavior that you want to address. Look at how these parents took the problems of "violence" and a "clean room" off the problem list and converted them into clear and concrete rules.

Combined Problem List	Converted Problems to Concrete Rules
1. Sam physically hits younger brother.	Rule #1 Sam's behavior toward his brother will be considered an act of violence if he does one of the following: ■ Pushes, shoves, hits, thumps, kicks, squeezes his brother or anyone else. ■ Threatens to hurt his brother or anyone else. ■ Any behaviors not on this list that may cause physical injury to someone else.

Combined Problem List	Converted Problems to Concrete Rules
2. Sam refuses to clean his room.	Rule #2 Sam's room will be considered clean only if: ■ Every piece of clothing is picked up off the floor, closet floor, and any other piece of furniture and placed in the hamper in the laundry room. ■ No food items of any kind in any part of the room. ■ The bed is made to parents' satisfaction. ■ Clean clothes hung up or put away. ■ Floor vacuumed on Monday and Thursday. ■ These tasks are completed and ready for inspection at 6:00 P.M. each day.

Different households will have different definitions of a particular problem. In this case, the family converted the problem of "hitting a younger brother" into a clear and literally stated rule with no loopholes. Sam was no longer able to bargain, demand an explanation, or point out his parents' inconsistencies.

These parents then went on to literally define a clean room in the same literal manner. Use the blank worksheets and other concrete examples of completed contracts offered through *www.difficult.net* to assist you in converting your problems into concrete rules with no loopholes.

You can convert the problems from your list (ditching school, not obeying curfew, running away) into concrete behaviors by asking yourself this question:

What are all the things that my teenager says or does that clearly indicate that they are exhibiting this problem?

For example, consider the rule about underage drinking that Martin's mother wrote to address the problem of a son who was abusing alcohol:

> Martin will not use alcohol at home or drink and drive. This includes beer, wine, or any other form of liquor. At any time, I will conduct random spot checks of Martin's room as he stands by his door and watches me. In addition, if I suspect alcohol use, Martin will be asked to submit to a breath alcohol test. If he fails to submit to this test voluntarily, he will be presumed guilty and this rule will be broken.

Strategy #3: Create a Well-Written Consequence

Once you have a well-written rule, you must produce a well-written consequence if that rule is broken or followed. By revealing the top ten consequences that teens care about, I will show you how to come up with consequences that will work to stop even the most extreme behaviors. Teens all across the world will be very angry at me for showing you these secrets, but it has to be done.

A Word of Caution

Before I reveal these consequences, I ask that you please use the consequences contained within this book with great care and responsibility. Some of these consequences are tough. They are included because it can take this kind of toughness to get your teens' attention and stop their problems. Please adhere to these guidelines when creating your consequences:

- **Make sure your teen's misbehaviors are persistent and repetitive.** Use the tough consequences in this book only if your teen is committing the same problem behavior over and over again. If not, use more traditional consequences such as a stern talk, grounding, or sending the teen to his or her room. It is normal for a teen to play hooky from school occasionally, become disrespectful, or even run away when upset or angry. Never use the consequences listed in Step 5 for a first-time offense. You should never use a hammer to kill a mosquito. If you do, you will make the situation much worse. I remember one family in which the father went to school dressed like a nerd after his son had skipped school for the first time in his life. The son was so angry and embarrassed that he started ditching on a regular basis. Use your big guns only if necessary.

- **Read the entire book.** Once I tried to put together a filing cabinet after only reading part of the directions. As soon as I put my television on it, the whole thing collapsed. In the same way, each step in this book supports and builds on the other. Therefore, if you try to pawn your teen's CD collection before you understand the concept of button-pushing, things will quickly escalate out of control. It is not just the make and model of the consequence that's important, it is when and how it is delivered.

- **Please follow the counselor recommendations.** When you see this icon, it means that you need to seek an outsider counselor for guidance. This icon signifies that the consequence is a big gun and should be used only in conjunction with the help of a mental health counselor. Some of these consequences will require nerves of steel and the ability to think on your feet when your teen countermoves with even more extreme behaviors. A qualified and competent counselor will help guide you through this process and provide the support you need. Please check the Appendix for concrete suggestions in picking the best counselor for you.

■ **Make sure you have a Plan B if Plan A fails.** Use the trou-

Backup Plan

bleshooting strategies in Step 3 to predetermine a backup plan if your first consequence falls flat or fails. As I stated earlier, you must think two steps ahead of teenagers. Otherwise, they will eat you alive. The backup plan icon should remind you that it is time to create a Plan B.

■ **Employ a love-and-limits approach.** Please understand that both you and your teen have been through a lot. There will be scar tissue on both sides. The years of conflict and confrontation have deeply bruised your love for one another. Because of this fact, your teen will need a healthy dose of limits through negative consequences *and* love through positives. One without the other will not lead to long-lasting and positive change. I implore you to apply the positive consequences outlined in this step and the strategies recommended in Step 7: "The Fine Line Between Love and Hate."

Locate Your Teenager's Achilles' Heel Using the Top Ten List

There is not a teenager alive who does not have an Achilles' heel—a consequence that he or she would rather not face or a reward that can motivate that teen to greatness. On the surface, such consequences are difficult to find.

Negative consequences that work are not immediately obvious because your teen works from the pleasure principle, preferring to face your punishment rather than give up the immediate gratification of skipping school, getting drunk, having unprotected sex, or staying out all night. Therefore, you must find a consequence that is so distasteful to your particular teen's "taste buds" that he or she would rather give up the pleasure than suffer the consequence. Sometimes those consequences have to be extremely creative as the cartoon on the next page illustrates.

A TEENS WORST NIGHTMARE:
MOM ON A MISSION.

Created by Brenda Paige.

The other Achilles' heel is rewards, or positive consequences. These can be hard to find because so many teens act as if they don't care. In reality, your teen cares very much. You just have to find the right reward. I will show you how this is done in the next section.

Based on my focus group interviews with both parents and teens during my four-year research study, I came up with a list of the top ten consequences—both positive and negative—that truly matter to teens. The list is limited to ten because the number of consequences dramatically decreases as children enter adolescence. As a nine-year-old, your child probably responded to many different punishments— taking away a toy, denying dessert, imposing an early bedtime. By age thirteen, however, these same consequences no longer worked. This number of consequences grows smaller and smaller as your teen gets older.

Top Ten Consequences

1. Money	Giving money or taking it away is a powerful incentive.
2. Telephone	Friends are extremely important to teenagers. Therefore, restrictions from talking to friends or the opposite sex can get their attention quickly.
3. Freedom	A loss of any kind of freedom (grounding, not being allowed to go to a party, see friends, watch television, go on the Internet, etc.) can quickly get a teenager on the right track if used correctly.
4. Clothing	Clothing makes a statement and represents an identity. Taking away certain clothes or making them wear "nerdy clothes" can be a great motivator.
5. Cars	This one has not changed since cars were invented. At sixteen and seventeen the ability to drive becomes critical to your teen. Parental transportation is very important. Taking the car away or forcing the teenager to take public transportation can be a powerful consequence.
6. Loosening Restrictions	When a parent modifies past rules such as extending curfew or bedtime, this communicates your willingness to treat your teenager like an adult. This is a tremendous motivator.
7. Trust	Earning and keeping trust with you is very important to your teen. Finding ways for teens to earn back trust slowly can make all the difference in the world.
8. Appearance	Looking good in front of peers is very important and goes beyond the type of clothes you wear. It becomes a matter of how you talk, who you are with, and looking cool. If you take your teenager who is ditching school to class and you sit next to him or her with pink rollers in your hair or a pocket pencil holder, your teen's appearance is threatened and motivation to do the right thing increases.

9. Materialism   More and more, material things (CDs, pagers, cel-
                   lular phones, jewelry, etc.) are becoming important
                   to teenagers. Removing these items can be a great
                   motivator.

10. Spending   Many teenagers will not admit it, but reconnecting
    Time   and spending quality time with a parent, mentor,
                   or caregiver is extremely important to them.
                   Most parents miss this one because teens are
                   so busy trying to act tough, they don't seem to
                   want or need any soft time with "uncool" parents.
                   Most of the time this is just an act and a smoke
                   screen.

After you study the top ten list, use the worksheet below to
rank which consequences are most important to your teen. Let's
return to Jill's case at the beginning of the chapter to see how I used
the top ten list to turn my initial failure with this family into a
success.

A Second Chance with Jill's Family

After the third straight cancellation, I called Marcia and asked
her and Jill for a second chance. I asked Marcia if she could
come in alone. At the meeting, I listed all the reasons why I had
failed, including the unwritten contract, the lack of troubleshooting, and rules and consequences that were not literally
defined.

Another reason for failure was the fact that we had selected
a set of consequences that Jill could care less about. Jill wasn't
worried about grounding. She could see her friends at school
and they could come over while Marcia was at work. There were
also no incentives for going to school or getting decent grades.
To avoid these same mistakes, I asked Marcia to evaluate top ten
consequences that teens care about. Here is what Marcia's list
looked like for Jill.

Rank Order	Consequence	Does He/She Care About This Consequence? Yes	No	If you answered "yes," what specific things does he/she care about?
#5	Money	XX		Jill liked to spend her money as soon as she got it.
#4	Telephone	XX		Jill loved the phone. She had her own phone.
#6	Freedom	X		Freedom to stay out late and hang with friends.
#2	Clothes	XXX		Jill loved clothes and liked to go shopping.
	Cars		X	
	Loosen Restrictions	X		Wants curfew extended.
	Trust	X		She wants trust around school and no checking up.
#1	Appearance	XXX		How Jill looked in front of her friends is extremely important to her.
#3	Materialism	XX		Jill loved her clothes and prized CD collection.
	Spending Time	X		Probably wants more alone time with Mom but will not admit this.

This list was a revelation to Marcia. It opened her eyes to a whole set of new possibilities around both positive and negative consequences. She told me:

"Looking at my list, I can't believe all the things that Jill cares about. I should have zeroed in on consequences around clothes, appearance, money, phone, and materialism. Even though freedom is important to Jill, grounding her doesn't work. I see what you mean now."

Once we zeroed in on appearance we used the Attending School strategy described within the truancy ace in Step 5. After mom attended school in hot pink curlers, a hair net, and a bathrobe we never had another problem with Jill being tardy or ditching school.

Please rank each possible consequence as it pertains to your son or daughter. You can order these blank worksheets at *www. difficult.net* or create your own based on the one I used for Jill. Please remember to place two or more X's in the "yes" column to highlight consequences that are particularly meaningful to your teen.

Strategy #4: Use Both Positive and Negative Consequences

Use the following worksheet to list both negative *and* positive consequences for each area you checked off. For example, if you checked off "money," you might list a positive consequence of an increase in allowance for doing chores and a negative consequence of fines for not doing them.

Once again, if your teen is having really serious behavior problems, you will find further ideas for specific consequences in Step 5.

Positive consequences are as important as negative consequences, for the following reasons:

1. **Negative or Positive Attention: "It's All the Same to Me."**
    Children and teenagers need and crave attention. Attention says

Positive and Negative Consequences for Your Teenager		
Consequence	Does my teen care about this?	If yes, what specifically does he/she care about?
Money	Yes No	
Telephone	Yes No	
Freedom	Yes No	
Clothes	Yes No	
Car	Yes No	
Loosen Restrictions	Yes No	
Trust	Yes No	
Appearance	Yes No	
Materialism	Yes No	
Spending Time	Yes No	

Use the list above to construct possible consequences to use.

	Positive	Negative
1.		
2.		
3.		
4.		
5.		

"I am noticed" and "I am somebody." Kids prefer positive attention or rewards for their behavior. However, if positive attention is in short supply, they will willingly accept negative attention. The end result is the same: being noticed. Out-of-control teens have a bad habit of getting used to negative attention. They may have brought it on themselves, but they are now so deep in the mud that it is impossible to see daylight. Because of this fact, they need a heavy dose of positive attention to rewire their brains.

2. The Real World Offers Positive Rewards and Negative Consequences.

Receiving both positive and negative consequences gives your teenager a choice—either to follow the rule and be rewarded, or to receive a negative consequence until the rule is followed.

The real world offers reinforcement of this kind all the time. For example, you will receive a paycheck if you go to work on time and do your job; if not, you will receive a negative consequence, such as having your pay docked or getting fired. It's up to you: You can follow the company's rules and get a paycheck, or you can choose not to and put your job at risk.

What do you think would happen if your job offered only negative consequences (no paycheck or any positive incentives like time off)? Under those conditions, how long would you be willing to do your job and cooperate with company rules and policies? The answer is probably not long. Your teenager's cooperation level will also continue to decline rapidly if he or she receives only negative consequences.

Strategy #5:
Put the Written Contract Together

Once you have created your consequence list, it is time to construct your first written contract with both rules and consequences. This first contract should be called a "working document," because you will refine it later after adding your teenager's input in Strategy #6 and troubleshooting any possible problems in advance in Step 3.

An example of how both negative and positive consequences can be written together is illustrated in my work with thirteen-year-old Jerry and his family. The problem was that Jerry refused to obey curfew.

Curfew and Consequences

Jerry's dad had previously tried everything from grounding him for weeks at a time to taking away all phone privileges. Nothing worked. Jerry told me privately that he had given up. "Even when I do come home on time, nothing happens. I only get s**t when I am late."

Dad was skeptical when I spoke with him alone. He told me, "Why should I reward Jerry for something he already should be doing?" I told his father that Jerry needed a nudge in the right direction. It is important to "bend a willow branch, but not snap it into two pieces," or there would be no incentive for him to keep trying.

Dad would lose nothing by trying this approach. Dad could still incorporate punishments if Jerry was even one minute late for curfew. The only difference would be that Jerry would also receive a reward for coming home on time. The choice of receiving a positive or negative consequence would be up to Jerry.

Jerry could also help generate ideas for a good reward and even a good punishment. Dad would have final veto power, but Jerry would be part of the plan.

Dad was still skeptical, so we agreed to a three-week experiment. If his dad did not see any progress in three weeks, he could go back to the old way of doing things and lose nothing. Here is what we came up with.

Jerry's Contract

Jerry's curfew time will be 5:00 P.M. on school nights (Sunday through Thursday) and 10:00 P.M. on weekends (Friday and Saturday). If Jerry returns home even one minute past the curfew hour, he will be considered late. These times will not be changed or altered until I (your dad) decide otherwise. Trying to change them on your own breaks this rule.

Consequence A

If Jerry comes home on time, he will receive one hour added to his curfew time the next night. If it is on a school night, the temporary curfew the next night will be 6:00 P.M. and, if it is on a weekend, it will be 11:00 P.M. Jerry keeps these hours as long as he comes home on time. If not he receives Consequence B and loses this extra hour until he finishes his punishment. He can then start all over again to get his extra hour, if he comes home on time for an entire week without being late.

Consequence B

For every night Jerry is late, he is grounded the next weekend night. If he is late again that same week, the same thing happens. If he runs out of weekend nights it will be tacked onto the following weekend.

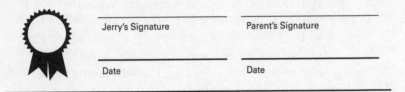

Jerry's Signature	Parent's Signature
Date	Date

In this example, the father constructed his list of top-ten consequences and discovered that the top-ranked consequence centered around "freedom." Therefore, Jerry had a choice: Follow the rule of curfew and receive the reward or positive consequence (one extra hour of curfew) or choose not to and receive a negative consequence (grounding the next day plus one weekend night).

Both the rules and the consequences were extremely concrete. Jerry's father stated what the consequence would be (one hour added to curfew or grounding), how it would be monitored (even one minute late by the kitchen clock), who would deliver it (Dad would enforce or grant the extra curfew time), when it would be enforced (each night of the week), and how long the consequence would last (until Dad decides otherwise).

With this kind of detail, it was next to impossible for Jerry to find a loophole. Jerry also helped write his own consequences in Strategy #8. He came up with the idea of extra curfew time. At first he wanted three hours, but his dad and I helped him modify it into something reasonable. Although Jerry initially refused, he finally agreed to try the contract out for three weeks as an experiment. He liked the idea that his dad was no longer trying to ground him for a month at a time and that it was up to him to lose or keep his extra hour of curfew.

Please make sure that you stick to the contract and avoid changing it midstream. For example, Jerry's contract almost got derailed the first week. On Wednesday, the father got angry at Jerry for "giving him the finger." Dad was about to remove the extra hour of curfew time for disrespect.

Fortunately, I talked to the father by phone and told him that it was normal for Jerry to test the waters. Jerry did not believe that his father would really give him positive rewards. The father agreed and took away the phone for disrespect, but left the contract for curfew intact. Jerry's dad realized that disrespect and curfew were two separate issues and should have a different set of consequences. Making new rules as you go along flies directly in the face of fairness and what was agreed to beforehand. Moreover, it takes an average of 30 straight days to change a bad habit. You need to wait out your teen for four straight weeks to give the contract a chance to work.

Strategy #6: Include Your Teenager's Input and Expertise

After you write down your first contract, it is important to try to elicit your teen's input and ideas. If your teen's ideas seem reasonable, you can incorporate them directly into the contract. Remember that you retain final veto power and can approve or disapprove their ideas. However, you lose nothing by asking for their expert opinion to solve their own problems. Research studies show that when people are co-owners of something, their motivation and cooperation increases.

You will be surprised by how clearly your son or daughter can define what consequences work best for him or her. Many times kids are harder on themselves and come up with stricter consequences than you would, as Matt did in the following example.

You Want to Do What??

Thirteen-year-old Matt would stubbornly refuse to do anything his parents asked. His total lack of respect often left his parents speechless. His father tried all kinds of consequences but could not stop the problem. As a last resort, the father decided to ask Matt's expert advice and think of the worst punishment he could imagine. Matt responded by stating that, for the first offense, he should be required to pick up stones in the backyard for one hour in the hot sun. Each additional offense would add one hour to his time of picking up stones. This would continue until he stopped being disrespectful. The father thought this was absurd but was desperate for a solution. Within weeks the problem ended. Matt did not like sweating in the August heat while picking up rocks.

Some out-of-control teenagers will not be helpful, especially if they see no advantage to doing so or if they are so out of control that they are unable to listen to reason.

It's Not What You Say But How You Say It

Most of the time your teenager does not help because of the way you ask the question. Out-of-control teens tell me, "I want to talk, but my parents don't know how to listen." Here are some examples. Close your eyes and go back to your teen years. Imagine for a moment your parent coming to you and asking the following questions. Which one would make you want to help?

A (*In a gruff voice*): Why do you think you are so disrespectful to me?

-or-

B (*In a soft voice*): Can I ask your expert opinion? How can we solve the problem of swearing when we get into a fight?

A (*In a sarcastic voice*): Why can't you get your act together? I am out of ideas. If you're so smart, why don't you think of something?

-or-

B (*In a straightforward tone*): I really need your help. What would you be doing differently if you stopped breaking curfew? What would I as your parent be doing differently starting tomorrow to help you to not want to break curfew?

Obviously, the B questions tend to get better results. How you ask the question and your tone of voice are 90 percent of the battle. The other 10 percent is looking interested and using some of your teenager's ideas.

Initially your teen may act as if he or she does not want to participate in helping with the contract. This is usually their way of acting tough and projecting an I-don't-care attitude when underneath they are just too guarded and scared to open up.

Try laying the groundwork by using some version of the following opening statement, which you can adapt to your particular parenting style:

I know this may sound strange, but I really need your expertise and help in writing this contract. I don't feel comfortable making decisions that affect your life without your input. Everyone can change, even me. I am sorry about the past. I wish I could change it, but I can't. All we can do is change the future. A first step is to get your opinion of how to best solve these problems [list the problems] one at a time.

I need your expert ideas to stop each problem cold in its tracks. As your parent, I will still need to have final approval, but I will do everything I can now or later to use your expert ideas. Can I please begin with the first question?

These statements suggest you are taking a one-down position, while still communicating clearly that you are the parent and leader of the household. You are not getting caught up in the sins of the past but looking forward to changing the future with your son or daughter's help. You are also coming to your teen with a clear working contract on paper and the behaviors you want to stop. This prep work will pay off.

What Questions to Ask

When you're both in a good mood and the television is off, ask your teen the following four questions. While you probably have never thought of asking most of them, I have seen them work magic with countless out-of-control teens who want the adults in their lives to listen to and really hear them. Please ask them in the order they are presented here.

1. **"How come you have not thrown in the towel yet and given up on yourself and our relationship with one another? What keeps you going?"**
   This is a refreshing and effective question because it focuses instantly on any and all positives in your teen and in your relationship with one another. Your teen is probably so used to hearing you emphasize the negatives that he or she might start opening up when you ask this. If, however, he or she gives one-word or abstract answers like "We just don't talk," gently say "What do you mean?" or "I don't understand" to get more detail.

2. **"I have told you in the past how you can be helpful to me. Now I want to know how can I be helpful to you?"**
   If your teen asks, "What do you mean by helpful?" respond with things like: helpful in getting people off your case, helpful in making our relationship better, or helpful in not getting grounded all the time. If your teen says, "I don't know," ask him or her to start guessing. If that does not work, *you* start guessing. Your teen will begin to correct you if you are off base. He or she will not be able to help it.

3. **"What things have I done or said in the past that were not helpful or turned you off? I ask this question because I don't want to repeat the same mistakes in the future."**
   It will be hard not to defend yourself at this point or take the answers personally. An old saying goes, "It is helpful to understand before trying to be understood." Therefore, at this point, ask only for clarification. For example, if your teen says, "You never listen," do not come back with "Yes, I do!" Instead, reply, "What

do I do or say that makes you think that I am not listening?" This question gives you concrete information and provides clarification. If your teen says, "I don't know," start guessing with things like Have I listened enough? Been fair enough? and so on. Your teen will correct wrong guesses and give you the right answer.

4. **"If we were on track to getting everyone off your back and solving this problem [name one problem at a time], what would you be doing differently? What would I be doing differently to help this happen?"**

-or-

"Suppose while we were sleeping a miracle happens and your problem [name the problem] is solved. How will we be able to tell the next day that a miracle happened? What will be different? How will you have done it? Who will be most surprised by this miracle?"

Once again, be patient and nondefensive. This is merely a fact-finding mission. Make sure you try to get your teen to be as concrete as possible. Thinking about what the future will look like instead of getting stuck in the past is a much better way to solve your teen's current problems.

These questions should establish an atmosphere of cooperation in which you can ask specific questions about consequences:

- If you could stop this problem [name the specific problem] tomorrow, what positive consequences or rewards do you think would help end the problem or decrease it?

- If you could stop this problem [name the specific problem] tomorrow, what negative consequences or punishments do you think would be in place to end the problem or decrease it?

- What would you say is the single worst punishment that would stop you cold in your tracks or slow you down if you broke this rule [name the specific rule]?

Ask your teenager if you can write down ideas as he or she talks. Writing down the responses will not only make the teen feel important but also helps you remember what was said. Continue to ask for clarification as you receive answers. For example, if your teen says, "The worst punishment is not getting to go out," you would then say, "What do you mean by not going out? What does not going out look like to you?"

Parent Alert: When Should My Teenager Not Help Write the Contract?

Most parenting books emphasize that teens should always have an equal voice and help write the contract. This works fine with most kids, but extreme teens require special handling.

Behaviors like violence, drug use, or running away are so severe and have gone on for so long that your teen will not give up without a fight. As a result, initially your teen may try to sabotage the contract to keep his or her current position of power or refuse to cooperate with you on any level.

Sometimes you have to establish order and authority before collaboration with your teen becomes productive. You also may have to stop the extreme behaviors (running away, the truancy, the violence) first before things are calm enough for collaboration. The goal is to move your teenager into a position of cowriting the contract, but *only* after things in your house have settled down.

After you finish taking notes, conclude with some version of the following statement:

[Teenager's name], thanks for all your help. I (we) will now take your ideas and try to see where I can combine some of your consequences with ours. I (we) may not use all of your ideas right now. I may take some now and some later. As time goes on, I (we) will look at how the contract is working. I may tweak or modify parts that are not working but will tell you beforehand. Like all teenagers, you may not agree with everything I put down. I will explain the final contract if you ask in a calm voice. If you get angry or still do not agree, we will stop explaining and exit from the conversation. You will get the final draft of the contract no later than [state the date and time]. I will slide it under your bedroom door. I will ask you to sign it next to my signature. If you refuse to sign the contract, that will be your choice. However, I will still move forward and the contract will be put into place.

You may want to review Step 4, on "Button-Pushing," before you present this final statement. Your teen may act like an angel until he or she actually sees the written contract; then all hell may break loose. Teens typically say, "You better put everything I said down on that contract or else," "I ain't signing no contract," or "You tell me that I'm grounded and I'm moving out." Intentionally your teen will do everything to push your buttons and throw you off track. If you do not understand how button-pushing works, you can be defeated even before you begin.

Luann reprinted by permission of United Feature Syndicate, Inc.

A Final Note: Teens Will Play Possum

Both possums and teens are great actors: A possum can convince you it is dead, and teenagers can convince you that they could care less about the consequences. If you don't get a reaction from your teen, you may automatically think that the consequence is not working and shift gears. This is what your teen wants you to think when he or she keeps saying "I don't care." Don't be fooled; stick to the contract, and to the consequences, for at least four consecutive weeks to give them a chance to work.

But first, you will need to come up with a Plan B in case Plan A doesn't work. Step 3 shows you how this is done.

Strategy #7: Be Consistent in Following Through

Before you put your contract into practice, please remember these two golden rules:

1. Do not say anything to your teenager that you can't do or don't want to do, and do everything you say you are going to do.
2. The more you can follow number 1, the less you will need to punish.

Please say these golden rules over and over again until they are burned into your memory. Put them on your bathroom mirror and look at them every day. Parents tell me that if they read these statements in the morning, they are more consistent the rest of the day.

If you are inconsistent, your teenager will see your rules and consequences as optional, not mandatory. If this happens, your teen will become even more disobedient and the need to punish will be that much greater. How many times have you been inside a supermarket or department store and overheard a mother or father threatening a young child to stop misbehaving? When the threats are empty, does the child act out more or less? The child acts out more and screams even louder when the parent doesn't follow through.

Watch out for the six pitfalls that undermine many parents' ability to be consistent with their teens:

Six Common Pitfalls

1. Empty statements
Do you find yourself making threats that you can't or won't carry out: "I won't give you any money until you get a job" or "If you

do not straighten up, pack your bags and leave"? If the answer is yes, you must stop yourself; you can also ask a spouse or best friend to take you aside and alert you when you are falling into these old habits.

2. Overstatements

Do you ever make overstatements when you get angry and come up with a consequence that is too extreme: "You are grounded for six months" or "You cannot talk on the phone the rest of the school year"? You then back yourself in a corner because you cannot monitor or enforce overstatements. To reverse this trend, try to stop yourself from making such statements. If you slip up once in a while, go back to your teen when you have calmed down and explain that the consequence was said in anger—then calmly state the real consequence.

3. Changing "no" to "yes" and "yes" to "no"

How often do you say no but change it to yes if your teen harasses or irritates you long enough? This change gives your teen a clear message that you will give up your authority if he or she applies enough pressure; it also indicates that you cannot be trusted to mean what you say.

4. Not checking on behavior

Do you frequently tell your teenager to do something, and then not check to see if it gets done? For example, if you ask your teen to clean his or her room, you need to follow through later that day. You should either apologize or not punish misbehavior if you didn't monitor it on the day the rule was given.

5. Lack of a unified parental voice

If the adults in your household have different approaches to parenting and discipline, there can be big trouble. If one is too strict and the other too soft, your teen will go to the softer parent when he or she wants something. If you are the "strict" parent, you will become angry and resentful toward your partner as well as toward your teen. While you are angry or frustrated with one another, your teenager is having the time of his or her life. Your teen will take charge of your household until you and your partner can set aside your differences and become a united front.

6. **Different reactions at different times to the same behavior**
Do you treat the same behavior in different ways depending on your mood that day? For example, do you lecture your teenager for not doing chores one day and then ground him or her for the same behavior the next day? Many parents do this when they come home from work and they are tired and worn out. If this happens, your teenager will realize that the rules are optional and refuse to obey them.

Construct a Nonverbal Sign to Remind You

In order to avoid these pitfalls, sit down with your significant other and study this list. Determine who makes overstatements and changes a "yes" to a "no" and who makes empty statements or fails to check up on the teenager's behavior. Make a private agreement to use some supportive, nonverbal sign to warn each other when you are falling into old habits.

For example, some parents will open their mouths wide to signal an overstatement, while others make a check mark in the air to symbolize the act of not checking up on behavior. If you are a single parent, perhaps you can ask one of your older children to give you a sign. Try to make the signs playful and noncritical. If the problem persists, please consult a counselor to help you through the rough spots.

Strategy #8: Catch Your Teen Doing Something Right

I saved the best for last. This final strategy in contracting is my #1 secret weapon to turn your teen around. If you follow these procedures to the letter for two consecutive months you will see unbelievable positive changes in your teenager.

The secret weapon is called a Positive Incident Report (PIR). It was developed several years ago by the Buckeye Ranch in Columbus,

Ohio, to successfully turn around even the most troubled teenagers. It is a simple procedure that will allow you to focus, reinforce, and reward any and all positive behaviors in your teenagers.

You will use the PIR in conjunction with your contract. The PIR will act like a booster shot and give your contract the rocket fuel it needs to really take off. Here is how it works.

Use Your Imaginary Magnifying Glass

Pretend that you have a magic high-powered magnifying glass that you carry at all times. This magnifying glass will allow you to see even the smallest positive changes in your teenager.

Throughout the day, use your imaginary magnifying glass to look for anything that your teen does to follow the contract or exhibit some strength. For example, if the rule is "no ditching school" and your son does not ditch, tell him that you notice the effort and how proud you are of him. If he displays strengths outside the contract (such as doing what he is told the first time, not fighting with his brothers or sisters), tell him. Try to decide ahead of time what strengths you want to focus on. It will help you see them as they happen. Examples of strengths include but are not limited to the following:

Excelled in Academics	Excelled in Artistic Expression
■ An A or B on a tough test	■ Wrote a poem or story
■ Completed homework on own	■ Drew an expressive picture
■ Remained focused on homework	■ Performed in a play

Excelled in Job Performance	Excelled in Concern for Others
■ Completed extra chore	■ Listened to another's problems
■ Did chores without being told	■ Helped brother or sister
■ Went to work outside the home	■ Visited a nursing home

Excelled in Sports	Performed Well Under Stress
■ Lost but was a good sport	■ Was rejected but talked about it
■ Tried a new sport	■ Comforted another in pain
■ Scored a touchdown, home run	■ Did not lose cool when stressed

Performed Beyond the Call of Duty	Used Self-Control
■ Helped cook	■ Avoided a fight
■ Did something unexpected	■ Took a time out on own
■ Made a positive leap	■ Talked through anger

Deliver the Positive Incident Report

After you see one of these strengths, fill out and hand your teen the PIR certificate below. Your teenager will be shocked but do not let this stop you. Copy as many certificates as you need. Make sure you sign it.

Please remember this critical point as you deliver your first PIR. Rules will be broken less often if you catch your teen doing something right by praising him or her for even the smallest improvement. Praise motivates but criticism crushes the human spirit. Dale Carnegie in his classic book, *How to Win Friends and Influence People,* said it best:

"Criticism is futile because it puts a person on the defensive, wounds a person's precious pride, hurts his or her sense of importance and arouses resentment. . . . Instead, the deepest desire in human beings is the craving to be appreciated. It is an unfaltering human hunger."

Positive Incident Report

For: _____

You Did It! _____ Academics _____ Athletics _____ Creativity

_____ Concern for Others _____ Performed Well Under Stress

_____ Performed Well Under Tough Circumstances

_____ Did Chores Without Being Asked _____ Avoided an Argument

_____ Job Performance _____ Respectful _____ Other

You earned this PIR because: _____

You are being recognized for going beyond the call of duty!
Keep moving forward!
You're fantastic!

I Saw It!

_____
Parent Signature

_____
Date

A Word of Caution

Before you present the PIR to your teen, I want to warn you about some things to watch out for. These are very common reactions that your teen might give you when you present them with a Positive Incident Report.

1. This Will Feel Mechanical or Forced at First.

In the past, there has been so much tension between you and your teen that giving your teen a PIR will initially feel phony, forced, or mechanical. This is normal and to be expected. At first, "You will have to fake until you make it." Over time it will begin to feel more real and authentic.

2. The PIR Will Also Feel Strange to Your Teenager.

At first, your teen will not know how to react when you give him or her a PIR. Your teen may think that you have an angle or want something. At first, he or she will not trust your good will and may be scared. Because of this, he or she may act in anger by ripping the PIR up, refusing to accept it, or saying "I don't care" and throwing it away. Again, this is normal. Do not take it personally. It is a big risk to let your guard down and trust again. Please try to understand. If you are consistent and give the PIR's unconditionally, it will begin to break down your teen's walls of anger.

3. No Appreciation

The PIR stuff will be so weird to your teen that he or she may be unable to say "thank you" or appreciate your kindness. This is normal. Your teen will thank you months or even years later when he or she is old enough to see the big picture. Right now your teen cannot, so please be understanding and patient. The PIR is good for teenagers even if they don't know it yet.

How Often Should You Give PIR's

For the first month, give your teenager a PIR every time you see a strength. You may want to do this for two straight months depending on your teen and how long the problem has gone on.

After a month or two, start giving the PIR certificate intermittently—some times and not others. Research studies by B. F. Skinner in his classic book *Science and Human Behavior* show that positive reinforcement works better if the person is off balance and doesn't know when his or her next behavior will be rewarded.

This principle has made the casinos in Las Vegas very rich. When adults use slot machines, they get rewarded with just enough coins to keep them playing for hours. However, for this principle to work with your teen a foundation of constant positive reinforcement must be laid down consistently for the first one to two months.

Wall of Fame or a Mini-Store

Once you give your teen the PIR, ask their permission to tape them on the wall or the refrigerator and call it the Wall of Fame. Even if your teen is shy about it, please try to tape it up anyway. This is just so new to them that it is normal for them to be initially resistant.

Most teens will like this gesture even though they may "play possum" and act as if they don't care.

After doing the Wall of Fame for several weeks you might want to add a little extra bonus. You can set up a mini-store where your teen can cash in their PIR certificates for fun or prizes. For example, if your son receives three certificates, he can choose between M&M's and three packs of Snickers. If your daughter receives ten certificates, she might be able to choose from a sleepover or a CD. Please do not go to the mini store idea until you have tried the Wall of Fame. Otherwise, your teen may associate praise with having to always get a reward.

One family had four shelves in a locked storage area. Each shelf represented a different level of certificates:

1. *Level 1 Shelf* (3 PIR certificates): M&M's, Snickers Bar—Choose one.
2. *Level 2 Shelf* (6 PIR certificates): Coupon for: ice cream, one extra hour of phone time, baseball trading cards, makeup—Choose one.
3. *Level 3 Shelf* (8 PIR certificates): Coupon for: 3 extra hours of phone time, 1 CD, curfew extended 1 hour on the weekend—Choose one.
4. *Level 4 Shelf* (10 PIR certificates): Coupon for: one approved sleepover, 2 CDs, or 1 pizza party—Choose one.

Modify these levels as you see fit and stock your shelves with things that your teen likes. You might be thinking that a mini-store is for little kids or that it will not work with your teen. This is simply not true. Trust me on this one.

Experiment with the idea for at least one month. You will be amazed at the results. You like to be rewarded with bonuses in your job and so will your teenager. The story of Micki and her mother demonstrates how powerful this approach can be.

"Why Try, Nothing Will Ever Be Good Enough"

Fifteen-year-old Micki complained that her mother was constantly negative. From the moment she got up, her mom was nagging that Micki was "too slow moving," "not pretty enough," "too lazy," or "not good enough." Micki told me that she was now at the point of giving up. Nothing would ever be good enough. Her motto became: If I don't try, I cannot fail in my mother's eyes.

I learned from the mother that she had received the same messages from her own mother when she was growing up. When I showed the mother the PIR certificate strategy, she was very skeptical: Surely her daughter was too old for a store.

Nevertheless, she agreed to give it a one-month trial. If she did not see even small changes, she could go back to the way things used to be. The mom and I then practiced this strategy: I played Micki, and the mom looked for positives with her imaginary magnifying glass. She pretended to give me a signed PIR certificate for each positive action. After a half-hour of practice, the mother began to catch on.

Imagine my surprise when Micki ran into my office and proudly displayed six signed certificates. The mother was also smiling and said that she had to hand it to me. Everything I predicted came true. Micki's overall behavior was better, and her mom noticed that she was trying harder. She felt closer to her daughter than she had in years. At that moment, Micki chimed in and said, "My mom told me that she was proud of me twice."

Step 3

TROUBLESHOOTING

How to Think Two Steps Ahead
of Your Teenager

After your contract is written, it is time to troubleshoot everything that could go wrong ahead of time before you fully implement your rules and consequences. You need a set of backup or contingency plans to counter anything that your teen might throw at you. For example, when fifteen-year-old Marie was grounded for ditching school, her parents decided ahead of time what they would do if Marie decided to (a) run away and disobey the grounding consequence, (b) continue to ditch school, or (c) call child protective services to claim abuse.

Most parenting books and contracts fail to teach you troubleshooting when you go to battle. You are not shown what to do if the contract fails or if your teen does something unexpected. There is no Plan B if your Plan A fails. Every great battle in history is won before the first shot is ever fired. Generals carefully anticipate the opposite side's every countermove before the battle begins. If they are right, victory is achieved. If they are wrong, defeat is certain.

Other parenting books also tell you how to fix your kid without telling you how other problems in your family (marital problems, depression, lecturing, etc.) directly affect your ability to enforce the contract. This step addresses both of these concerns by showing you how to create backup plans and how to address underlying family problems.

Strategy #1: Coming Up with Plan B When Plan A Fails

Warning! Do not let your teenager read this step! Give your teenager a copy of the ironclad contract but keep a copy of your written troubleshooting plans out of sight. Use your backup plans only if your teen tries to derail the contract.

The steps will help you to create secret backup plans that will take teenagers completely by surprise. When they ask you what you've been reading, simply smile, nod your head, and tell them that you have no idea what they're talking about.

Generate a List of What-Will-I-Do-If Scenarios

After you complete your written contract, go back over every rule and consequence, asking yourself this question:

What are all the things that could go wrong with this rule or consequence?

For example, let's say your rule was "no ditching school" and the consequence for breaking this rule was that you would attend school with your teen. On a separate sheet of paper, list what-will-I-do-if scenarios such as

- **What will I do if** I try to go to school and my teen refuses to go with me?

- **What will I do if** my teen screams and makes a scene when I walk into the classroom?

You must troubleshoot not only what your teenager might do or say to undermine the contract but also how other professionals might intentionally or unintentionally do the same thing. For example, the parents of thirteen-year-old Mitch thought that the consequence of calling the police for throwing a chair through the window was an air-tight plan. When they called the police, however, it took them forever to arrive—by which time, Mitch had already run away. The police officer did not do anything but take a report. When Mitch heard this, he literally laughed in his mother's face and said, "See, I told you the cops couldn't do anything. You can't stop me."

To help you get started with contingency plans, I have listed the most common what-will-I-do-if scenarios for each of the extreme behaviors that worry parents most: disrespect, ditching or failing school, running away, sexual promiscuity or teen pregnancy, alcohol or drug abuse, threats or acts of violence, and threats of suicide.

Disrespect

- **What will I do if** my teen continues to swear even after I tell him that he will lose his phone, will be grounded, fined, and so on?

- **What will I do if** my teen continues to follow me around the house and yell at me when I try to exit from the situation before losing my cool?

- **What will I do if** my teen refuses to obey my simple request to clean his room, wash the dishes, take out the trash, and the like?

- **What will I do if** my teen starts to get so disrespectful and angry that he begins to threaten to hit, push, or shove me?

Ditching School or Failing Grades

- **What will I do if** the teacher or school principal refuses to back me up?

- **What will I do if** my child refuses to do any homework even after the consequence is administered?

- **What will I do if** my teenager gets suspended or expelled from school?

- **What will I do if** I try to go to school and he (or she) refuses to go with me?

- **What will I do if** if my boss will not let me off work to attend school?

Running Away

- **What will I do if** I try to ground or stop my teen from leaving and he or she simply walks out the door?

- **What will I do if** my teen finds a friend to stay with and the parents do not require them to leave?

- **What will I do if** my teen calls the police or child protective services and claims that there is abuse going on in the home?

- **What will I do if** my teen refuses to come back home?

Sexual Promiscuity or Teen Pregnancy

- **What will I do if** my religious faith will not allow me to advocate birth control and I know my teen is sexually active?

- **What will I do if** my teen keeps having unprotected sex?

- **What will I do if** my teen gets pregnant or gets a sexually transmitted disease?

- **What will I do if** my son gets a girl pregnant and refuses to accept responsibility or provide financial support?

Alcohol or Drug Abuse

- **What will I do if** I suspect that my teen is using drugs or alcohol?

- **What will I do if** I know that my teen is using drugs or alcohol on a regular basis and he or she refuses to acknowledge it as a problem?

- **What will I do if** my teen refuses to take my drug screen or blow into the BreathScan tube?

- **What will I do if** my teen has a relapse and refuses to change his (or her) lifestyle?

Threats or Acts of Violence

- **What will I do if** my teen threatens to push, shove, or hit someone?

- **What will I do if** my teen actually commits an act of violence like hitting someone or putting a fist through a wall?

- **What will I do if** I call the police or the probation officer and they refuse to back me up or take any action?

- **What will I do if** I call the police or probation office and my teen turns it around and tries to claim that I was the one abusing him (or her)?

Threats of Suicide

- **What will I do if** I place my teen on twenty-four-hour watch with my counselor and he (or she) still verbally threatens to hurt him- or herself?

- **What will I do if** I cannot take the time off necessary to place my teen on a twenty-four-hour watch?

- **What will I do if** my teen tries to commit suicide for real?

- **What will I do if** my teen has to be placed in the hospital for a threat of suicide?

Most of the answers to these questions can be found in Step 5, "Stopping Your Teenager's Seven Aces." The goal in troubleshooting is to rewire your brain so that you can begin to think like your teenager. Here is how one mother won the battle even before the first shot was ever fired.

Picket Signs

Fifteen-year-old Lucius ran away repeatedly. Any time he didn't get his way, he simply walked out the door. When his mother tried to enforce curfew, Lucius would come home when he pleased. Before giving Lucius a copy of the contract, she secretly thought two steps ahead and generated this what-will-I-do-if scenario: What will I do if Lucius refuses to accept his grounding and just walks out?

This is what had caused previous grounding consequence to fail. Lucius would bolt out the door every time his mom tried to enforce grounding. This time, however, Mom formulated the following backup plan.

The mother contacted her pastor and asked him to organize a meeting with several members from the congregation. At this secret meeting, the mother outlined her dilemma and asked for everyone's help if Lucius refused to obey his grounding. Here is what was planned:

- Lucius was able to run away because he had a safe house to stay at. The family at this safe house loved to have Lucius stay over and refused to put him out.
- If Lucius ran away, the congregation would meet with the mother at the church and construct picket signs. The signs would be painted with sayings like:

> My son is being housed illegally by these parents [list
> their names].
> Lucius, come home. Your mommy loves you!!!
> Why are these parents doing this to my son?

- Local television stations also would be called. The parent and church congregation would picket on the public streets or sidewalks in front of the home so as not to violate trespassing laws.

As predicted, Lucius did walk out the door when his mother tried to ground him for missing curfew. However, this time the mother countered with her backup plan. Words cannot accurately describe the shock in Lucius's face when he saw his mom and eight members of the church congregation standing outside his friend's house. The parents were so shocked and embarrassed that they asked Lucius to leave and never return. Without a safe house to run to, Lucius suddenly began to obey the consequence of "grounding."

Develop a Comprehensive Backup Plan

It is now time to develop a set of contingency backup plans for each

Backup Plan

of your what-will-I-do-if scenarios.

This process is like taking out an insurance policy on your teenager. As with insurance, you hate to purchase something you may never use, but if disaster strikes, you're relieved and thankful that you have the insurance in case the unexpected happens. Many people wished they had had flood insurance when Hurricane Andrew hit back in 1992. If Hurricane Teenager hits, you will be glad you had insurance.

As you create your own contingency plans, please remember these rules of thumb:

- **Develop these plans in private.**
  You have two written documents: an ironclad contract that your teen reads and signs and a backup plan that the teen does not see. The rationale is that you may never have to use it. If you show the

teen the contingency plan prematurely, he or she may get angry and retaliate on purpose—or think of ways to outsmart you. There is no reason to awaken a sleeping rattlesnake unless you have to.

■ **Write down your plans.**
When and if your teen makes a countermove to overturn the contract, you will naturally be upset or angry, and your judgment may get clouded. Having a written backup plan hidden in your sock drawer can help you stay calm and effective.

■ **Draw from the top-ten list in Step 2.**
These are the consequences that your teenager cares about. If you've figured out the top two consequences that matter to your teen and have included one of them in the contract, make sure you include the other in your contingency plan.

■ **Be creative and playful whenever possible.**
The mood in your household is likely filled with tension, anger, or frustration. Therefore, try to make your backup plans playful. It will lighten the mood and make you and your teen laugh. For example, as her backup plan, one parent bought a high-powered squirt gun and doused her son if he started screaming and yelling. The son cracked up, the mood changed, and the crisis was over. Many of the consequences in Step 5 are extremely silly and playful. Use them whenever possible.

Two Sample Backup Plans

As you read these and other consequences, please remember my five guidelines under Step 2. Remember that you should administer these tough consequences only if all other attempts have failed and the same behavior happens over and over again.

Backup Plans for Ditching School

Fifteen-year-old Keith refused to go to school. Previous contracts had failed. However, this time the rules and consequences were literally defined and Keith's mom troubleshot everything that could go wrong ahead of time. Here are her backup plans:

- **What will I do if** Keith refuses to go to school with me?

    A. I will go to school anyway but this time wear a ratty pink bathrobe and slippers. I will wear a sign that says "Keith's mommy" with his nude baby picture on it. I will do this again, if Keith refuses to go the next day.

    B. If Keith still refuses, I will start pawning his material items starting with five CDs per day until he starts to go to school. If Keith tries to steal or take my items in retaliation, I will press formal charges with the police.

    C. If Keith starts ditching a second time, I will come to school dressed in a rented clown outfit and ask the mother of Keith's girlfriend to join me. The number of pawned items sold this time will equal the minimum-wage value of the number of hours I had to take off work.

- **What will I do if** my boss will not let me off from work.

    I will tell Keith and the school that I will attend school the first day I am able. The impact will not be as powerful, but it will still have the desired effect. (I will also gently remind my boss that if my teen gets suspended or expelled, it will cost the company more money if I am forced to take off work to attend teacher conferences.)

    These backup plans came in handy. When Keith refused to go to school, the mother calmly got her coat and pulled out Keith's baby pictures to put on her homemade sign. When Keith saw that his mother was serious, he thought better about not going to school and changed his mind. His only request was that Mom leave the baby picture sign at home. Keith never missed school again. The boss supported the mother and she never had to use that part of the backup plan.

I believe Mom's contract with Keith worked for three reasons. First, the mother had a plan if Keith tried to derail the original contract. It also took Keith completely by surprise. Second, Keith cared about his appearance and about looking good in front of his friends. Therefore, the mother picked the right backup consequence for her particular child. Third, the baby picture sign was creative and playful. It was not abusive. Instead, it lightened the mood around a behavior (ditching school) that had been a constant source of conflict.

Backup Plans for Threats or Acts of Violence

Fourteen-year-old Jordan terrorized his mother by threatening to beat up her and his two younger sisters. In the contract, if Jordan threatened violence, Mother and sisters would play the theme song from *Sesame Street* and dance around the table. This was done to make Jordan laugh and lighten the mood in the household. If Jordan committed any acts of violence, the mother and sisters would immediately exit the house without saying a word and call the police to file charges from a neighbor's house.

His mother also developed the following backup plan:

What will I do if Jordan threatens violence even after we dance around the table?

A. We (Mom and daughters) will immediately exit from the situation and go into the safety of Mom's locked bedroom door. The mother will then call several neighborhood males that Jordan respects and would be embarrassed if called. They will come over and read him the riot act.

B. If this still does not work, the neighborhood males will come over and spend the night sleeping in Jordan's room.

What will I do if the police come over and do nothing but file a report?

A. I will immediately call the staff sergeant on duty while the officer is still in my house and demand that charges be filed.

B. If the staff sergeant refuses, I will tell him or her that I will call the local television and newspapers claiming that the police are unwilling to help me stop my teen's violence. I will then call the television station and newspaper.

What will I do if Jordan calls child protective services and falsely claims abuse.

A. I will remain calm and try not to take it personally because I am winning and Jordan is getting desperate with a last-ditch effort to regain lost power.

B. I will cooperate and realize that the CPS worker is just doing his or her job.

C. I will contact our counselor to advocate for us.

D. We will tell Jordan that the contract still stands.

Threats or acts of violence are so serious and potentially life-threatening that troubleshooting must be very detailed and concrete. You need a counselor who can assist you and advocate for your position.

With this kind of detail and preliminary planning, Jordan's problem quickly stopped. Jordan laughed so hard when his mother and sister danced around the living room table to the theme from *Sesame Street* that he could not stay angry. The dancing changed the mood of the household to one of playfulness. The mother told me she did this crazy intervention only because she had a firm backup plan in case her contract failed.

Jordan put his fist through the wall only once. He was so embarrassed to have the neighbors over and the police called that he never committed an act of violence again. In addition, he hadn't realized that he would have to pay for a brand-new door and was shocked to see how much it cost.

Strategy #2: Anticipate What Your Teen Will Do Next

The next step is prevention. It is important to try to anticipate what your teen will do in reaction to your backup plans and role-play it out. For every new action you initiate there will be an equal and opposite reaction by your teenager as a last-ditch effort to regain lost authority. Your teen is used to being in charge. He or she will not go down without a fight.

For example, from the age of seven, fourteen-year-old Maureen threw violent fits to get her way. If Maureen did not like something, she would start cursing and throw plates against the wall. Maureen was very materialistic and loved her antique collection of dolls.

After her parents started pawning her dolls, Maureen became enraged. Her parents, however, were coached to exit and leave the room when she started to throw a temper tantrum. Without an audience, Maureen was forced to yell at the wall and the houseplants. This lost its appeal very quickly.

With my help, the parents were asked to anticipate what Maureen might do next as a last desperate attempt to regain her lost power. The parents thought long and hard and decided that she might try to steal their property. I added that Maureen also might go so far as to intentionally create bruises on her body and then show them to another adult. She would then ask that person to call the police or child protective services. The parents could not believe that this would happen but agreed to put it in as a what-if scenario just in case.

We role-played both scenarios. First, the parents acted out what they would do if they came home and found personal items missing. They would tell Maureen ahead of time that if anything was missing, the police would be called and charges filed immediately. The father and I then played out what to expect if a child protective services worker got involved. I coached the parents on how to respond. Here is a sample of that role play.

> ME: John, when I play the part of the child protection worker, try to stay calm and show them our dated contingency plan that illustrates that we anticipated Maureen would create bruises intentionally to get you to back down. This should help—child protective service workers are starting to understand how some kids are abusing the system.
>
> JOHN: What if they are still skeptical and want to press charges?
>
> ME: It is highly unlikely, but if they do, give me a call right away. I will be there in a flash to back you up and go to the worker's supervisor if we have to.

It was fortunate that we anticipated this move and rehearsed what to do. On her way to school the next day, Maureen intentionally threw herself against a brick wall to bruise her shoulders and arms. Maureen showed her teacher the bruises, and the teacher called child protective services.

As predicted, the CPS worker came to the home. When she read our troubleshooting plan, not only did she close the investigation against the parents, but she congratulated them on a job well done. She informed Maureen that future abuse of the system would not be tolerated. With no more cards to play, Maureen was forced to stop the temper tantrums and change her behavior.

The parents were able to be confident and effective because they had taken the time to anticipate Maureen's countermoves. If they had not done so, they would have taken Maureen's actions as a personal attack rather than a creative way to regain her lost authority. Instead, they were prepared for battle before Maureen's first shot was fired.

Strategy #3: Troubleshoot Underlying Family Problems

Your contracts and backup plans will be severely hindered or end in failure unless you also troubleshoot and solve such family problems as marital discord, different parenting styles, domestic violence, or alcoholism. For example, how effective will you be if you have marital problems and your spouse secretly takes satisfaction in undermining your authority by telling your teen that he or she doesn't have to listen to you? Or how successful will you be if one of you is severely depressed and the other one is secretly fighting a cocaine addiction?

If you are still skeptical, rent and closely watch movies like *Parenthood, American Beauty, American X, Jack the Bear,* and *When a Man Loves a Woman.* In each movie, you will see what happens when a parent tries to discipline children while their unresolved issues still exist. In theory, your contracts and backup plans look good on paper. However, they will break down quickly when unresolved problems rise to the surface. I emphasize this not to blame you; family problems occur in many households. But you need to address your own problems in order to be able to help your teenager.

"My Parents' Pain Is More Than I Can Bear"

Sixteen-year-old Lashon told me privately that she was very concerned about her father's drinking and her mother's depression:

"Dr. Sells, why should I start doing better in school and stop running away? Every time I start doing better, my mom starts to talk about being sad and lonely and starts nagging my dad about his drinking. My dad then says he is going to move out. When I'm bad they worry about me and not each other."

Sure enough, Lashon was right. She started running away again and the mom came to my office no longer looking sad. The father's drinking was no longer discussed. They were too busy being worried about Lashon to have time for their own pain.

Reprinted with special permission of King Feature Syndicate.

People do not live in a vacuum; what affects one person usually affects someone else. Our society emphasizes the individual, but this viewpoint is problematic if you have an out-of-control teenager. Teenagers' problems are heavily influenced by changes in their friends, changes in your parenting styles, and changes in your personal problems, such as marital conflict or alcohol abuse.

Don't get me wrong. I still believe that teenagers are responsible and accountable for their own behavior. If they run away, ditch school, or get disrespectful, they have made the choice to do these things regardless of their family problems.

My point is that your family problems are unintentionally "helping" your teen misbehave. They hinder your ability to stand firm and enforce any contract. For example, if you and your spouse disagree on how to parent, your teenager has no reason *not* to act out.

Where Do You Go from Here?

If what I am saying makes sense, please review the following checklist. If you check off one or more of these areas, I recommend that you seek outside help in the form of a competent counselor. Please check my Web site at *www.difficult.net* or the Appendix for suggestions on how to find the right counselor for you. Please ask your counselor to read this book to make sure you are working together to solve your teens' problems as well as your own.

Note that I divide the list into serious problems and severe problems.

Serious Problems

The distinction between serious and severe problems has to do with the risk of harm. Problems in the "serious" category, such as marital conflict, overly strict parenting, and stepfamily issues, will likely cause your teenager's behaviors to worsen but are not usually life-threatening in and of themselves. (In the "severe" category, things like violence or drug or alcohol addiction can lead to psychological and physical problems, even death.)

If you check two or more "serious" problems, I highly recommend that you seek outside professional help.

Severe Problems

The following problems are listed as "Severe" because of their potential to cause physical and psychological harm. In this environment, behavior problems like ditching school and running away thrive and become more dangerous. You must seek outside professional help because of the risk involved. Until these underlying problems are solved, your teen's out-of-control behavior will surface again and again, no matter what medication is used or what group home he or she is placed in. Seek outside help if you check one or more severe problems.

Checklist of Common Family Problems

Serious Problems

☐ **Marital Conflict**   You and your significant other have marital problems to the point that your kids are taking sides and there is a lot of tension in the air. Problems may include but are not limited to open and bitter fighting in front of the children, quiet fighting behind closed doors, putting the child or teen in the middle, bitter disagreements on how to parent, or arguments over alcohol, drug, or gambling abuse by one or both parents.

☐ **Overstrictness**   One or more adults goes overboard in disciplinary tactics. This includes but is not limited to hitting the teenager to the point of leaving marks, losing your temper quickly, rarely if ever compromising, grounding or other restrictions for months at a time, or threatening to beat, punch, kick, or slap your teen on a consistent basis.

☐ **Outsider Care**   Teenagers who have been institutionalized (in the care of a psychiatric hospital, group home, boot camp, detention facility, or foster care) for more than three months may get hardened inside and put up thick walls. It may be hard for them to attach to others, and they feel very angry and betrayed.

☐ **Lack of Nurturance**   Overall, there is a lack of softness among family members. This includes but is not limited to a lack of special outings between parent and child. Instead, there is constant bickering and arguing. Over time, this leads to severe behavior problems in both children and teenagers.

☐ **Constant Lectures or Sermons**   One or more parents constantly lecture to the point that your teen shuts down and stops communicating on a consistent basis. In turn, the parent-teen communication is characterized as very resentful and bitter.

☐ **Different Parenting Styles**   One adult in the household is much "too soft" and lenient and the other is "too harsh" and strict. This stylistic difference will allow your child or teenager to divide and conquer by playing one parent against the other. Such behavior eventually will cause a severe rift, conflict, or resentment in your relationship or marriage.

☐ **Difficult Divorce**   A difficult divorce occurs when both parents cannot control their disputes and place the children in the middle of their heated arguments, unresolved conflicts, and hostilities. The children are used as pawns when one or both parents tell them negative things about the other or try to recruit them to turn against the other parent. An ex-spouse undermining your authority or taking sides with your teenager is a problem.

☐ **Stepfamily Problems**   In stepfamily problems, the teenager and stepparent are at odds with one another and fail to establish a working relationship. The biological parent is then forced to take sides as the teen's behavioral problems escalate.

☐ **Single Parenting**   Single parenting becomes a problem only if your teenager acts out and you have no resources to stop the problem. For example, if your teen is violent, you are left alone to handle the problem. A good counselor can help you acquire the support and resources you need.

Severe Problems

☐ **Alcohol, Drug, or Gambling Abuse**   One or more adults or siblings shows signs of consistent abuse in one or more of these areas. Such problems can destroy your ability to think clearly and be an effective parent, especially when you have a difficult or out-of-control teen. For example, some adults who drink become verbally and/or physically abusive. If this happens, your teen's problems will only worsen.

☐ **Mental Illness**   One or more adults or siblings who live in the house has a serious mental illness, such as hearing voices, bipolar disorder, schizophrenia, or a severe eating disorder.

☐ **Depression**   One or more adults or siblings living in the household show signs of deep sadness or an inability to get out of bed to complete normal everyday tasks.

☐ **Domestic Violence**   If any of the adults in the household has hit, punched, or slapped another person, this problem must be addressed immediately. This also includes damage to property.

☐ **Sexual Abuse**   There are suspected or actual acts of sexual touching between siblings, between parent and child, between the child and an older teenager, or between the child and an adult outside the family.

☐ **Threats or Acts of Suicide**   Someone in the household threatens or attempts to hurt or kill him- or herself.

If some of these problems describe you or your household, you are not alone; these difficulties are common in families all over the world. The important thing is not to blame yourself or anyone else but to seek help—for your teen's sake if not for your own.

You are the best chance your teenager has to turn the corner. Teenagers tell me all the time: "The more I see my parents try to change and work on their own stuff, the more I want to change too."

Teenagers may not say this openly, but they know that change is not easy for you. They appreciate your efforts. No one likes to be labeled as the sole problem. Even if your teenager contributes 95 percent of the problem, if you work through your own 5 percent, you will see miracles begin to happen.

Step 4

BUTTON PUSHING
Why Your Teen Wins Arguments

Parents who come to my office cannot understand why perfectly good rules and consequences work well with their younger children but not with their out-of-control teenager. The reason is as simple as it is complex. Whenever you try to set down a rule or enforce a consequence, your difficult teenager pushes your buttons and/or you push the teen's. Buttons are words ("I hate you"; "You never let me do anything"; "You're such a disappointment") or actions (a whiny voice, a disgusted look, a lecture) that you or your teen intentionally or unintentionally uses to anger, frustrate, or belittle the other person during an argument. You may use the buttons of lecturing or criticizing on your teen, while your teen may use the buttons of swearing or rolling her eyes on you.

For example, fifteen-year-old Jennifer would yell "I hate you!" every time her parents tried to enforce the rule of not going out on school nights. Her parents got so upset by Jennifer's screams that they would forget about their contract and let her leave. The more often they did this, the more Jennifer used the tactic of screaming "I hate you!" to get her parents to back down.

This is why many contracts fail. They look good on paper, but when you deliver them, your teen pushes your buttons and gets you flustered and out of sorts. You then counter by pushing your teen's buttons. Soon the discussion turns so heated that your rules and consequences fail. You need both gears operating simultaneously. You need an ironclad rule, but you also need to deliver consequences without letting your teenager push your buttons.

To your out-of-control teenager, arguments and confrontations are a game. The object of the game is to be the first person to control the mood or direction of any argument through button-pushing. Whoever can do this first has the most power to control the other player regardless of size or weight.

If you do not believe me, go to a toy store next weekend and just observe. Soon you will see a small child whine to her father that she cannot live without a particular toy. The father says no but the daughter insists, her whines growing louder and more irritating. In response, the father gets visibly upset and frustrated. He makes idle threats, but the daughter only whines louder until she makes a scene. Soon thereafter you see the father at the checkout line buying the toy and the daughter smiling in triumphant victory. The daughter learns the rules of this game early in life—physical size or strength matters little. Whoever controls the mood of the other person through button-pushing is the winner. When we become grown-ups, we seem to forget these rules and how the game is played.

© Lynn Johnston Productions, Inc./Dist. by United Feature Syndicate, Inc.

The goal of Step 4 is to help you regain your lost footing and stop letting your teenager push your buttons. When you are in control of yourself, consequences that never worked before will suddenly be effective.

Strategy #1: Find Your Parental Buttons

Before you can change your methods of confrontation in the next step, you must identify the hot buttons that your teen pushes to make you vulnerable. Everyone is different. A certain word or action may have a profound effect on one parent but hardly faze another. In this step you will figure out what your hot buttons are and then determine which buttons bother your teenager the most.

Ask yourself this question:

> If I had big buttons with names on them all over my body that my teenager pushed to make me feel upset, manipulated, angry, or frustrated, what would they be called or look like?

Write down as many buttons as you can think of. Ask your spouse or significant other to make a list of his or her own buttons. After completing your lists separately, exchange them. Note which buttons were similar and which ones were different. For example, in one family, the mother was vulnerable to a whiny voice, while the stepfather became extremely angry when his stepson said, "You're not my real father; I don't have to obey you."

You may be surprised to recognize the types of buttons that make you feel angry, defensive, guilty, sad, or manipulated. You may smile or laugh when you complete this step because you may have never thought about confrontation this way. If this happens, you may begin to see that your teenager is not as mean or bad-spirited as you once thought. Rather, your difficult teen may simply see confrontation as a game that can be won if he or she can "get under your skin" by applying pressure to your hot buttons.

It may help you to take it less personally if you see how many of your hot buttons turn up on most parents' "top ten" list:

The following specifics about each button explain how teens use it to manipulate you. Understanding that it is a deliberate strategy and not a heartfelt expression of your teen's true feelings may help you see the bigger picture and avoid overreacting.

Top 10
Parent H🔥t Buttons

1. **"You never let me do anything!"**
2. **"You don't love me!"**
3. **"I hate you/this family!"**
4. **Swearing or verbal abuse.**
5. **"You're not my real mother/father; I don't have to listen to you!"**
6. **A disgusted look, improper gesture, or whiny voice.**
7. **"I'm gonna hurt myself/you/others."**
8. **Lying**
9. **"I hate school; I'm not going!"**
10. **"I'm gonna leave or run away."**

1. **"You never let me do anything!"**
This statement invites you to point out specific times that you have allowed your son or daughter to do what he or she wanted. The intended purpose is to steer you away from the real issue at that moment and give your teen an upper hand in the discussion.

2. **"You don't love me."**
Your teen uses this statement to induce guilt and make you question your worth as a parent. Unfortunately, many parents take this bait instead of recognizing that asking your teen to do something has nothing to do with love. You often have to administer medicine that tastes bad but is necessary for their growth. Teenagers use this phase to make you feel guilty and withdraw the punishment.

3. **"I hate you/this family!"**
These statements are meant to get you to lose your temper through personal character attacks. This anger clouds your

thought process and limits your ability to enforce consequences effectively.

4. **Swearing or verbal abuse**

Like saying I hate you, swearing and verbal abuse are designed to distract you from enforcing the contract by making you lose your temper.

5. **"You're not my real mother/father. I don't have to listen to you."**

This statement really unnerves stepparents, but it rarely has anything to do with whether the parent is biological or not. It is merely another tactic by your teen to get the stepparent flustered and angry so that he or she is unable to address the real issue—whether the rule was obeyed.

6. **A disgusted look, improper gesture, or whiny voice**

Body language, gestures, and tone of voice are some of the most powerful nonverbal tools your teenager uses to toy with your emotions. Unfortunately, if you take these barbs personally, it gives your teenager the upper hand. As long as your teen knows these nonverbal cues bother you, he or she will use them again and again.

7. **"I'm gonna kill/hurt/myself/others."**

Teens sometimes use such statements to scare you so that you will back off and lessen the rules and consequences. Teenagers may use threats of violence only as a last resort or if other buttons failed to work. For example, one teenager used this tactic only when swearing failed to make the parent back down. Difficult teenagers often are willing to go to this level if you will get scared and back down.

8. **Lying**

Lying is a pet peeve of most parents, and one that your teens know will get you angry and frustrated so they can win, win, win. You must be able to punish the lying behavior without losing your cool.

9. "I hate school."

Most parents value education. Therefore, this statement invites a lecture on how the teenager is throwing away his or her future. Teenagers normally cannot see past tomorrow, so they often do not see failing school as a problem. However, teens know how important education is to their parents and will use this statement to make them upset and gain the upper hand.

10."I'm gonna leave or run away."

This statement gets parents to back off from exerting their authority because they fear what might happen if their teen runs away or lives on the streets. Teens recognize this fear and often use this statement as another effective tactic to keep you from taking action or enforcing a rule or consequence.

A parent came into my office and told me the following story:

"I Took the Bait—Hook, Line, and Stinker"

Dr. Sells, this button stuff really works. Yesterday, as I was driving home from work, I thought to myself, Be prepared. As soon as you walk through the door, John will immediately ask you if he can spend the night with his best friend even though he's grounded. I then remembered our meeting and how I discovered how good John was at pushing the button "I Hate You" to make me feel guilty and back down. I prepared myself to do battle and not allow this button to throw me off track.

Sure enough, John immediately said, "I hate you" when I reminded him he was grounded. I was doing well and keeping my cool until the unexpected happened. When the "I Hate You' button did not work, John went to the button of "Preying on My Most Vulnerable Area" by refusing to speak to me. It was as if he knew how to set my hook with just the right bait. When I took the bait, he set the hook and reeled me in without a fight. What a stinker!

It is a challenge at first to avoid being hooked by your skillful teenager. You've been taking the bait for many years, and it takes time and practice to break old habits. But once you understand why your teen is really saying those awful things, you can learn to respond with detachment instead of falling for the same old tricks.

Reprinted with special permission of King Feature Syndicate.

Which Buttons Bother You Most?

Now that you know your hot buttons, use the following worksheet to assess how many times a day your teen gets to you. Place a check mark next to the button each time your teenager pushes it. You may have three or more checks next to several different buttons during the course of a day.

Beside each check briefly describe how you reacted (I got angry, I maintained my cool, I yelled back) or how you saw someone else react (spouse, siblings, teacher). This information will be very revealing.

After a week, count up the number of check marks next to each button and note how you and others reacted. A clear pattern should emerge to show you which buttons get to you most.

Through this analysis you also will learn what your teenager's favorite buttons are and how you or others typically respond. With this information, you will be able to find an anti-button-pushing strategy that works for you.

Your Personal Button Baseline			
Day	List the buttons pushed that day	Check each time pushed	Your reaction
Monday			
Tuesday			
Wednesday			
Thursday			
Friday			
Saturday			
Sunday			

Strategy #2: Find Your Teenager's Buttons

After you have discovered your personal hot spots, it is important to uncover the buttons that you knowingly or unknowingly push on your teen. This type of button-pushing can be comparable to putting gasoline on an open fire. The fire is already lit between you and your teenager during an argument. Adding gasoline in the form of lectures or criticizing will quickly make the fire rage out of control.

These buttons do not only lead to heated arguments. Sometimes you will push a button that makes your teenager withdraw, rebel, or seek advice and support from negative influences outside the family. When this happens, communication breaks down between you and your teenager and the misbehavior only gets worse. The following example illustrates how this can happen.

A Self-Fulfilling Prophecy

Fourteen-year-old Joey started having a difficult time in math. The farther behind he got, the more his father lectured and told him, "You will never amount to anything in this world unless you understand numbers. We live in a computer age." The more his dad lectured, the worse Joey felt inside. Joey desperately craved his father's encouragement through this difficult time. Instead, he received only criticism.

Joey soon lost his confidence and started failing his other subjects as well, which made his father criticize him even more. It became a self-fulfilling prophecy. Joey began to become what his father had said he would. Joey started to hate school and ditch all the time. To avoid the embarrassment of not knowing an answer in class, Joey acted out and became the class clown. The teachers were shocked because only one year earlier he had been an A student and a role model to other kids.

Joey started to hang out with other kids who were just like him. He started smoking pot on a regular basis and making fun of kids who used to be his best friends. Today Joey is a career criminal. People tell him all the time that "he has so much unrealized potential." No one can figure out what went wrong, including Joey.

Before you look at my top-eight list of teen buttons, take a few minutes to brainstorm all the possible buttons that you push on your teenager. Doing this will probably be more challenging than locating your own personal hot buttons; it's always harder to put yourself in someone else's shoes. Ask yourself this question:

What would my teenager tell his or her best friend that I do or say during an argument, or within a typical week, that makes him or her feel angry, frustrated, sad, upset, or hurt?

Write down as many buttons as you can think of, ask any other adults in the house to compile their own lists, then compare them to each other and to the following list.

While you may mean well when you use these buttons on your teenager, they don't work the way that you intend; in fact, they often have the opposite effect. The strategies later in the step will provide you with a set of tools that will allow you to throw these buttons in the trash.

Top 8
Teen H🌊t Buttons

1. **Preaching and using clichés**
2. **Talking in chapters**
3. **Labeling**
4. **Futurizing**
5. **Instant problem-solving**
6. **Questioning your teen's restlessness and discontent**
7. **Not tolerating experimental behavior**
8. **Collecting criticisms**

1. **Preaching or using clichés**

   As soon as teenagers hear lectures beginning with clichés like "When I was your age" or "As long as you live under my roof," they instantly go deaf. Your teenager does not want to hear how bad he or she is or how good others are by comparison. Instead, your teen will get angry, walk away, or ignore you. In turn, you will get angry and the argument will escalate. If you do not get rid of this button, your teenager will continue to tune you out or stop coming to you with problems.

2. **Talking in chapters**

   Instead of simply saying "Take out the garbage," have you ever "talked in chapters" and said something like "I have told you for weeks and weeks to take the garbage out. How many times do we have to go through this? I'm sick and tired . . ."? The longer the speech, the greater the risk that it will contain negative statements. If this happens, your teenager will become angry and feel personally attacked. Over time, this can lead to a total breakdown in parent-teen communication.

Reprinted with special permission of King Feature Syndicate.

3. Labeling

Teens hate when parents say they are "always" this way or that way. Labeling can also consist of an attack on your teen's personality or character. This happens if you use terms like "lazy," "worthless," or "pitiful." Long term, this kind of labeling can lead to a self-fulfilling prophecy. Your teenager may come to believe that these labels are true and consciously or unconsciously change behavior to fit the label. For example, thirteen-year-old Steven had stopped doing his homework. When asked why, Steven replied, "Why try? No matter how hard I work my dad still says that I'm lazy. I hear it so often that I began to think that I was just born lazy."

4. Futurizing

This happens when you talk about your teen's future in a negative light. Typical futurizing statements include: "You'll never get into college," "No one will hire you," or "You'll never get a date with that attitude." Futurizing often results in your teen shutting you out and feeling resentment and anger. As with labeling, your teenager may start to act and behave as you predict. In turn, this will seem to confirm your prediction and make you want to futurize more.

5. Instant problem-solving

Teenagers usually do not want instant understanding and problem-solving when they come to you with a problem. When troubled by conflicts, your teenager will feel different from everyone else. Your teen believes that his or her emotions are new, personal, and unique. You mean well by trying to offer instant solutions or by telling your teen that you went through the same thing and it was no big deal. However, your teenager often just needs to feel heard. If not, he or she will seek an understanding ear outside of the family.

6. **Questioning your teen's restlessness and discontent**
Developmentally, adolescence is a time of uncertainty, self-consciousness, moodiness, and suffering. These feelings usually pass over time. Until they do pass, you may only aggravate the situation when you constantly ask questions such as "What is the matter with you?" and "What has suddenly gotten into you?" These are unanswerable questions for a restless and discontented teenager. Even if your teenager would put it into words, he or she probably would not come to you and say, "Look, Mom and Dad, I am torn by conflicting emotions, engulfed by irrational urges, and confused by raging hormones."

7. **Not tolerating experimental behavior**
There is often a fine line between tolerating certain behaviors and not accepting them. Your teenager's changes in clothing and hair-styles are symbolic of his or her normal developmental need to establish a personal identity. If you use all your energy to stop these changes, you might win these battles but lose the war on bigger issues like drugs, alcohol, skipping school, and curfew violations. For example, the single mother of fifteen-year-old April spent the bulk of her time in arguments with her daughter over the type of clothing she wore. April called it her "black period" and preferred to wear all-black clothing. The more the mother protested, the more black April would wear. In the meantime, April was skipping school, too. However, the mother was so busy focusing on April's clothes that she had little time and energy to focus on school.

8. **Collecting criticisms**
Insults and criticisms cut deeper when they come from you. Criticisms can damage your teenager's inner spirit. Unlike physical bruises, they often take years to heal. If you push this button by

pointing out your teen's defects, no one benefits. You collect criticisms when you keep a mental scorecard handy and rehash your teenager's past behavior problems during current arguments. Doing so shuts down all communication. Instead of catching your teen doing something wrong, make a determined effort to catch him or her doing something right.

Retrain Your Mind

Button-pushing, like smoking, can become a bad habit. To change a bad habit, you must retrain your mind. One way to do this is to consciously remind yourself of these buttons when you wake up in the morning and your mind is most receptive to new information. Place both the top-ten list of parental buttons and the top-eight list of teen buttons on your bathroom mirror. If you review it each morning, I guarantee that the frequency of button-pushing will drop dramatically.

Another way is to turn it into a game. One family I worked with started a friendly competition. The parents went out and purchased two big Mason jars and cut holes in the top. They labeled one "Parent Buttons" and the other "Teen Buttons." They transformed the lists into two big poster boards and put both the jars and the posters in a prominent place in the kitchen.

The parents then went to the bank and got thirty $1 coins. Each time the teen pushed a parent button from the posted list, two dollar coins were placed in the parent jar. Each time the parent pushed the teen's button from the posted list, two dollars were placed in the teen's jar. The only rule was that you could not intentionally provoke the other person.

Since it was the parents' money, the teen had to work off any money accumulated in the parents' jar through sweat labor or extra chores (one hour for every dollar, or it could be paid back using the teen's own money).

Both the teen and the parents had so much fun with this game that they kept it going for six straight months! No one wanted to lose the money or the bragging rights.

> **Parent Alert! You Are Not to Blame!**
>
> It is important to note that most of us push our teens' buttons not because we want to hurt them but because we want them to learn from our mistakes. We often think that if we make our points long enough, loud enough, or strong enough, lecturing or criticism eventually will work. Our parents lectured and criticized us as teenagers for the same reason. Their parents did the same thing to them. Unfortunately, these tactics probably did not work on you as a teen, and they will not work on your son or daughter. There's a better way. The button-buster techniques below will enable you to keep your cool during arguments.

Strategy #3: Button-Buster Techniques

Parents frequently tell me, "I like this button-pushing idea. I finally realize how my teenager has skillfully baited me. But now what do I do? Show me how to change the way I argue and still get my teen to do what I ask the first time." I will answer this question by outlining button-buster techniques which will enable you to respond calmly during arguments.

These techniques will act like a shield against button-pushing. When you use these techniques, you are less likely to lose your cool, and your rules and consequences will suddenly work better than ever before.

Separate Button-Pushing from Personal Attacks

Most of the time button-pushing by your teen is not personal. It can feel that way sometimes but more often than not it is your teen just trying to get what they want. As a teen, you probably pushed buttons on your parents. How many of you would pout to push your mother or father's guilt buttons? If they were wise, your parents didn't take it personally; they understood that it was a game and a form of manipulation to get your way.

Any time you say to yourself, "Why is my child doing this to me?" you are taking button-pushing as a personal attack. If this happens, you will become hurt and lose control of your emotions. Over time, you may lose the ability to show tenderness because you will feel so wounded and angry that it poisons your entire relationship.

"I Really Love You, But You Don't Know It"

Sixteen-year-old Lisa never did what she was told. Her father took this defiance very personally and described Lisa as mean, spiteful, and ungrateful. Lisa, however, reported that she was just pushing her father's buttons to get her way. To Lisa, button-pushing had never been personal.

Over the years, Lisa's father stopped giving Lisa hugs or any signs of affection. Lisa reported that it had been years since they had done anything special as father and daughter.

When Lisa tried to explain that she loved her father and was simply pushing his buttons, the father responded by saying that this was just another form of manipulation. The father was unable to separate Lisa's button-pushing tactics from their father-daughter relationship. Over the years, this emotional distance turned into deep resentment on both sides and led to walls of bitterness that could not be torn down.

Of course, years of anger and bitterness usually will not go away overnight. Therefore, you may have to use other button-buster techniques listed here before you can stop taking button-pushing so personally. For example one husband painted a posterboard that read "It's just a game, sweetie." When his son began pushing his wife's buttons, he would step behind his son's back and hold up the poster. She began to laugh and say, "I get it."

Exit and Wait

Since it's difficult to act calmly and in control if you are angry or frustrated, the two most important four-letter words to remember are exit and wait.

The best thing about this technique is that by saying nothing, you never have to take back harsh words or criticisms said in anger. As the adult, you are older and wiser than your teen. Therefore, you are the designated role model. *Exiting* a heated confrontation before you lose your cool and *waiting* until you are calmer to enforce the consequence shows great wisdom on your part.

The old school of parenting states that you must administer a punishment immediately after the misbehavior. This is good advice up to a point. You should give a punishment as quickly as possible—but only if you are in a calm state and it is convenient for you to do so. Otherwise, let your teen wait until you are calm and ready. As you'll see in the following example, this can be an hour, two hours, or a day.

"But Jason Is Late for School"

Sixteen-year-old Jason did not get up in time to go to school. Instead of leaving for work and letting Jason suffer the consequence for missing school, his stepmother began to get into a heated discussion. Jason then had the opportunity to push her buttons by calling her a "bitch" and a "whore." The stepmother got angry and pushed Jason's buttons by labeling him a "troublemaker" and futurizing that he would go to detention for violating probation. With gasoline on the fire from both parties, the argument quickly raged out of control.

The tide of battle did not change until the stepmother learned the art of exiting and waiting to enforce the consequence for ditching on her own terms. Two weeks later Jason was again late for school. This time, however, his stepmother calmly began to head for the door and leave Jason behind. When Jason started to mumble under his breath that she was a "bitch," the stepmother simply turned to Jason and said in a calm voice, "That comment constitutes disrespect and we will deal with that later." The stepmother left for work and called Jason's biological father, as planned. When the father returned home, he backed up his wife by placing Jason in time-out for six hours for disrespect and grounding him for an entire weekend for missing school. In this way, the consequences were enforced at the parents' convenience and when the situation had calmed down. Jason was never late for school again, and the disrespect tapered off.

Here are the steps Jason's mother followed to design and implement the Exit and Wait button buster! Please follow the same mini-steps.

1. Define Get-in-Your-Face Behaviors

Write down all the things that your teenager might do to create a need to exit and wait. These usually center around four areas: (1) disrespect, (2) stubbornly refusing to comply with your requests, (3) threatening to hurt you or others, or (4) committing violent acts such as property damage. I call these get-in-your-face behaviors because your teenager will literally get in your face to try to get you to back down. If you or your teen does not exit and wait, arguments will quickly escalate out of control. By exiting and waiting, you are in effect pouring water on the fire before it gets started.

To do this successfully, you must concretely define what each one of these behaviors looks like. Once these get-in-your-face behaviors have been clearly defined, the need to make decisions under pressure and the risk of losing your cool decreases dramatically. Instead, you can tag each behavior as unacceptable and exit before the argument escalates. You can then administer the consequences for these inappropriate actions at your convenience.

For each behavior, ask yourself this question:

> What would my teenager be doing or saying that would tell me that he or she is being disrespectful, stubbornly refusing to comply, threatening violence, or committing an act of violence . . . ?

Here is a sample list of clearly defined in-your-face behaviors.

Unacceptable Behavior #1: Disrespect

- Swears
- Uses obscene gestures such as giving the finger
- Yells or screams

Unacceptable Behavior #2: Stubborn Refusal

- Refuses to clean his room
- Refuses to stop fighting with brother
- Refuses to obey my requests to stop nagging me

Unacceptable Behavior #3: Threats of Violence

- States the he will hurt you
- States that he will kick the door in
- States that he will punch his sister

Unacceptable Behavior #4: Acts of Violence

- Punches the wall
- Hits his brother
- Pushes you

Now, using the same format, write down your own definitions. Your teen should not be present while you make this list; otherwise he or she will only try to argue and throw you off track. You should show the list to your teen only after you have all the steps firmly in place.

2. Set Up Exit-and-Wait Procedures Beforehand

Once you concretely define the unacceptable behaviors, it is time to write down how you will deliver the exit and wait procedures. For example, are you going to give your teenager a verbal warning to stop arguing before you exit? Or are you going to tell your teenager that he or she is disrespectful and must go to time-out?

Whatever your decision, it is important to let your teenager know ahead of time that the reason you are exiting is not that you don't want to listen. Instead, say that you will exit because:

- The argument is getting too heated to be productive.

- The teen is disrespectful or displaying one of the other three unacceptable behaviors (stubborn refusal, threatening violence, or committing violence); or

■ The teen is using language and a tone of voice that is unacceptable.

Your teen should be clear on these points ahead of time and understand that exiting will prevent the argument from getting out of hand. Most teenagers will see the logic in this reasoning.

Once your teenager commits an unacceptable behavior, you should state:

What you are saying [name the statement] and/or doing [name the behavior] is disrespectful. I am gong to exit now and talk to you later.

You should then exit from the situation as quickly as possible. Pick out your exit place (your bedroom, a walk in the neighborhood, the porch, etc.) beforehand. This spot should be designated as off limits to your teenager during your exit and wait times. If possible, your exit room should have a lock on the inside to ensure privacy.

If your teen follows and enters your designated area, the punishment should be severe. Tell your teen this in advance. You can administer the punishment for following you when you receive backup from a friend or spouse or when you are in a state of calm.

Use the following worksheet to custom-design your own exit-and-wait strategy.

Your Own Exit-and-Wait Strategy

Unacceptable Behaviors

Exit-and-Wait Statement
What you are saying _____ and/or doing _____ is disrespectful. I am going to leave right now and talk to you later.

Your Cooling Off Spot(s)

Punishments or Rewards

What is my planned *punishment* if my teen follows me into my cooling off spot after I exit?

_____

_____

_____

What is my planned *punishment* if my teen continues the unacceptable behavior after I exit from the conflict?

_____

_____

_____

What is the planned *reward* if my teen shows restraint and immediately stops the misbehavior after one warning?

_____

_____

_____

My Backup Supporters

_____

_____

_____

3. "My Teen Needs to Exit, Not Me"

Some parents have told me they are reluctant to exit because their teen may take it as a sign of weakness. Just the opposite is true. Exiting calmly is a quiet but powerful way of demonstrating how serious the situation is while role-modeling self-control. You are controlling the mood of the argument, *not* your teenager.

In addition, if your teen is yelling and swearing, a calm exit takes the wind out of his or her sails. Without an audience, teenagers learn that they cannot get their point across using disrespectful language. Yelling at a houseplant gets old very quickly. Your teenager is now faced with a choice—either change the unacceptable behavior or be ignored.

If your teen is physically stronger than you are or prone to violence, always exit and enforce your consequences when the mood is calm. If possible, enforce the punishment with help or backup in the form of a spouse, a significant other, or a friend, neighbor, or minister.

Depending on your teen, sometimes it is a good option to let him or her take a time-out and exit from the argument. Work this out ahead of time with the teen following ground rules:

- You—*not* your teenager—should determine when your son or daughter needs to take a time-out. As the parent, you are responsible for determining the mood and direction of any argument, not your teen. If teenagers are allowed to exit at will, they may abuse this privilege by leaving the discussion anytime it is not going as they hoped.

- Explain to your teenager beforehand that time-outs are mandatory, not optional, when the discussion becomes too heated. If your teenager refuses to go into time-out, you will still exit. If you have to exit, there will be consequences after both parties have cooled off.

- Predetermine the teenager's cooling-off spot and the length of time he or she will be required to stay in time-out. The teen's bedroom is *not* the best place for time-outs; usually bedrooms contain too many sources of entertainment.

4. Use Role-Plays to Pull It All Together

The final step is for you and your teen to practice or role-play each of the exit-and-wait steps. I call these dry runs or dress rehearsals. Like a play, if you practice before opening night, you can work out the kinks or trouble spots beforehand. You do this to prevent anything from going wrong when the real-life performance takes place.

Backup Plan

To conduct a dress rehearsal, pick out one of the unacceptable behaviors on your list. Ask your teen to pretend to have the problem. For example, if the behavior is disrespect, ask your teen to pretend to yell at you. Then pretend to exit and wait or make your teenager exit, if that is your predetermined arrangement.

The rule of thumb is that anyone in the family can raise a hand to critique the other's performance. The critiques should only consist of positive suggestions. You may have to go through several takes until the dress rehearsal is a success. Please try these role plays. You will be surprised by how much fun they can be for the whole family.

In some cases, your teen will be particularly stubborn and unwilling to participate. He or she may start yelling as soon as you try to set down a new rule. In these cases, I recommend that you rehearse with your spouse, significant other, best friend, or counselor, as Monica's parents did in the following example:

"It's Easier to Be Calm When My Parents Stay Calm"

Fourteen-year-old Monica was particularly skillful at pushing her parents' buttons whenever they tried to enforce a rule. When this happened, Monica would swear, call her parents names, and cry uncontrollably. The mother would give in, while the father became extremely angry.

Because of the severity of the problem, I decided to go through a number of role-plays with the parents before Monica came back into the room. I played the part of Monica while the parents practiced their exit and wait strategy as soon as the girl started to yell. We went through three dress rehearsals until both parents felt battle ready. Monica was then asked back into the room. As predicted, she began to scream and cry as soon as her parents told her she was grounded for missing school.

Instead of giving in this time, however, her mother told her in a firm voice to stop. When Monica refused, her mother stated:

> "Yelling and talking to me in that tone of voice is not respectful, so I'm going to leave right now and talk to you later."

After this, her mother quickly exited, and Monica sat back, speechless and stunned. She calmed down. Over the next week, both parents experimented with this technique, and Monica stopped her temper tantrums. Later in treatment, I asked Monica why she had suddenly stopped. She replied that she did not like to be ignored. Her parents were also calmer—which made it easier for her to be calmer too.

Stay Short and to the Point

Lecturing or offering long explanations only gives your teenager a chance to push more buttons. You also run the risk of pushing your teen's buttons and throwing more gasoline on the fire. Think of it this way: The longer you spend arguing or trying to justify your actions, the greater the chance that you will regress to your teenager's chronological age.

The rule of thumb is that for every two minutes you stay in an argument with your teen, deduct five years from your present age. For example, a parent who is forty years old automatically regresses to age twenty after only ten minutes of arguing. After a while, it will be difficult to determine who is the parent and who is the child.

Staying short and to the point is extremely difficult for many parents. Many feel that they owe teens an explanation or a justification for their actions.

Explanations are helpful up to a point. If your teenager continues to argue even after you try to explain, it is time to stop. No explanation will ever be good enough. You do not owe your teenager an explanation. One parent posted this familiar saying on their refrigerator door: "What part of the word 'no' don't you understand?"

Before you implement this strategy, take a few moments to tell your teen about how you will use staying short and to the point in the future. Again, you're doing this not to ignore your teen but to avoid button-pushing and heated discussions.

Here is a sample statement that you can use:

From now on, I refuse to argue or bicker with you. If you break our contract, I will simply remind you what the punishment is and enforce the rule instead of offering long explanations. It will be short, sweet, and to the point. I will try to keep these conversations to less than two minutes. Arguing will only cause us to push each other's buttons and create more hard feelings between one another. If you break a rule that is not on the contract or argue end-lessly, I will exit quickly and tell you that I am going to my cave to think about what to do. I do this to give me time to gather my thoughts. You are not allowed to follow me into my cave.

When I ask teens "Would you rather have a lecture explaining the consequence or just get the consequence?" what do you think they overwhelmingly answered. You guessed it. Teens would rather just receive the consequence without the lecture. Something to think about.

Backup Plan

As with the exit-and-wait strategy, I recommend that you and your teenager or spouse rehearse the short-and-to-the-point strategy. Pick out an unaccept-able behavior and ask your teen to pretend to argue with you. If your teen will not play along, ask your spouse to play your teen.

Ask the person playing your teen to push your buttons and demand an explanation as to "why" you are grounding him or her, not letting him or her go to a party, taking the phone away—what-ever. The teen should try to get the parent to stay in the argument as long as possible. If your age starts to drop, have someone hold flash cards up that say:

- You Are Now at 25 Years Old.

- You Are Now Rapidly Dropping to 20 Years Old.

- You Are Now the Same Age as Your Teenager.

- You Have Now Dropped Below Your Teen's Age.

These cards will remind you in a playful way that the discussion is getting too hot. Your teen is beginning to gain the upper hand by making you lose control of your emotions and controlling the direc-tion of the argument. Then pause the role-play to get feedback from everyone as to what you can do better the next time. Keep repeating the role-play until you have mastered this new strategy.

Reflectors

Use reflectors to help ensure success with exit-and-wait and short-and-to-the-point techniques. Reflectors are words or phrases like "nevertheless," "regardless," "that is the rule," or "no exception." These words are called "reflectors" because they help you reflect or direct the conversation back to the issue at hand.

Whenever your teenager tries to push your buttons to take you off track, you can simply say "Regardless, the rule still stands," or "Nevertheless, you cannot go to your friend's house." Each of these statements automatically brings you teenager back to the real issue, whether he or she obeyed or broke your rule or not. This is the bottom line. Everything else is just a smokescreen.

For example, suppose your daughter tries to change the rule of no phone use after 9:00 P.M. Instead of arguing the matter, you would simply say *"The rule is 9:00 P.M., no exceptions."* Your daughter may refuse to accept this answer and try to bait you by saying "You never let me use the phone when I want." When this happens, you can counter by saying *"Nevertheless,* you may not use the phone after 9:00 P.M." In each situation, reflectors will help you return the conversation back to the real issue: Phone time will not be extended.

Billy's story provides a good example of how to use reflectors.

"That's Not Enough of an Explanation"

Thirteen-year-old Billy was an expert at pushing his father's buttons and taking him off track. Billy would wait for the father's most vulnerable moment—walking in the door after a long day at work. Billy would then relentlessly ask his father for an extension on his curfew.

The father wanted to stay short and to the point and not give in. However, he needed a reflector shield to protect him from getting drawn into long explanations. The following is a brief transcript of how the father used reflectors to keep the conversation on track and avoid button-pushing. The reflectors are italicized.

BILLY: I want to go out with my friends to a concert next week, so I need to extend my curfew from 11:00 P.M. to 2:00 A.M.

FATHER: *The rule is 11:00 P.M.—no exceptions. (Rather than try to argue with Billy, the father used reflectors of "the rule is" and "no exceptions" to let Billy know immediately that there would be no negotiation on this rule.)*

BILLY: Why not? That's not enough of an explanation! You never let me do anything! *(Here Billy was still trying to test the waters by seeing if his father would take the bait and explain times when he did allow Billy to do things he wanted.)*

FATHER: *Nevertheless,* you may not go. *(The father does not take the bait but uses the deflector of "nevertheless" to stay focused and maintain his authority.)*

BILLY: I hate you! *(Billy refuses to give up and shifts his tactics to personal attacks.)*

FATHER: I hear that you are angry, but *regardless,* the rule still stands as written in the contract. *(The parent acknowledges that Billy is angry but uses the reflector of "regardless" to return the discussion back to the issue at hand.)*

Sometimes the best reflector is to say nothing at all. Most of the time, your teen knows what to do. They simply want to engage you in an argument to throw you off track or back down. You can say something like, "You know what to do, there is no need for further discussion." You can then exit and wait.

As with the other techniques, I recommend that you and your teenager role-play the reflector strategy. Pick out an unacceptable behavior and ask your teen to pretend to argue with you and try to take you off track. Practice using the reflector statements until they become second nature to you. Again, if your teen will not play along, ask your spouse or friend to play the part of your teen. Evaluate your performance and modify this strategy as needed.

Secret Signals

When your buttons are pushed, you do not have to face these challenges alone. If a spouse or significant other is living with you, he or she can help. Together you can develop a set of secret signs to alert one another that your teen is skillfully pushing your buttons or that it is time to exit and wait. For example, one parent held up the word "Stop" on a sign, while another used a cutting motion across the throat as a sign to exit and wait.

Custom-design your signals and keep them secret from your teen, so he or she stays off balance and guessing. These signs are for you, *not* your teenager. If he or she finds out, that's OK, but don't volunteer the information. Some families I worked with used the following signs:

- Every time the mother was losing control, the father walked over without saying a word and kissed her on the cheek to remind her to calm down.

- One mother pretended to cast out a fishing line and reel in a big fish as a signal to the other parent that he was being hooked like a fish by the son.

- When one father wanted to encourage his wife to get firmer with their daughter, he drew a line in the air with one finger, to remind her to "draw the line" and stop giving in to the daughter.

- In another family, since the father took the button-pushing as a personal attack, his wife would start to hopscotch on the floor to remind him that it was just a game.

Use any sign you want, but make sure it's lighthearted and playful. It should never signal criticism or a lack of support. One husband read about this technique and thought that a good signal would be a frustrated sigh. The husband never bothered to ask his wife if his sign signaled support or criticism. He was surprised when she started to cry. It was not until the husband began using a hug as a sign that she felt supported and could change her parenting style.

If you are a single parent or have an unsupportive spouse, modify this approach by creating secret signs with the oldest of your children who is not having the behavior problem. That child could give you a sign each time your buttons are being pushed or the conversation is getting overheated. However, only use this as a last resort. You do not want to risk creating more bad feeling between siblings.

For example, one mother asked her twelve-year-old son to give her a thumbs down each time his brother Derrick was whining and getting her off track. The mother then used the strategy of reflectors to regroup.

Speaking in One Parental Voice

Teenagers will often take advantage of the softer or less consistent parent. When the stronger parent is gone, the teen takes the opportunity to persuade the more lenient parent to overturn existing punishments or award special privileges. This tactic is successful if both parents fail to work together as a team or have different parenting philosophies. See how fourteen-year-old Nancy exploits this inconsistency to divide and conquer her parents.

"I Love to Play One Parent Against the Other"

Nancy's parents had radically different parenting philosophies. The mother felt that the father was too strict and the father felt that the mother was too soft. This allowed Nancy to play one parent against the other. When Nancy wanted something like extended curfew time, she would go to her mother when the father was not around. The mother would say yes without consulting the father. This only made the father angry. Both parents would then blame the other, and their marital relationship suffered. When this happened, Nancy began to take her mother's side against the father. The mother was more than happy to have an ally. Nancy could then manipulate the situation even more.

Over time, the father observed this special relationship and became even more resentful. He began to openly criticize his wife for giving in to the daughter, thus reinforcing the wife's view that he was too strict and that Nancy deserved special treatment. Nancy would sit in the corner and smile as this real-life drama unfolded. Nancy realized that as long as her parents disagreed, she could push buttons all day long and get exactly what she wanted.

You do not have to live in the same household for the divide-and-conquer tactic to work. If you are divorced, your teenager can simply pick up the phone and tell your ex-spouse all kinds of lies to get them to side with him or her. If you are already angry with each other over the divorce, your ex will not need much convincing.

If your teen does this, you and your ex will be unable to work together as a team and subsequently will undermine each other's authority. Your teenager may even threaten to move out of the house to live with the other parent to scare you into submission. (If this is the situation in your house, please see the section on difficult divorces entitled "A Final Step" for possible solutions.)

To start working together as a team, you and the other parent should identify your individual parenting philosophies. Write down your answers to the following questions. Do not compare answers until after you have answered each question on your own.

1. What is the typical punishment you use when your teenager breaks a rule?
2. On a scale of 1 to 10 (1 = not consistent at all; 10 = consistent 100 percent of the time), rate how consistent you are as a parent.
3. On a scale of 1 to 10 (1 = no similarities in your parenting styles; 10 = identical parenting styles), how similar and consistent is your parenting style with that of your spouse or significant other?

If your answers are significantly different, it is time to make a list on the areas in which you will compromise and those that you will agree to disagree. Depending on the degree of disagreement, you may want to seek a counselor to help you with this list and keep you focused on the bigger issue: the well-being of your teenager.

If you agree to disagree, you must lay out the ground rules of how, when, and where you will use one parenting philosophy over another. You may agree to flip a coin or alternate between punish-ments (e.g., one week we try your way, the next week we try mine) until you find out which style works better than the other or that both styles work equally well. Please do this with the help of your coun-selor.

Finally, you must agree that you will not allow one another to be cornered. If your teenager tries to corner you by demanding an answer or trying to change your mind, you must agree to wait until the other spouse returns or you can contact him or her by phone to make the decision together.

Parents have told me that the closed door policy works best. Instead of openly disagreeing in front of their teen or within earshot, they take their differences behind a locked bedroom door. For exam-ple, if one parent observes something she doesn't agree with, she asks to speak to the husband in private. After negotiation, both of you should emerge as one voice. When you present a united front on a regular basis, your teen's ability to manipulate you through button-pushing will become less and less.

Step 5

STOPPING YOUR TEENAGER'S SEVEN ACES

Disrespect, Truancy, Running Away, Teen Pregnancy, Alcohol or Drug Abuse, Violence, and Suicide Threats

The best poker players seem to have a hidden ace up their sleeves to defeat their opponents just when they appear to be winning. In the same way, your difficult teenager will use the seven aces—disrespect, truancy/poor school performance, running away, teen pregnancy, alcohol or drug abuse, violence, or suicide threats—to defeat you and make you back down. You get defeated because each of these "aces" causes traditional rules and consequences to fail. For example, if you attempt to ground your teenager for disrespect, he or she can use the "ace" of running away to leave the house as soon as your back is turned or you go to sleep.

In addition, aces like suicide threats, violence, or drug abuse are potentially deadly or risk physical harm to you or others. You often back down out of fear—fear that if you push too hard, your teen might commit suicide, become violent toward others, or suffer a drug overdose and die. Teens understand these fears and the limits of traditional consequences better than you do. These seven aces cause parent abuse or teen terrorism and are the single biggest reasons why you are unable to keep your authority long enough to stop your son or daughter's extreme behaviors.

To stop these seven aces, you must come up with consequences that are so bitter tasting to teens that they would rather give up the payoff of the ace (total freedom, special attention, controlling your household) than continue to suffer the punishment.

The goal of this step is to provide you with a menu of consequences that your teenager will care about. I have assembled the best consequences that I could find to help you stop each ace.

Each ace has its own set of consequences to choose from. For example, under the ace of truancy, you will see a consequence called "Working Collaboratively with Your Teen's School" along with a set of step-by-step instructions.

Some of the consequences are exclusively designed to stop one ace while others can be modified to work for several different aces. For example, you can use the pawn broker strategy to stop running away; you can also modify it to stop disrespect, truancy, and threats or acts of violence.

A Hierarchy of Aces

The aces presented go from least to most extreme. For example, a disrespectful teen is much less dangerous than one who tries to commit suicide. This progression of aces can mirror what goes on in the mind of an out-of-control teenager. Here is an example of what some teens tell themselves.

> Level 1. Disrespect. "I want to go to this party and I don't like to be told what to do. If they tell me something I don't want to hear, I am going to start cussing or rolling my eyes. This will push their hot buttons and get

them upset. If they get upset, there is a good chance that they will get frustrated and back down. I will win."

Level 2. Truancy or Failing School. "Cussing does not seem to be working. It doesn't faze her and she won't back down. I think I need to up the ante a bit. She values my education a lot. It would drive her crazy if I start to ditch school or come home with straight Fs."

Level 3. Running Away. "At first, the ditching school and failing grades stuff was working great. But then my mom started talking to the teachers on a regular basis and decided to go to school with me if I ditched. She even came to school in curlers and a ratty bathrobe. That was way too embarrassing. So now I have to up the ante again."

Level 4. Teen Pregnancy. "My mom is worried that I am not using protection and that I will get pregnant. When I am running away and out all night, she worries even more. She is so scared that she is afraid to stand up to me for fear that I might have unprotected sex or get pregnant. Her fears allow me to do what I want."

Level 5. Alcohol or Drug Abuse. "While I am running away and having unprotected sex, I am also smoking pot on a regular basis. Now my mom does not know what to do or where to turn. She handled the disrespect and ditching school just fine, but now she seems overwhelmed. It is just too much for her to handle."

Level 6. Threats or Acts of Violence. "Something happened. Mom must have gotten a second wind or something. She videotaped me smoking pot and turned it over to the police. She is also requiring that I get a birth control shot once every three months. I must act fast. I threatened her with a knife the other day, and it seemed to do the trick. She is scared again and has backed down."

Level 7. Threats of Suicide. "The threats-of-violence thing was working great until Mom started to walk away, call the police, and press charges against me. I have now decided to throw down the gauntlet. A friend of mine went into a mental hospital for depression. She told me that if I threaten to kill myself, everyone gets scared and backs off. I think I will try this tomorrow."

This teen has what I affectionately call "multiple ace disorder." Most teens will not go to such great lengths to defeat their parents. However, many teens will quickly go from one level to the next if their current ace is not working. These are not bad kids; they just are extremely creative and skillful in getting you to back down. One teen I worked with never gave threats of violence a second thought until his parents skillfully shut down his running-away ace.

Some teens genuinely are in serious emotional pain and depression. When I talk about the ace of suicide, I provide a checklist of warning signs and recommendations to determine if your teen has severe psychological problems. If that is the case, you *must* seek professional help.

What can you do to stop the seven aces of a teen who doesn't have a serious psychological problem but is seriously out of control? Below is an overview of some of the consequences that can be amazingly effective.

| Sample Consequences to Stop Your Teen's Seven Aces

The Stealth Bomber	Learn how to tap into your teen's weakness of being extremely materialistic and turn it into your advantage. Your teenager may choose to stop ditching school, running away, or committing threats or acts of violence if his or her material possessions are pawned or if you post a "wanted poster" with an unflagging picture all over school.
The Prime Suspect	Learn how to stop alcohol and drug use cold through careful monitoring using home drug kits and using home camcorders to catch them in the act.

Working with the School System	Learn how to work collaboratively with school personnel and receive their help to stop your teenager's truancy or poor school performance.
The Old MacDonald Strategy	Learn how being silly and playful will catch your teenager off guard and make it extremely difficult to stay disrespectful.
Shutting Down Safe Houses	Learn how to find the homes of peers that harbor your teenager when he or she runs away and create ways to prevent your teen from running to these homes again.
Attending School Together	Learn how to tap into your teenager's need to look "cool" in front of friends and how going to school in fuzzy slippers and curlers will make him or her think twice about ditching school ever again.
24-Hour Watch Strategy	Learn how to stop the threat of suicide by safely watching your teenager 24 hours a day until the danger has passed.
5 Levels of Teen Aggression	Learn how your teen can go from Level 1, Whining and Complaining, to Level 5, Acts of Violence, very quickly and how to stop the teen at each level.
A Town Meeting	Learn how to conduct a special town meeting to recruit the help and support of family, friends, and neighbors.
Hierarchy of Consequences	Learn how to use traditional consequences like grounding in a creative but different way to stop disrespectful behavior.

Some Warnings Before You Begin

■ *For every consequence you put into place, there will be an equal reaction by your teenager. Bottom line: It will get worse before it gets better.*

This is normal and to be expected. Teens immediately sense that you have "struck gold" and finally come across a set of consequences powerful enough to shut down their biggest aces. Since they are not likely to give up control of the household without a fight, they may increase the intensity of their current ace, resurrect an old ace, or come up with a new one.

■ *If I recommend that you seek an outside counselor before implementing an extreme consequence, please follow my recommendations.*

I will clearly tell you which consequences require an outside counselor and under what circumstances. Once again, when you see this icon, it means that you need to seek an outside counselor for guidance, or you may risk harm to both yourself and your teenager.

■ *Use extreme consequences only after lesser consequences have failed and the misbehaviors are happening over and over again.*

In battle, you resort to your biggest weapons only if the lesser ones fail. Otherwise, you have no backup in case of emergency and lose any leverage you might have. In the same way, you must use your big guns solely as a last resort. I will make it very clear which consequences are extreme and when and how to use them effectively. As discussed earlier, you should make sure that the misbehavior is not just a one-time thing. As a teen, we all did crazy things, and overreacting to an isolated incident can make things worse.

- *Don't back down, no matter how difficult and tempting it is.*
  Just as an army that is on the brink of defeat will use the last of
  its arsenal in a final effort to defeat the enemy, your teen's negative reaction actually means that you are turning the tide and
  winning the war. But all will be lost if you waver.

- *Some of the consequences may seem controversial when
  you first read them.*
  Parents with seriously out-of-control teens need practical solutions when everything else fails. You need tough and very creative consequences when your teen's behaviors, such as suicide
  or violence, are potentially dangerous.

- *Address family problems for long-term success.*
  As I discussed at the end of the troubleshooting step, any success will be short-lived if there are unresolved problems such
  as marital discord, conflicting parenting styles, drug or alcohol
  problems, domestic violence, sexual abuse, or depression.
  Unless these issues are addressed and solved, your teen will
  relapse and go back to old behaviors. The behaviors may even
  get worse the second time around. Both you and your teen may
  get discouraged, frustrated, and lose hope. Once hope is gone,
  despair sets in, and your teen feels less motivated than ever to
  improve. Therefore, if you have family problems, please seek
  out a qualified counselor to solve them at the same time you are
  helping your teenager.

ACE #1: DISRESPECT

What most parents want is what Aretha Franklin sings: a little R-e-s-p-e-c-t. The number-one complaint that I hear from parents every day involves such disrespectful behavior as teens' rolling their eyes, talking under their breath, refusing to obey, and swearing. Not only does disrespect drive parents crazy, but if it is not stopped, it can lead to more serious problems. For example, a disrespectful teen may escalate into one who threatens to punch your lights out. Disrespect also may make *you* lose your cool by screaming or even pushing your teen against the wall.

No one wants to be treated with disrespect; it may even be the primary reason for revenge and bitterness between two people. Parents often tell me that disrespect must stop before they will even consider an act of nurturance or softness toward their teen. Use the following strategies to clearly define for your teen what "disrespect" means and what will happen if things go on this way.

Strategy #1: Clearly Define Disrespect

Start by clearly defining what you mean by disrespect. What might be disrespectful in one household may not be in yours. A common pitfall is to simply tell your teen "From this point on, there will be no more disrespect." This definition is too broad and open to interpretation, as you'll see in the following example.

"Telling You No Was Not Disrespectful"

Thirteen-year-old Jackie did not like to follow rules. When her mom asked her to do something like homework or clean her room, the first answer was usually no. Jackie also liked to roll her eyes and mumble under her breath.

Each of these behaviors irritated her mother to no end. One day the mother decided to take action and wrote up a contract. At the top it read "No More Disrespect." At the bottom it stated that the consequence would be no phone use for that day.

After dinner that evening, the mother asked Jackie to wash the dishes. Jackie crossed her arms, rolled her eyes, and said, "No." Her mother immediately pointed to the no-disrespect contract posted on the refrigerator and told Jackie that she had just lost all phone privileges for the evening. Jackie stormed out of her chair screaming that saying no was not disrespectful. Saying "no" was not written on the contract. A bitter argument then ensued over the definition of respect.

Mom learned her lesson. The next day when Jackie woke up, she saw the following version of the disrespect contract posted on the refrigerator:

D-I-S-R-E-S-P-E-C-T
The New & Improved Definition

Jackie,

I will now literally and exhaustively define the term "disrespect."

You will be considered disrespectful if you do any of the following things:

1. Use the word "no" or refuse to do what I ask the first time—like clean your room, wash the dishes, feed the cat, etc.
2. Swear, yell, or use gestures like rolling your eyes or mumbling under your breath.
3. Mimic me in an unflattering manner.
4. Follow me all over the house nagging me when you don't get your way.
5. Tell a lie (that I can prove is a lie).

As your mother, I reserve the right to add to this list at any time if you come up with new disrespectful behaviors in the future.

Love, Mom

The definition of disrespect was so clear that Jackie no longer had room to haggle over the definition of respect.

To come up with a similar definition of your own, write down your answers to the following question: What does my teen do or say that is disrespectful or displays a bad attitude? Like Jackie's mother, use those answers to come up with a clear definition of disrespect that starts "You will be considered disrespectful if you do any of the following things," then lists the behavior you want to change. (It's also a good idea to add a note at the end reserving your right to add to this list.)

Strategy #2: Choose Your Battles Wisely

Did you know that research shows that most parents ask their children or teenagers to comply with their requests an average of 50 times per day, or 350 times per week? Anyone—even adults without behavior problems—would probably balk at following so many orders.

Therefore, it is essential to choose your battles wisely. If you try to take a stand and punish every single disrespectful act or gesture, both you and your teenager will be overwhelmed.

I recommend that you start out with the two or three disrespectful behaviors that bother you the most. You can always add to this list or subtract from it when your teen stops swearing or giving you the finger. It's important to conserve your energy for the big things rather than sweating the small stuff. Please remember this principle: *The more you try to control, the less control you have.*

If you try to control other people, it is human nature for them to rebel. They will stubbornly resist the more you persist. This is especially true for teenagers: The more you try to control every little thing they do, the more often they will become disrespectful.

It took ingenuity to overcome this dilemma in the case of Patrick and his mother.

"My Mom, the Control Freak"

Sixteen-year-old Patrick told me that he constantly felt controlled by his mom. Ever since his dad died suddenly in a motorcycle accident five years ago, his mom was constantly on him. From the moment he walked in the door, she pounced.

Mom's single biggest complaint was Patrick's "total disrespect." He would constantly say "F**k you," walk out when she was talking, and get in her face. Recently it had gotten so bad that Patrick had actually shoved her into the wall.

Mom admitted that she was "a bit controlling" but that Patrick had to make the first move by being respectful and pulling his grades up. Patrick told me that he would agree to these terms but only if Mom made the first move and stopped controlling. They were at a standstill with neither one agreeing to make the first move.

To break this stalemate, I had to get creative. They both had to make a first move at the same time. Based on this objective, Mom and Patrick created the following contract around disrespect.

Mom's Agreement

I will agree to stop nagging and showing disrespect in the following way:

a. I will not nag Patrick about his homework. Instead, he will present a weekly progress report to me on Friday no later than 3 P.M.
b. I will not say a word about his daily chores of cleaning his bedroom and the bathroom. Instead, I will merely check to see if they are completed by 5 P.M.
c. I will refrain from calling my son names and putting him down through statements like "You are good for nothing," "lazy," "a disappointment," and "worthless."

Consequence

A violation of either a, b, or c will result in an automatic fine of $10.00 out of my own pocket. This money will be placed in a big fine jar on the kitchen table for all to look at and see. Patrick will receive this money on Friday.

Patrick's Agreement

I will agree to stop showing disrespect to my mom in the following way:

a. I will show respect to my mom by bringing the weekly progress report on Friday and lifting my percentage average for every class by at least 10 percentage points until I attain at least a C average or better. I cannot fall below a C average.

b. I will show respect to my mom by cleaning my bedroom and bathroom without being asked no later than 4:59 P.M. each day.

c. I will show respect for my mom by not swearing, getting in her face, pushing or shoving, or walking out on her in the middle of a sentence.

Consequences

A violation of a) will result in the removal of the car until Mom receives a weekly progress report that shows a 10 percent rise in each and every subject. The distributor cap will be removed from the car to make it undriveable and ensure compliance.

A violation of b) will result in one weekend of grounding for each night either one or both chores are not completed by 5:00 P.M. EST.

A violation of c) will result in the loss of the car for an entire weekend. If the car has already been removed for school reasons, you will be fined $10.00 for each incident. If you do not have the money, personal items will be sold or you can pay the fine through extra chores. If you are violent on any level, the police will be called and charges filed.

To stop disrespect, sometimes both parent and teen have to change at the same time. If you are not respectful, why should your teen have to change when you don't? It becomes hypocritical. In Patrick's case, the contract was written so that both Mom and he had to change simultaneously. Both had something to lose if they refused.

Mom chose her battles wisely. She kept her focus on the top three behaviors that she felt were disrespectful. She also had much to lose if she started to control or nag Patrick. Ten dollars per incident was a lot of money. She also dreaded the thought of looking at a jar filled with her hard-earned money each day. For Patrick, the stakes for disrespect were just as high. He dreaded riding the bus or losing any weekend time. He also did not want to pay back any fine money.

Old habits like control and disrespect are hard to break. It takes strong leverage to make someone want to stop. In Patrick's family that leverage was money, freedom, and transportation. In your family it may be something else. Finding the right leverage is the key ingredient.

Strategy #3: Two Can Play at That Game

This strategy is fun for parents and will definitely catch your teen off guard. It goes like this: If your teenager is disrespectful to you, why can't you be playfully disrespectful back?

You can do this by being disrespectful to teens when their friends are over or when they are watching television, talking on the phone, or trying to be alone in their room. It works especially well when your teen's boyfriend or girlfriend can see or hear you.

As teens ourselves, we all wanted to look cool in front of our dates and would be mortified if our parents embarrassed us. Are you starting to get the picture? Here are some tactics other parents have used:

- **The Cross Dresser** When Rob had his girlfriend over, the father immediately went into his wife's closet and put on one of her dresses over his clothes even though they did not fit. He also put on a wig, which he had bought for the occasion, and applied some lipstick. He then went up to Rob in front of his girlfriend and kissed him on the forehead. The son was horrified and embarrassed. The father told the girlfriend that he did this because Rob was so disrespectful. He then got down on his knees and begged the girlfriend to talk some sense into him.

- **The Loudmouth** The daughter had all her friends over to watch a movie. Throughout the movie, Mom sat in front of the television in a ratty robe and hair curlers. She kept talking loudly over the movie. When the girls went into another room, she followed. She then stuffed her face with popcorn and started to drool all over herself.

- **The Picket Sign** In one household, the disrespect got so bad that the single-parent mom had to do something drastic. She got together with another girlfriend in the neighborhood and made picket signs. They blew up a picture of her son and plastered it on the sign. Underneath the picture it read "This is my son Jeff P. He refuses to treat me with R-E-S-P-E-C-T so I am on strike. Will you talk some sense into him for me!" The mother and her friend then picketed up and down the street in front of the school and at the places the boy hung out. In the background, they brought a tape player that blasted out over and over again Aretha Franklin's song "Respect." It was the talk of the school, and Jeff was relentlessly teased all day.

- **Phone Interruptus** Monica loved to talk on the phone. For a solid week, Monica's mom got on the phone every time she was on to sing, talk to her friends about world events, or make strange animal noises. The girl had no privacy.

Reprinted with special permission of King Feature Syndicate.

In each of these examples, it was amazing at how quickly the teens wanted to call a truce on disrespect. Some of the teens even admitted that until the shoe was on the other foot, they had no idea how disrespect could be so irritating. They did not like the embarrassment or how it made them feel.

Strategy #4: A Hierarchy of Consequences

See Counselor for Direction!

To extinguish a behavior like disrespect, you may have to get tougher each time your teen commits a disrespectful act in a single day. This is called a hierarchy of consequences. For example, the mom and dad of seventeen-year-old Roby used the following hierarchy of consequences on their contract:

First Offense: Grounding the next weekend day (no phone, TV, friends)

Second Offense: Grounding another weekend day (no phone, TV, friends)

Third Offense: Fine or loss of car or any transportation for next day and the weekend day

Roby was told ahead of time that, for every complete day he was respectful and followed directions, he could have a one-day reduction of these offenses. For example, if he was grounded for being disrespectful the day before, he could gain that weekend day back for being respectful the next day. This is done to incorporate both positive and negative consequences. Roby was also told that if he committed two straight days of disrespect, he would not be able to receive any reductions that week.

Roby's parents did not go past the third offenses on any one particular day. They started fresh each day with the first offense. They realized that they would only get into a power struggle if they went past the third offense. One parent made the mistake of escalating his consequences and ended up trying to enforce two straight months of grounding after a single disrespectful incident. Each time the teen mouthed off, the parent replied, "If you make another peep, you will be grounded another week." The teenager was so ticked off that he kept saying "peep" until he had eight straight weeks of being grounded.

The father was left with the job of trying to enforce and monitor eight weeks of grounding. Otherwise, he would lose face with his son. The father was able to monitor only two weeks before he gave in. This failure empowered the son to be even more disrespectful the next time. The moral of this story is, never make any consequence harder on you than your child.

If your teen insists on pushing your button of disrespect long after the punishment is administered, exit and wait. If your teen tries to follow, either go to a locked bedroom or take the other children out for ice cream or to the park. Make sure you tell the kids to giggle and say that they had "the best time ever" as you walk through the door. It will demonstrate that you refuse to play the game on your teen's terms and allow him or her to control the mood of the entire household.

Strategy #5: Lavish Praise and Appreciation

As discussed under "Catch Your Teen Doing Something Right" in Step 2, I cannot overemphasize how lavish praise and appreciation will decrease the number of acts of disrespect. If teens do not receive positive attention, they will seek your attention any way they can get it—which is often through disrespect. At least it gets them noticed. In fact, though, all human beings—including your seemingly indifferent teen—crave praise and appreciation in order to thrive and grow.

If you don't believe me, try using this strategy *consistently* for eight straight weeks. You can see what happened in Trudy's case.

"What Has Gotten into My Father!"

The father of fourteen-year-old Trudy was skeptical but agreed to try this approach as a time-limited eight-week experiment. He agreed because he still did not have to give up punishments for acts of disrespect. He only had to look for things that were positive and catch her doing something right.

He started the experiment by leaving notes on her pillow, the bathroom, and her cereal bowl that simply praised her for specific things in the present and the past. For example, Trudy would start to pour her milk in her cereal bowl and stop because there was a Post-it note that said "Have I told you lately how lucky I am to have a daughter like you?" At night she might receive a note on her pillow stating "I appreciate the fact that you did not yell or swear when I asked you to take out the trash. Thank you."

These notes started to mess with Trudy's brain. She was still being as disrespectful as ever, yet her dad did not seem to be taking it as personally as he once did. How could she verbally attack him one minute and the next minute receive a card and a carnation on her pillow. Trudy thought, "There has to be an angle that Dad is trying to play." When she asked him point blank "Why?" he just smiled and said, "Because I love and appreciate you."

When Trudy doubled her disrespectful efforts, Dad still maintained a course of praise and appreciation. He exited and waited and refused to let his hot buttons get pushed. This only made it harder and harder on Trudy to be disrespectful.

She was now getting Positive Incident Report certificates taped to her door. What was really weird is that she was almost starting to look forward to them when she woke up in the morning. She started to collect them with pride instead of ripping them up. The strangest thing of all was that she was actually starting to feel a new emotion. This emotion was guilt; she began to feel guilty when she was disrespectful to her dad. She was finally getting noticed and receiving the kind of attention that she had only dreamed about. Trudy couldn't help it; she started treating her dad with more respect.

You should still hold teens accountable for disrespect, but look for moments to praise them and catch them doing something right. Smother them with honey and remove the vinegar. Doing so will make it harder for them to be disrespectful. If you try this strategy for eight consecutive weeks and still don't see even a small change, e-mail me and I will personally send you a check for the cost of this book.

Strategy #6: Do the Unexpected

In some ways, this strategy is similar to Strategy #3, "Two Can Play at That Game." This act of playfulness, though, is directed to stopping your teen cold rather than as an act of retaliation.

Create a private list of all the crazy and wacky things that you can think of that will take your teen completely off guard and change the mood in the room. Disrespectful arguments poison the air and make your entire household tense. If you counter this poison and tension with unexpected playfulness, you change the mood. When you control the mood, you regain control. Besides, a teen who is laughing usually can't get angry and swear at the same time.

For example, one parent did something completely startling when his son Ernie started to swear. In the past, the father would swear right back and the argument would explode. This time the dad immediately broke into a musical rendition of the song "Feelings" and walked out of the room. The boy was left with his mouth wide open in disbelief.

This strategy actually can be fun. Please try it. Your teen will not understand it, but you are the only one who has to see the bigger picture. Here are some other ideas to get you started:

- **Say something completely off the wall.** You can take your teen completely off guard if you say something unexpected. For example, if your teen says "You're a jerk," you can say "You're awfully cute when you're mad." This will stop your teen cold in astonishment.

- **Do something completely off the wall.** If your teen is disrespectful, take him or her off guard by doing something playful, like soaking the teen with a squirt gun, reciting a sentimental poem, or putting on a wig—the stranger, the better.

Try this strategy off and on for at least one month. It is good to be playful and keep your teen off balance, wondering what you can possibly think up next. Doing so takes some of the darkness and tension out of the air.

Strategy #7: The Pawn Broker

See Counselor for Direction!

Like a pawn broker, you can confiscate one of your teen's prized possessions (stereo equipment, tennis shoes, makeup, roller blades, CD collection, or telephone) if he or she is disrespectful. Give your teenager a pawn ticket (see the sample provided later) stating that items will be sold or given to charity if he or she is disrespectful again that same week. The catch is that once these items are sold or given away, you must never replace them (or you may replace them only after an extended period of time, say one to three months). That decision will be yours to make based on your particular teen.

Use this strategy only as a last resort and under the supervision of a qualified counselor. Why? This strategy will anger your teen. It works extremely well, but you need to know how to troubleshoot and prepare with backup plans.

You can also use this strategy effectively with the aces of running away, alcohol and drug use, violence, and truancy. Please follow the instructions to put the pawn broker consequence into place.

Defining the Terms

If your teen continues to be disrespectful, clearly define what behaviors will be considered disrespectful and how the pawn broker strategy will work:

[Name of your teenager], if you are disrespectful again this week, the punishment will be severe. Disrespect in our house is defined as refusing to do as I ask, such as clean your room after one warning, swearing, yelling at me, rolling your eyes, and mumbling under your breath. I will not tell you what the punishment will be ahead of time. You will never have to find out unless you are disrespectful. If you break the rule of disrespect, I will simply hand you a piece of paper with the punishment written out. Or the note may be waiting for you on your pillow or taped to your bedroom door. I will try not to yell or lecture. It doesn't work anyway.

I recommend that you do not reveal the punishment ahead of time for two reasons. First, teenagers can hide their prized possessions if they know about your plan. Second, it is to your advantage to keep your son or daughter off balance and wondering what will happen next. Keep the teen guessing.

Practicing Your Delivery

Before you hand a pawn ticket to your teen, take thirty minutes to an hour and rehearse the scenario with your spouse, significant other, or best friend. Ask your partner to play the part of your teenager and pretend to push all your buttons as you try to deliver the pawn ticket.

Go through as many different scenarios as you can think of ahead of time. For example, have your spouse or best friend rip up the pawn ticket, swear at you, call you names, follow you around the house, or search through the house to find the pawned item. Practice reacting to each possible scenario. Repeat the role-plays until you feel confident and prepared. A little preparation now will go a long way toward ensuring that you will be ready for any curve ball your teenager might throw at you.

Troubleshooting and Backup Plans

After you have finished the role-play, you must create backup plans for everything that could go wrong. Before you deliver the pawn ticket, answer the following troubleshooting questions

- **What will I do if** my teen tries to rummage through the house to find the item I have hidden away?

- **What will I do if** my teen tries to retaliate by stealing my things?

- **What will I do if** my teen keeps nagging me about getting his or her stuff back?

- **What will I do if** my teen says that these items are his or her property?

There are more what-will-I-do-if questions, but these examples will get you thinking in this direction. Here are my recommendations for these questions.

If your teen tries to rummage through your house looking for the pawned item, say that if he or she continues, this item will be sold immediately. (You can also take the item to work or give it to a friend to hold.) There's no point in looking for an item that is simply not in the house.

If your teen tries to steal your things, say ahead of time that you will press formal charges with the police. In addition, you will immediately sell the teen's items and never replace them.

If your teen nags you, you can say he or she has a choice. He or she can either stop or add three more days to the pawn ticket. Most teens will stop at this point.

If your teen tells you that personal items cannot be touched, say: "Personal items are used all the time to pay back debts. You owe me for breaking this rule"; or "When you want to start paying for rent, utilities, and phone, I will not touch your property. Until then, these items can be pawned." If your teen continues to argue, exit the conversation without saying another word since no explanation will ever be good enough.

Delivering the Pawn Ticket

When your teenager is disrespectful, walk away calmly and say nothing except "You have now broken the rule of disrespect. You will receive your piece of paper describing the consequence later."

When the teen leaves the house, remove the item that you have decided upon in advance. *Do not take everything at once:* Pawn just enough so it will sting but not so much that your teen will have nothing left to lose. For example, if you decide to pawn a CD collection, take just enough CDs (five or six) to make an impact. One mother made the mistake of taking all her daughter's clothing and stereo equipment. Her teen got so angry that she just shut down.

If your teen rips up the ticket in anger and refuses to comply, simply state, "The consequence still stands." Calmly walk away without another word. It is important to deliver the ticket and exit quickly to avoid a bitter argument. You do not have to deliver the standard lecture. The ticket is powerful enough on its own.

Please photocopy the following pawn ticket. Fill in the information, and deliver it to your teenager:

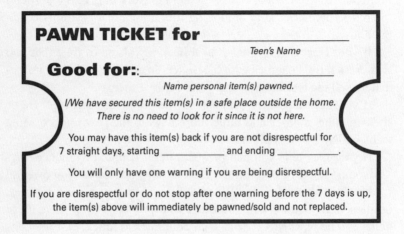

PAWN TICKET for _____

Teen's Name

Good for:: _____

Name personal item(s) pawned.

I/We have secured this item(s) in a safe place outside the home. There is no need to look for it since it is not here.

You may have this item(s) back if you are not disrespectful for 7 straight days, starting _____ and ending _____ .

You will only have one warning if you are being disrespectful.

If you are disrespectful or do not stop after one warning before the 7 days is up, the item(s) above will immediately be pawned/sold and not replaced.

A seven-day time period is recommended, because it's long enough to have the intended impact. If you go more than seven days, teens will begin to feel that they have nothing to lose and stop trying. Start small to give both you and your teenager a chance to be successful. Momentum can then take hold, and your teen will be able to "hold it together" and stop the disrespect for longer periods of time.

If the seven-day period does not work after several attempts, you have the option of extending the time limit past seven days. Or, depending on your teenager, you might choose to pawn the item for fewer than seven days if you know that a one- or three-day removal will have the same impact.

If your teen is disrespectful again within your seven-day time period, the pawned item that you took to work with you or hid at a neighbor's house is immediately sold.

Depending on your teen and situation, you may want to put in the contract beforehand that once this item is sold or given away to charity it will not be repurchased by you. You have no control over whether or not your teen purchases the item again, but you will not purchase it yourself.

Once the item is pawned, you can repeat these same procedures again with an additional item until the behavior stops. Your teen would receive another pawn ticket for a different item.

A Special Case

Even if your teenager does not have many material possessions to begin with, most teens have at least one special item, such as a jacket or shoes, that they value. In this case, I recommend the temporary removal of the teenager's cherished item for seven to ten days and the substitution of something less attractive. This is how it worked for Markel.

"I Love My Jacket"

Thirteen-year-old Markel was disrespectful to both his mom and his teachers. Markel's mom lived below the poverty level, but Markel had one possession he cherished, a designer "Charlotte Hornets" jacket. Instead of pawning this jacket, Markel's mom took it and replaced it with an old and nerdy-looking jacket from Goodwill. Markel was given a pawn ticket that stated the following:

> Markel, your Hornets jacket is safely hidden outside this house. You will get it back unharmed and untouched after 7 straight days of doing what your teacher asks the first time, no swearing or yelling, and doing your chores at home. Until this time, you will be required to wear the jacket I picked out for you. You can exchange this jacket for your Hornets jacket after you successfully complete the terms of this agreement.

Markel wanted his jacket back, so his disrespectful behavior quickly stopped.

This is an example of how a consequence can be altered to be effective regardless of whether the family is rich or poor. You can always find ways to work with what you have.

ACE #2: TRUANCY OR FAILING GRADES

I have combined truancy and failing grades into one ace for two reasons. First, they both involve the school system on some level. Second, both behaviors have the effect of neutralizing your authority. Missing school makes you anxious and fearful because your teen is unsupervised. Getting Ds and Fs makes you so angry and frustrated that you will lose your cool.

Before assuming that your teen is simply failing school due to a bad attitude, stubbornness, or laziness, it is often a wise first step to rule out the possibility of learning disabilities.

Once you notice a downward trend in your teen's tests or grades, you may request intellectual and achievement testing at any time during the school year, which the public school is legally obligated to complete. In most states, the public school system is required to test your teen within 90 days of receiving a formal request in writing. This requirement does not hold true for private school systems. In private schools, you must pay for testing.

Once the tests are completed, the teacher is required to explain the results to the parent and make recommendations and modifications based on the results of the tests if the teen meets the criterion for a specific learning disability.

Once a learning disability is ruled out you can proceed with the strategies recommended in this step. The first thing you should do is work in close collaboration with school personnel.

This is often easier said than done, because in the past teachers, guidance counselors, or principals may have blamed you or you've blamed them. One parent told me, "It's like this. My son's teacher thinks I am to blame for his acting out in class. She doesn't tell me to my face, but I can see it in her eyes." Similarly, you may also blame the teacher. As one teacher told me, "With so many kids in the classroom, it's all I can do to keep order. I know that a lot of these parents blame me but I am really doing the best job I can. I need the parents' involvement to back me up."

Without a united front between you and the teachers, your son or daughter will divide and conquer. Read about what happened to the parents and teachers of thirteen-year-old Dennis.

Divide and Conquer

When Dennis started to get failing grades, he knew he had to act fast. If his parents received warning notices in the mail or talked with his teacher, he might actually have to start doing homework. To stop this from happening, Dennis designed an ingenious plan.

Each day he checked the mailbox for notices and hid any that arrived. Still, in the back of his mind, Dennis knew that his parents eventually would see his report card. Someone would have to be blamed. To make sure it would be someone else, Dennis started a smear campaign.

The next day Dennis went to school and told his teacher, Ms. Jenkins, that his mom said that she was a bad teacher who didn't know what she was doing. Ms. Jenkins was so angry and hurt that she replied, "Your mother has no idea what she's talking about. If she thinks she can do a better job, I'd like to see her try. If she made you do some homework, I'm sure you wouldn't be failing most of your subjects."

When Dennis got back to his desk, he immediately wrote down all these juicy quotes. Of course, he modified them to suit his own needs. The quotes he wrote down read: "Your mom is not a good parent. She has no idea what she is talking about when it comes to schoolwork. She doesn't take the time she needs with you."

At the dinner table, Dennis let his mom know what his teacher supposedly had said about her. Dennis's mom retaliated by spouting obscenities and character attacks. Dennis was quick to relay these statements to Ms. Jenkins the following morning. This went on until both parent and teacher had such hard feelings toward one another that they stopped communicating on any level. Dennis had successfully divided his mother and teacher. The scene was now set to conquer.

When his mother finally got his report card, she was stunned by how bad Dennis's grades were. Instead of blaming Dennis, she immediately blamed Ms. Jenkins: "She never sent me grade warning notices in the mail, she never bothered to call, and she never sent home warning notices with you. What kind of teacher does that!"

There are more masterminds like Dennis out there than you might think. Teens are very smart, creative, and resourceful. They realize that they will not be held accountable for their behavior if they can pit you against the school and keep you from communicating with the teacher.

Once your teen's divide-and-conquer plan is exposed and a collaborative plan established, the school usually becomes more cooperative. The following strategies illustrate step-by-step how to transform your teen's school from a nonhelper into your best advocate and supporter. You can either hire the services of a counselor to act as a mediator or do it yourself. I recommend a counselor, but these strategies will work even if you go solo.

Strategy #1: Work Collaboratively with the School

When you meet with the school, ask your teen to wait outside the room while you initially go over the written plan. (See the example that follows.) Pass a copy out to each teacher or school counselor present.

Do not let your teen see the plan beforehand. Witnessing any disagreements between you and the school personnel provides your teen with more ammunition to successfully divide and conquer. Because teachers usually have only fifteen to twenty minutes to spare, you must get to the point quickly. Your plan must clarify the teachers' roles and explain how it will benefit each teacher and make their job easier.

Remember that your teen's teacher sits through hundreds of parent-teacher conferences a year. Usually they are all the same: dismal and nonproductive. They begin with the teacher taking out a grade book and going around the room to report how badly your teen is doing academically and/or how disruptive he or she is in class. Your child or teen looks down and slumps in the chair as you look more and more defeated. The same exact meeting repeats itself all over again at the next parent-teacher conference.

"Your daughter is a pain in the ass."

At this meeting, however, teachers will be curious and energized. You are presenting something unique and different. You are presenting concrete solutions in a written format.

What follows is a copy of the plan that Kevin Smith, the father of thirteen-year-old Jason, presented to his son's teachers. It is reproduced to help you create your own plan. As you read it, look for three key things: (1) how the first two sentences tell each teacher how this plan will make their job easier; (2) how the tone is looking at solutions, *not* strictly problems; and (3) how Mr. Smith clarifies everyone's role.

Kevin Smith   January 20, 2001
55 Buckhead Road
Savannah, GA. 31415
(912) 555-1234 home   (912) 555-6789 office

7th Grade Teachers of Jason
Ms. Watkins   Ms. Bixler
Ms. Gordon   Ms. Rucker

Dear Teachers,
We do not expect you to perform a baby-sitting service for our child. We want to support you and make your job easier. The plans contained within this letter are designed to do just that.

The purpose of today's meeting is to coordinate our actions and set up guidelines for Jason. During this trimester Jason's mother has been kind enough to allow Jason to live with me so I can concentrate my full attention on helping him improve at school.

I will not stand by while Jason is being disruptive in your classes or not turning in his assignments as he did last trimester. I am therefore requesting your help as follows:

1. I am giving each teacher two stamped postcards with my return address. If you have any behavior problems with Jason or if he misses any assignments, please drop these cards in the mail and I will respond immediately.

2. Place any comments about Jason's behavior, lack of attentiveness, or missed assignments in his daily planner. I will review this planner with him on a daily basis. This planner will serve as a way for us teachers and (me) to communicate with one another.

3. If Jason will not settle down, call me at any of the numbers listed above and I will come to school the next day. I will sit with Jason in class to assure that he does not disrupt your teaching.

Jason knows ahead of time that there will be consequences at home for receiving any negative comments in his planner or on the postcards. I have asked Jason to have each of you initial his planner every day to assure that he writes down the assignments correctly. It also allows you to make any comments about his behavior in the classroom.

I thank you in advance for your extra efforts. I want to work collaboratively with you to make this Jason's most productive trimester. I would like to meet again in a month to discuss his progress and review this plan.

After you present your plan, the teachers will have questions. Try not to get defensive. Ask them what they think, and, if possible, add their input into the plan. Like everyone else, teachers gain a sense of pride and co-ownership from helping to formulate the plan. Co-ownership breeds cooperation and costs you nothing in return.

After you have the details worked out, ask your teenager to come into the room. Read the contract to the teenager, explain everyone's role, and outline how it will be monitored. Ask your teen to repeat back what was just said. If you have a counselor, ask him or her to be present at the meeting to keep both you and the school on track and focused on the bigger picture.

Before this meeting, Jason's teachers had been negative and uncooperative. At the conclusion of this meeting, there was a noticeable change. The teachers were energized, cooperative, and helpful. They stopped looking at their watches and gave the father an extra fifteen minutes. The letter kept the meeting focused and everyone on track.

With a well-organized plan, Jason suddenly became accountable for his actions on a day-to-day basis. Problems could now be identified and immediately addressed before they became chronic or resulted in suspensions or expulsions.

Suspensions have become a kind of reward system for many teens, who tell me, "I like to act out in class because I get suspended. I can stay home, watch television, and raid the refrigerator. Even an in-school suspension is better than sitting in class all day." Plans like Kevin Smith's can prevent suspensions or expulsions from happening.

Strategy #2: Positive Praise and Recognition

Instead of focusing on what your teen is doing wrong in school, focus on anything he or she is doing right—even if it is as small as simply attending school. Although they may act as if they don't need it, teens flat-out crave positive recognition and praise when it comes to school.

Behavior problems tend to spill over into school performance. When teens start acting out in the classroom, teachers often become more concerned with stopping their disruptive behavior than educating their minds. The teens then fall farther and farther behind. The farther they fall, the more their confidence is shaken. Once this happens, they will act out even more to distract both teachers and classmates from learning the truth—that they don't understand the work. Their pride and self-esteem are now at risk. Their view of school is as negative as their teachers' view of them.

While it helps to provide careful monitoring through your written plan in Strategy #1, it won't work unless you give your teen significant praise and recognition for even the slightest effort.

Listen to what these teens have to say on the subject:

I wish my mom would encourage me in school. She just pays attention when I mess up. She yells at me all the time and tells me how stupid I am and that I will never amount to anything if I don't get my ass in gear.

—Sean, age 13

I know that I will never be as smart as my older brother, but just once I wish my dad would say that he is proud of me for trying. I have just shut down. When I try to tell my dad that I am having problems, it's always "Well, you should have studied this way" or "Matt never had these problems." I want to pull my hair out and scream.

—Marlene, age 15

I basically stopped doing homework on purpose just to give my dad the finger. He is always pressuring me to excel and do better. But nothing was ever good enough. If I got a B, his response was always "Why isn't it an A?" If I got an A, it was "Why didn't I get an A+?" Just once I would like to hear "I'm proud of you," "Way to go," or "Keep up the good work." Don't parents get it? We need praise and encouragement. Criticism doesn't work with us.

—Tracy, age 16

These teens represent the voices of thousands of other teens all over the country. For the next two months, try using negative consequences in conjunction with lavish praise and appreciation for what he or she is doing right. The results will astonish you. Use the Positive Incident Report as a way to accomplish this goal.

Find Out What Your Teen Needs

Custom-fit your encouragement around what your particular teenager wants and needs. Here are two questions to get you started:

[Teen's name], in the past I know I have focused on what you were doing wrong in school and not what you were doing right. But I want to try hard to change these habits, and I need your expertise to do that. Please tell me what you need or desire for me to do to encourage or praise you, more often when it comes to school. For example, do you want me to start focusing on improvements like attending class or doing homework? What other things can you think of?"

If you catch your teen in a good mood, he or she will be pleasantly shocked by this question. It sets an entirely different tone and a way of communicating with one another. I recommend this follow-up question:

[Teen's name], in the past what have I said or done that has seemed overly harsh or critical? Could you give me some concrete examples from the past? I need to see it in my mind to change it for the future.

Depending on your teen, you may want to begin with this question first. Try not to get defensive. Do not make excuses or say that your teen's examples are untrue. There is no right or wrong here, just different points of view.

Try Switching Roles

Take a few minutes to try this fun and thought-provoking exercise. Pretend that you are your son or daughter and have your teen pretend to be you. Take on each other's mannerisms and tone of voice. In the first role-play, ask your teen to mirror exactly how you would criticize or find fault. Ask him or her to exaggerate those criticisms so that you can really see them. In the second role-play, ask your teen to continue to play you, but this time show what it would look and sound like if you were giving encouragement and praise. Do this as many times as needed until you get it.

Finally, go back to playing yourselves. Show your teen what you have learned from watching him or her in the second role-play. Ask your teen to rate your performance.

Strategy #3: Grounding

Grounding is more effective when it is implemented on a one-to-one ratio: one day of grounding for each school violation. For each school violation (ditching, no homework, class disruption), your teen is grounded for one weekend day and night beginning Friday. Grounding should be done on the weekends because these are the times your teen cares about. It is also typically easier for you to monitor grounding on the weekends rather than when you are in the office.

For example, if your daughter violates her contract on Monday, she is grounded on Friday. If a second violation occurs that same week, she will be grounded on Friday and Saturday. If subsequent violations take place in the same week and you run out of weekends, you can tack in onto the next weekend.

Backup Plan

Your teen should be told beforehand how you define the term "grounding." Most often this means no television, no phone, no car, no stereo, and no friends. Please do not forget to troubleshoot all the ways that your teen might try to unravel your grounding consequence. Some of the most common problems include attempts to sneak out of the house or make your life miserable while they are grounded.

Strategy #4: The Pawn Broker for School Issues

If grounding is not working, you can go to the bigger gun of the pawn broker strategy outlined under Ace #1, "Disrespect." No matter how tough you get, however, please do not abandon the positive reinforcements of praise and appreciation. Your teen may think that you are a hypocrite for trying to praise and punish him or her at the same time. You can answer this concern by saying that you will hold the teen accountable when he or she does well and also when he or she does not.

You can give your teen a pawn ticket for any school problem. Use pawn tickets sparingly, and only after you have tried milder consequences.

The procedure is the same as for Ace #1, except that you would substitute "ditching" or "failure to complete homework" for "disrespect."

Charlie Pawn Ticket—Ready for Use

Here is an example of a pawn ticket that was written for fifteen-year-old Charlie after he repeatedly skipped school.

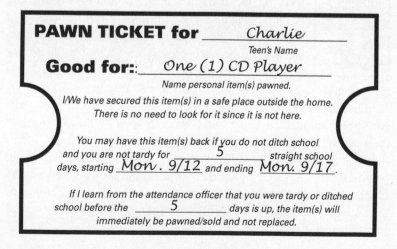

PAWN TICKET for _____Charlie_____

Teen's Name

Good for::___One (1) CD Player___

Name personal item(s) pawned.

I/We have secured this item(s) in a safe place outside the home.
There is no need to look for it since it is not here.

You may have this item(s) back if you do not ditch school
and you are not tardy for ___5___ straight school
days, starting __Mon. 9/12__ and ending __Mon. 9/17__.

If I learn from the attendance officer that you were tardy or ditched
school before the ___5___ days is up, the item(s) will
immediately be pawned/sold and not replaced.

Charlie had been ditching school for such a long time that five straight days was a major first step. The parents gradually extended the number of days he had to be at school from five to seven days, then to ten days, and so on.

Charlie was motivated to improve when his mom or dad took on the role of the pawn shop. In other words, Charlie received two chances. If Charlie ditched school before the five-day limit was expired, the item would go to his parents' imaginary pawn shop. A dollar amount value was placed on the item. (It was not the true value but a percentage of the total dollar amount.)

Charlie had one week of extra chores at an hourly minimum wage to work off that dollar amount. If he was successful, Charlie would receive his CD player back from Mom and Dad's pawn shop. If not, the CD player would be sold immediately.

You can use the same variation with your teen or immediately choose to sell the item with no second chances. Experiment with both variations. What works best all depends on your teen and what you think will be the best motivator.

Strategy #5: Attending School

A very effective strategy is to attend school with your teen. You can use this strategy if your teen is ditching school, being disruptive in class, or failing because of laziness. This intervention is one of your biggest guns and should be used only if the school problem has gone on for a long time with no end in sight. I also recommend the help of a counselor for this strategy.

This strategy is effective because teens are extremely self-conscious about their image and want to look "cool" in front of their friends. Teenagers will definitely not like the idea of their mommy or daddy following them to each class and sitting right next to them. They may pretend not to care, but they do—especially if Mom comes to school in fuzzy slippers with rollers in her hair or Dad comes dressed in colorful golf pants, nerdy glasses, and greased-back hair.

"I Could Never Go to School"

As you read this strategy, you may object because you do not have the time or energy to take off from work or going to school will embarrass your teen and possibly damage his or her self-esteem. Try looking at it this way before you make up your mind.

First, consider the pure economics of taking off from work. Wouldn't it be better to take a few days off now and stop the problem then let it drag on until you can barely concentrate on your work? Think about all the required parent-teacher conferences that you will have to attend and what it would cost you to pay someone to watch your teen if he or she gets suspended or expelled. You can pay now or pay more later.

When I call parents' employers on their behalf and make this point, most agree and let the parent take some time off. Besides, if you implement this strategy exactly as planned, you will only have to miss a few days of work. Strong medicine does not need much time to take effect.

As for the effect of this strategy on your child's self-esteem, teens are stronger and more resilient than you think. No matter how embarrassed they may be at first, their friends will quickly move on to other things.

Besides, your teen's self-esteem will definitely suffer if the school problems continue. I have yet to see a child or teen with strong self-esteem who is failing, dropping out, or being expelled. You have two choices: Embarrass your teen a little now and solve the problem quickly, or let it drag on for years and only get worse.

Preparation

In order to use this strategy successfully, you will need to work closely with your teen's school.

Before you escort your teen to school, set up a face-to-face parent-teacher conference with both the teachers and the principal. As in Strategy #1, prepare a letter that explains your plan. If you are working with a counselor, ask the counselor to be present to help mediate the meeting and keep it on track.

If the principal or teachers are uncooperative, tell them that you will call the Board of Education, the local media, or seek legal counsel. They will quickly change their minds. However, play this card only after you have exhausted all other resources. You want to establish a partnership, not an adversarial relationship.

In your written plan, ask each teacher if he or she would phone you during break or contact the school secretary to call if your teen is absent, tardy, or disruptive. Determine ahead of time how many tardies equal one absence and a trip to the school. I recommend that two tardies should equal one absence. You also can ask the teachers to call and let you know if your teen is not turning in homework assignments or mail the pre-stamped postcards you give them. As a backup, tell them that you will contact the school attendance officer to find out this information each day.

State on the plan that you will accompany your teen to class the next day or the first day you are able to get time off from work. Use the element of surprise in your favor. Show up unannounced to make your teen constantly wonder when you are going to walk through the door.

The first offense can be a "warning shot." You only have to attend a few classes and sit right by the teen's side. If it happens a second time, you would attend more than one class. Only this time you would be dressed in fuzzy slippers and hair curlers or flood pants and a pocket pencil holder.

Attending school for a third violation includes eating lunch with the teenager in front of his or her friends. The idea here is that the consequences will get more extreme if the behavior continues. This procedure works best if both you and your spouse can attend together, if only for the first time. Doing so turns up the heat and shows your teen that you are a united front.

If your teen has severe behavioral problems (hitting other kids, destruction of property, swearing at teachers) in the classroom, define these ahead of time on your written plan. Determine when and how often these behaviors have to occur before you get a call from the teacher to back him or her up. For example, one teacher preferred to try handling the problem herself with one warning. The plan read:

"Ms. Johnson will give Jerome one verbal warning to stop. If this same behavior happens again that week, Mom will be called."

If your teen refuses to do homework, you can go to school the next day or the first day you get off work. Determine how many missed homework assignments will constitute a trip to the school. As I stated earlier, you must first rule out any learning disabilities and determine if your teen's behavior is just laziness. Otherwise, you will be punishing your teen for something he or she cannot help, such as dyslexia.

Troubleshooting

Backup Plan

Troubleshoot with the teachers before your teen sees the written plan. Go around the room and ask everyone what your teen might do to try to sabotage this plan. For every what-will-I-do-if scenario they come up with, create a backup contingency plan. Here are two of the most common problems, along with the backup plans that both teachers and parents have come up with.

- **What will I do** if my son flat-out refuses to attend school with me?

Plan A: I will take it in stride and say, "I appreciate your concern, but that is not optional." I will then ignore the "white noise" and just get up as planned and take my son to school. If it is going to be a power struggle, I will make sure he gets on the bus. I will show up unannounced later that morning.

Plan B: If Plan A fails and my teen runs away, I will tell him that he has a choice. Either he goes to school with me tomorrow and in the future, or I will go without him and sit in my child's seat. Only this time, I will be dressed in everything from a rented clown suit to wearing no makeup, curlers, or flood pants. I will also talk to his friends at lunch and tell them embarrassing stories.

- **What will I do if** my daughter throws a fit in class when I arrive?

Plan A: I will immediately yank her out of class and give her the following options. Either she goes back into class and behaves or I will leave. If I leave, two things will happen immediately. First, I will go home and take some of her personal property and sell it at a pawn shop in order to cover lost time and wages at work. Second, I will be back the next day in a crazy outfit and sit in her chair.

Plan B: If Plan A fails, my daughter will work off my time in the form of sweat labor. Extra chores at a minimum wage per hour will be posted on the refrigerator along with specific date and time deadlines. If these deadlines are not met, I will sell personal items to cover these debts and she will be grounded until the debt is paid off.

After the troubleshooting is complete, ask your teen to come into the conference room with you and the teachers. Go over the plan and ask your teen to repeat it so that there is no misunderstanding. Ask your teen any ideas that might improve the plan (besides not having a plan to begin with). If your teen has some good suggestions, incorporate them into the plan. If not, conclude the meeting quickly so that your teen does not have an opportunity to sabotage it.

Strategy #6: Home Schooling or Switching Schools: A Last Resort

When given the chance, some teens will make pie-in-the-sky promises to entice you to try home schooling. The problem is that if they are unable to change their behavior in a regular school setting, they will not miraculously change it at home.

After an initial honeymoon period, your teen's behavior probably will get worse. In home schooling, teens often have too much time on their hands and are left unsupervised. Once the taste of freedom sets in, it can be nearly impossible to get your teen back into regular school.

Other teens will think that switching schools will magically solve their problems. But the problems follow teens no matter what school they attend. Switching schools should be considered as an option only when it can be determined that a teenager is in danger of being physically hurt and school officials are unable or unwilling to get involved.

Consider home schooling or switching schools as a last resort under these conditions:

■ All the strategies described in this step have been tried and have failed on a consistent basis.

■ Your teen maintains a part-time or full-time job and pays you the equivalent of one semester's charges before home schooling begins. Your teen is not allowed to pay after the fact or as he or she goes along. Often schools provide home schooling at little or no charge. If this is the case, the money your teen pays you can go into a savings account and be used as a future reward or punishment. For example, if your teen attends every class and achieves a grade of C+ or better, your teen will get the money back and can begin home schooling. If not, you get the money and there is no home schooling.

■ If regular school is not working out and your teen is between sixteen and eighteen years old, he or she must obtain and hold down a full-time job for one full quarter before being allowed to drop out. He or she also must pay for and pass a high school equivalency examination and obtain a General Education Diploma (GED).

With many of our public schools failing to make the grade, sometimes the idea of home schooling is quite tempting. Home schooling is one thing for teens who have no extreme behavior problems. If teens are out of control, however, it is a completely different story. Such teens are all too ready to blame others and give up on solving their own problems. It is important for out-of-control teens to try to work through their school problems before jumping ship, since self-esteem improves when we stick things out and overcome adversity.

ACE #3: RUNNING AWAY

The ace of running away is a powerful weapon. Your teen realizes that even the threat to run often makes you back down out of fear. Frightened that if you push too hard, your teen may leave and come to harm on the streets, you are held hostage by this threat and stop enforcing rules.

Often a teenager is truly running away from something. For example, a teen might run from a parent who is overly harsh and punitive or from a parent who is abusing drugs or alcohol. Sometimes teens will run just because they want to or because they don't want to follow rules. Such teens are the exception, however.

Most teens run *from* something that genuinely bothers them. What often bothers your teen the most is the perception that they are not wanted or needed anymore. I am not saying this is true, but it is still your teen's perception. In addition, other family members may want to run away, like a parent, but it is never openly talked about. You have to be willing to look in the mirror and find out what issues your teen is running away from.

Strategy #1: Figure Out Why Your Teen Runs Away

First you must determine if there are any underlying problems contributing to your teen's desire to run. Some families do not have underlying problems; they just have a teenager who enjoys running away. In most cases, I believe a combination of the two is at work: Teens may enjoy running away, but they also do so because of unresolved family issues. In order to help your teen, complete the following lists.

- List all the reasons you can think of why your teenager might want to run away.

- List any problems in your household that may make life stressful or uneasy (disagreements in parenting, inconsistent discipline, drug or alcohol problems, sudden death in family, etc.).

- List everything that would need to change to make your teenager want to stay at home on a permanent basis.

Here Are Issues That Often Prompt Teenagers to Run

- One or both parents are overly strict, punitive, or focus on the negative to the extent that the teen feels that nothing he or she does will ever be good enough.

- Parents and teens push each other's buttons to the extent that the home front becomes so negative or violent that the teenager runs away or is asked to leave.

- There is undisclosed sexual abuse in the family. If your teenager has an extreme or negative reaction to being alone with another parent, adult, or sibling, you may need to consider sexual abuse. Chronic running away is a common response to sexual abuse.

- There is a severe lack of softness or a nurturing bond between parent and teenager. Both parties cannot remember the last time they hugged or went on a special outing together. Communication is 75 to 100 percent negative or filled with tension.

- At least one parent is an addict of some type (alcohol, drugs, gambling, etc.). Because of these addictions, the parent can become violent, inconsistent, or verbally abusive.

- A high degree of marital tension makes everyone uneasy. Both you and your spouse cannot control your disputes and place the children in the middle of your heated arguments, unresolved conflicts, and hostilities. Children are used as pawns when you try to recruit them to turn against the other parent.

If your family is struggling with any of these issues, please follow these three recommendations:

1. *Seek out a counselor.* You will need a counselor to work through any underlying family issues. Otherwise, your teen will keep running and may come to harm on the streets. The stakes are sufficiently high that you need a counselor to guide you through this complex set of issues. Please see the appendix or go to *www. difficult.net* for tips in finding the right counselor for you.

2. *Stop the running away.* Use the rest of the strategies in this section to temporarily stop the running away and keep your child safe. These strategies are tough and likely will stop your teen's running immediately.

3. *Solve the problem.* While these strategies may stop the immediate problem (the running away), you still must cure the long-term problems by identifying and healing whatever your teen is running away from. Otherwise, the bleeding (running away) will start again as soon as the bandage (temporary solution) is removed.

Once you temporarily stop the running away, it is time to collaborate with your counselor and your teenager to discover what the underlying issues are and how to solve them.

Strategy #2: Use Your Teen as an Expert

Before you jump into the "stealth bomber" strategies in the next section, pause to get your teen's input. Ask your teen why he or she runs and what everyone would be doing differently in the future to stop it from happening again.

Your teen may refuse to help you on your first attempt, but please continue to try until you crack through the ice. Teens tell me that one of the biggest mistakes parents make is to take their resistance at face value. As one fourteen-year-old put it:

"We are just kids. Nothing works the first time. Parents give up way too easy. Sometimes we just want to test them to see if they care enough to keep trying. Sometimes we are just in a bad mood. Just keep trying. We will open up eventually."

Try asking these questions calmly and gently:

- "I know this may sound strange, but I really need your expert advice and help on how to stop you from wanting to leave home without permission in the future. Can you please tell me everything that I am doing or saying to put pressure on you to run away?" (If your teenager says "I don't know," ask him or her to guess. Try guessing what it might be and asking the teen to accept or correct your guess.)

- "If we were to kick this running-away monster out the door, what are all the things you and I would need to do differently to rally together and defeat it once and for all?" (At this point, you may see your teenager smile and puff up with pride because no one has ever shown so much respect for his or her opinion.)

- "If you were a parent to someone just like you, how would you stop the problem of leaving the house without permission?"

- "On a scale of 1 to 10, with 1 meaning that you will run away the first chance you get and 10 meaning that you will never run away, what number are you currently at? What needs to happen for you to go from a 1 to a 2, from a 2 to a 3, and so on?"

If your teen opens up, incorporate his or her ideas into your no-running-away contract. For example, fifteen-year-old Mark told his mother that he was currently at a "3" on a scale of 1 to 10. However, that number would go from a "3" to an "8" if his mom would stop yelling and screaming at him constantly. The mother countered with "What would I be doing instead of yelling and screaming to get you to do what I ask the first time?"

With the help of the counselor, Mark told her that it would work better if she wrote everything down on a piece of paper with specific dates and times. If the dishes needed to be washed, she should write down what time they needed to be done by and the consequence if they were not washed by that time. This would avoid the need to remind, yell, and scream. Good counselors can really be helpful in negotiations of this type, acting as mediators and helping both parent and teen to compromise.

If your teen refuses to cooperate, immediately proceed to the stealth bomber consequences to shut down the running away. Sometimes you need to stop the bleeding before your teen is ready and willing to negotiate terms. Things also may have to settle down long enough for you to be able to address your own issues.

Strategy #3: The Stealth Bomber Consequences

As with the stealth bomber, your teenager will not see these consequences coming.

Stealth bomber consequences include:

- Using a "wanted poster" with an unflattering picture of your teen and a small cash reward for information leading to his or her whereabouts. Hang these flyers all over your teenager's school and around town.

- Shutting down your teen's safe houses—the places the teen goes when running. Use picket signs, notarized letters, and other means to turn up the heat on the parents of these safe houses to make your teen unwelcome.

- Using the pawn broker strategy to sell, pawn, or remove your teenager's prized possessions (stereo equipment, tennis shoes, makeup, Roller Blades, or telephone) if he or she continues to run away.

Many teenagers will choose to stop running away rather than face these kinds of consequences.

The Wanted Poster

If your teen cares about status and looking good in front of friends, this consequence will be very effective. Most teens would be mortified if you put up "wanted posters" like this one in their school and their favorite hangouts:

WANTED

Jill McCaffery

$$$ REWARD $$$

For any information leading to the whereabouts of Jill McCaffery

Please call her Mommy at 555-4982

How would you like it if your most unflattering picture was posted all over town? If you have a daughter, I recommend a picture of her without makeup. If you have a son, include a cute baby picture of him next to a recent picture. This consequence works because your teen would rather give up running away than go through the embarrassment of having the picture posted.

Prepare and Troubleshoot

Tell your teen ahead of time that the consequences will be severe if he or she leaves the house again without permission again, but do not reveal the consequence ahead of time. If the teen is not back within twenty-four hours, call the police and report the teen as a runaway.

Photocopy your flyer with the unflattering picture on it and tape it wherever your teen hangs out. Also give a set to the police department. In big print place the words "Reward for Information Leading to the Whereabouts of [Teen's Name]" at the bottom of the flyer. Do not put a dollar amount, just your phone number.

Show your teen's principal this section of the book, and ask for permission to hang the flyers up all over school. Also ask if you can come back to replace any flyers that are "mysteriously" taken down.

The following are some of the what-will-I-do-if scenarios you may encounter:

- **What will I do if** my teen rips up all the flyers or has friends do it?

- **What will I do if** the principal refuses to let me post flyers at the school?

If your teen or friends rip up the flyers, try not to take it personally. Simply replace them with the help of friends or neighbors.

You also can go to school the next day and personally hand them to your teen's friends as they get off school buses. I recommend you do this dressed in your bathrobe and slippers.

If the principal refuses to let you post or distribute the flyers at school, you can hand them to the teenagers as they leave school property. You also can ask the principal to reconsider before you take your cause to the local press.

Wait and Record

Now sit back and wait for the calls to come in. You do not usually need to offer a large reward; usually an amount between $30 and $60 is enough.

You will be surprised how many of your teen's so-called loyal friends will phone if money is involved. Sometimes even the parents of your teen's friends will call. One parent told me that she was taken completely off guard when the mother of her son's best friend called. Ironically, the teenager was "secretly" staying over in the mother's basement. For a sum of $35, the mother kicked the teenager out of her home for good and never allowed him to return.

When you receive a call, record the caller's voice by pressing the "record" button on your answering machine or require that the person meet you face to face to receive the reward money. When your teen returns home, you can play the call back or tell who ratted the teen out. After this, chances are your teenager will no longer want to be friends with these people or hide out in their homes. This action also helps to eliminate at least some of your teen's safe houses. The more difficult it becomes for your teen to find comfortable shelter, the more likely it is that he or she will quickly return and stay home.

A Personal Note

Some parents worry that what I suggest is too embarrassing or harmful to their teenager's self-esteem. Please consider that when teenagers are running away, there is a serious risk that they may die on the street. A little embarrassment now can save your teenager's life long enough for you to work on raising his or her self-esteem.

The following example shows how one mother overcame her doubts in order to help her daughter.

"Look at That Hair"

Fifteen-year-old Lesha continued to run away no matter what her mother tried. The mother was on her own and had little support. Despite her concerns, her mother decided to try the "wanted" poster out of desperation. I asked her to locate the most embarrassing photo of Lesha that she had, which turned out to be a picture of the girl taken after she had gotten out of bed, with her hair sticking straight up and no makeup on. The mother then used the photo to create a "wanted" flyer, which she photocopied and posted all over town.

Within days, the mother received a call from some of Lesha's friends. Ironically, before the mother called the police, she received a call from Lesha herself during which Lesha demanded that her mother take down "those embarrassing pictures," which were "ruining her reputation."

The mother responded that Lesha would have to come home for this to happen. If Lesha tried to take the posters down herself, the mother had plenty of extras. If Lesha did not return home the next day, the mother would go to the school and hand the flyers out personally in a pink robe, pink slippers, and hair rollers! Lesha was home before nightfall.

Shutting Down Your Teen's Safe Houses

One reason teenagers can continue to run away is that they have one or more "safe houses" to go to. How many teens would run if they had to sleep on the cold pavement outside or eat out of garbage cans?

Often the parents at these safe houses do not know that your teen has run away. They might think that your teen has permission to sleep over, or your teen may have been able to convince them through lies that they are being abused.

To stop your teen from running away, you must do everything in your power to find these safe houses and make your teen no longer welcome there.

Many parents ask me if they have a right to bother or impose on other parents. They have somehow gotten the message from society that anything that has to do with their teenager's peers is off limits or a violation of their civil liberties. This message is wrong. Parents not only have the right to impose but are required to do so when safety is an issue. Here's how to proceed.

The Black Book

Keep a secret "black book" with the addresses and phone numbers of your teen's friends. Sometimes teenagers like to be secretive about their friends and will tell you it's none of your business. When you are battling for your teenager's safety, however, their friends are definitely your business. Even if your teenager is not currently running away, you can construct this black book as an insurance policy for the future.

There are several ways that you can obtain these numbers and addresses. First, you can change the rules in your household and make it mandatory that you meet each one of your teenager's friends before he or she goes out. Give your teenager a choice: Either you meet the friends and get their addresses and phone numbers, or the teen does not go out. Your rationale is that, in case of emergency, you need a way to contact your teenager.

Second, give your teenager a carbon copy message pad to use. Every time your teen receives a phone message, the name and number will be carbon copied. When your teen is not around, you can copy the information left on the carbons into your black book.

If your teen runs, you now have a list of phone numbers and addresses to call. Tell each parent you call that your teenager is missing without your permission. Say that the police have asked you to call to find out who is illegally harboring your teenager. If they have any information, they should let you know. If you find out personally, the police will not not need to get involved.

These statements may be an idle threat, but most parents will not know that. If they are harboring your teenager, the chances are that they will not want to be involved with the police and will ask your teen to leave.

Approaching a Cooperative Safe House

Once you locate the safe house, initially assume that either the parents are unaware of your teen's presence or have been given misinformation. With this assumption, make a surprise visit after work to talk to these parents. Do not try to blame them or threaten them; simply explain the situation calmly and clear up any misinformation. You will be surprised at how many parents are receptive to this approach and will gladly turn over your teenager.

Tell the safe house parents in front of your teenager that if he or she should run away again, you will call these parents immediately. Then exchange phone numbers. Seeing this collaboration between parents will warn your teen that this house is no longer a safe harbor.

Approaching a Noncooperative Safe House

If the safe house parents are uncooperative, tell them that they are illegally harboring your teenager and that, if the situation continues, you will contact the police. One parent even picketed on the sidewalk in front of a stubborn parent's house with a sign that said "Joe and Mary Smith are housing my daughter without my consent." This embarrassed the safe house parents so much that they soon gave up the daughter.

You also can hand the safe house parents a certified letter stating that they have now been officially informed that they are illegally harboring your son or daughter. The letter should also state that if the safe-house parents do not immediately release your teenager, a copy of the letter will be delivered to the police.

Most families will give up the teenager at this point rather than deal with the police. The more safe houses you make off limits, the more difficult it becomes for your teenager to run. In addition, word will spread that you will harass anyone who harbors your teenager in the future. This is what happened with Darien and his father.

"You Can't Harass My Friends"

Fifteen-year-old Darien hung out with a crowd of older friends. Many of them were drug dealers or in trouble with the law. Whenever Darien wanted to run, he had a safe place to stay. The father did not know what to do. Previous counselors had told him that he had no right to choose Darien's friends. As a result, the father took a hands-off approach and watched helplessly as his son drifted deeper into a life of crime.

When the father consulted me, I told him that I disagreed with that advice. It was fine to take a hands-off approach if his son's friends were even halfway decent. However, when the peer group is harboring Darien illegally when he runs or is using drugs, it is time to step forward.

After receiving the green light from me, the father took the following steps. The next time Darien ran, his father immediately phoned the parents of Darien's best friend. Their attitude was that they didn't care about the father's concerns, so he drove to their house.

Since Darien's father was a police officer, I recommended that he approach the house in full police gear. The father told the parents and their son that if they ever harbored Darien again, he would personally see to it that their son was searched for drugs and the parents would be charged for illegally harboring a minor.

The parents quickly turned Darien over to the father. Since Darien had no place to stay, the running away quickly ended.

The Pawn Broker Consequence

This step has been discussed under the aces of disrespect and truancy. If you think that your teenager is at risk to run away or has done so in the past, tell him or her the following:

[Name of your teenager], if you decide to run away again, the punishment will be severe. Running away means going somewhere or leaving the house without a parent's permission or not coming home at the appointed curfew time. I will not tell you what the punishment will be ahead of time. You will find out when you return home. If you leave or do not come home within one hour after your curfew time, I will call the police and report you missing. When you return, I will hand you a piece of paper with the punishment written out. The note also may be waiting for you on your pillow or taped to your bedroom door. I will try not to yell or lecture when you return. We have much to work out on the home front. Everyone has to change, not just you. However, this will not happen unless the running away is stopped long enough to make a difference.

If your teenager still runs, call the police and report the teen as a runaway. The police will do nothing except log your teen's name into their computer. Nevertheless, informing the police is important, because if your teenager is stopped by the police or picked up for a crime, his or her name will be in the computer and you will be called.

After notifying the police, select the item or items you plan to pawn and take them to work or place at a friend's house before your teen returns home. Don't forget to troubleshoot any backup plans ahead of time. Photocopy the pawn ticket, fill in the information, and deliver it to your teenager.

PAWN TICKET for _____

Teen's Name

Good for::_____

Name personal item(s) pawned.

I/We have secured this item(s) in a safe place outside the home.
There is no need to look for it since it is not here.

You may have this item(s) back if you do not leave the house
without permission for _____ straight days,
starting_____ and ending _____.

If you leave the house without permission before the _____ is up, the
item(s) above will immediately be pawned/sold and not replaced

Alert

Please understand that your teenager probably will run away the first
or second time you put the pawn ticket in motion. He or she will want
to test the waters and see if you will be consistent and follow through.
This behavior is normal and to be expected. If you understand this
beforehand, you may not take this testing so personally and abandon
this consequence at the first sign of trouble.

Strategy #4: The Gandhi Consequence

**See Counselor
for Direction!**

This consequence was named after the Indian leader
Mohandas Gandhi, a noted advocate of nonviolent
protest, because you can commit to all-day nonviolent sit-ins with your teenager if the teen continues to
run away. Using this consequence, each of you would
be required to sit and stare silently at one another. Dr.
Neil Schiff, a colleague of mine, developed this consequence. It may
sound strange, but it works.

Teenagers want their space and would rather stop running away
than endure an all-day sit-in staring at you. If you use this consequence correctly, I can almost guarantee that you will never have
another problem with running away again. However, to be successful,

you must have the guidance of a competent counselor. Please follow the following instructions to put this consequence into place.

Preparation and Setup

Before your teenager runs away again, inform him or her about this consequence. In previous consequences, I instructed you not to tell your teen ahead of time, to keep him or her off balance.

In this case, I want your teenager to recoil at even the thought of the two of you spending an entire day staring at one another. The very idea may be enough to stop your teenager from running away again, provided that he or she is totally convinced that you are willing to follow through if necessary.

The length of time for a sit-in should be double the time your teenager has been gone without permission. For example, if your teenager was away without permission for three hours, the sit-in time would be six hours. If your teen was missing for five hours, the sit-in time would be ten hours, and so on. Because longer time periods are a hardship on you, you might want to set the maximum sit-in time at fourteen hours, even if your teenager was gone longer than seven hours.

How well behaved your teenager is during the sit-in can also determine the time limit. You can agree up front that the total time is extended by thirty minutes each time there is yelling or swearing. In some cases, you may want to reduce the time by one hour for every hour the teen is quiet and not talking.

During the sit-in, neither party can listen to the radio, watch television, or make or receive phone calls. Instead, you are required to stare at one another without saying a word. If your teenager starts talking for more than several minutes, the hour starts all over again. Tell your teen this ahead of time.

The sit-in should physically take place in a small room with only one exit, such as a bedroom or small den. You should sit in front of the one exit door to prevent your son or daughter from leaving abruptly. Use the following sample statement to warn your teen about this consequence:

[Teenager's name], if you run away again, the consequence will be severe. To keep you safe, we will use what is known as the Gandhi Consequence. This means that we will sit in a room together all day and stare at one another. There will be no television or phone. If you try to leave or talk during this time, there will be consequences. The time we will sit and stare will be double the time you were gone, up to fourteen hours. This time may be reduced for good behavior or extended. The choice is yours. Remember that this consequence will not have to be enforced unless you choose to run away again.

The Gandhi Consequence can be effective if only one parent can take off work; however, this consequence is much stronger if both parents are present. In addition, if things should get heated, one parent can coach the other to calm down. For a single parent, it is absolutely necessary for another adult to be present to make it more difficult for the teenager to act out or become verbally abusive.

Troubleshooting and Backup Plans

As with the other consequences, you must troubleshoot with your counselor everything that could go wrong ahead of time. The following are some of the common what-will-I-do-if scenarios you may encounter:

- **What will I do if** my teen tries to get up and leave?

- **What will I do if** my teen throws a temper tantrum and starts yelling and screaming?

One way to prevent your teen from leaving is to have him or her strip down to underwear and a T-shirt before the watch begins. You also can lock their other clothes in a safe place before they come home. Your teen is not likely to run out of the house half naked. If this is a problem, block the one exit door in the bedroom with a huge dresser. If the teen gets violent or tries to push you away, let him or her go. You can use some of the other strategies in this book to stop this behavior.

If your teen throws a temper tantrum, ignore it. DO NOT LET YOUR TEEN BAIT YOU. No matter how many buttons are pushed, you must stay calm and not respond except to say "Your time begins when you are quiet."

Here is how the Gandhi Consequence worked with one family.

"You Want to Do What!"

Sixteen-year-old Katie was referred to my office because of running away. When the parents attempted to stop her from leaving the house to see her boyfriend, Katie became hysterical and ran away. The police were called and Katie was taken to the hospital for observation.

At the first meeting, I recommended the Gandhi Consequence the next time Katie ran away. Katie immediately recoiled at the idea that she might have to sit in the living room with her parents for an entire day without talking. In fact, Katie said, "You want me to do what?" and "There is no way in hell."

The father reported that he would be unable to take off work to spend all day with his daughter. I then excused Katie from the room and told the father that nothing else to this point had worked and that this consequence was worth a try. In addition, I emphasized that Katie had recoiled at the idea. This alone was a good sign that the consequence would be effective.

The father was instructed to sit in front of the door to block the daughter from running away. The parents were also shown ways to be nonreactive to Katie if she started to scream or throw a temper tantrum. Two days after this meeting, Katie tested this consequence by running away. The next day the father took off work as promised, and the parents and daughter had an all-day sit-in. The daughter hated this intervention so much that she never ran away again.

Why the Gandhi Consequence Works

Parents have told me that this is a tough consequence on them. Having to sit with a teen and not talk for hours at a time causes a lot of anxiety. Afterward, though, they say it was worth it. Their teen was ready to negotiate new terms that did not include running away or being disrespectful.

I think this consequence is effective because of what it communicates to the teenager. A parent who is willing to go to this much trouble and take off work gives a son or daughter these powerful messages:

- "I am not going anywhere. We are going to work this problem out together."

- "I love you and I will not run away from this problem. I am willing to sacrifice my time to prove this love."

- "I am physically present and I will not leave you no matter what you do."

An intervention this intense communicates these messages loud and clear. Desperate times often call for this kind of desperate measure.

After you use these strategies to locate the underlying problem and temporarily stop the running away, it's essential to develop a plan to solve any underlying family issues that make your teen run.

ACE #4: TEEN PREGNANCY OR SEXUAL PROMISCUITY

I used to be remarkably naïve about sexual promiscuity and teen pregnancy. While I knew that teens had sex, the issue rarely seemed to come up in my counseling sessions. Parents and teens hardly ever mentioned it. It was like the old saying, out of sight, out of mind. That was before Robert and his father taught me that what you don't see can be worse than what you do.

After a year's work together, I was about to end counseling with seventeen-year-old Robert and his family. We had accomplished a great deal. Robert initially had been referred to counseling because he beat up a boy so badly that he had to go to the hospital. The father was a military officer who was extremely angry and bitter with his son. Robert had joined the household after his dad had remarried and fought constantly with his stepmother.

Robert and his father were getting into fistfights by the time they came to see me. The family followed the steps of this book to the letter. Dad was a quick study and figured out that Robert was pushing his buttons to play a game. Dad also used playful strategies such as using a squirt gun to cool Robert off when he got angry. In the end, Robert and his dad were hugging one another for the first time in years and going on special outings.

Things could not have looked more promising. But then, at the end of our last meeting, Robert asked to speak with me alone. He told me that he had gotten his girlfriend pregnant. When I asked Robert if his father had talked to him about sex and protection, he replied, "Not really. My dad gets uncomfortable about the subject." At that point, I realized I had done the same thing. During the entire year of counseling, we had talked about everything *but* sex and contraception.

When the family found out about the pregnancy, "the stuff really hit the fan." Everything that the family had worked for suddenly fell apart. The father refused to speak to the son, and all affection and special outings stopped. In turn, Robert moved in with some older kids and started smoking pot. Even after the baby was born, the father and son refused to speak. The mother is now on welfare and no one knows where Robert is.

This was a sad ending to what should have been a successful story. I made a mistake and learned three valuable lessons from this family.

First, no matter how uncomfortable it gets, parents and counselors need to talk openly to teenagers and children about sex and contraception. Robert told me, "In the black community, the more kids you father the better. It makes me look cool and makes me like a godfather." If either the father or I had talked about sex early on, we might have made a difference. The latest survey research from the Centers for Disease Control found that 78 percent of white and 70 percent of African American teenagers reported that poor communication between a girl and her parents is the main reason why teen girls have babies and boys get girls pregnant.

Second, a 1999 review of research studies on teen pregnancy by the Department of Health and Human Services confirms that teens with behavior problems are the most likely group to initiate sexual intercourse and have unintended pregnancies. Yet these teens are the least prepared group to become parents. Raising a child takes patience and resources that are acquired with age, education, and maturity. Extreme teens usually do not possess these resources.

Third, sexual promiscuity and especially teen pregnancy are powerful aces up your teenager's sleeve. If you fail to confront them, as Robert's family and I failed to do, positive changes can be undone in a single moment.

According to the most recent statistics from the Centers for Disease Control, we have a problem with teen pregnancy:

■ The United States has the highest teenage pregnancy rate of all developed countries.

■ About 1 million teenagers become pregnant each year; 95 percent of those pregnancies are unintended, and almost one-third end in abortions. This means that nearly 4 girls in 100, ages fifteen to seventeen, had a baby, and 13 percent of all U.S. births were to teens.

■ According to 1999 Youth Risk Behavior Survey data, 8.3 percent of students report having had sex before age thirteen—a disturbing 15 percent increase since 1997.

■ Public costs from teenage childbearing totaled $120 billion from 1985 to 1990; $48 billion could have been saved if each birth had been postponed until the mother was at least twenty years old.

■ Teens fifteen and older who drink are seven times likelier to have sexual intercourse and twice as likely to have it with four or more partners than nondrinking teens. More than half of teens (53.3 percent) say the main reason teens do not use contraception is because they are drinking or using drugs.

■ Children whose mothers were age seventeen or younger when they were born tend to have more school difficulties and severe behavior problems.

■ Teens have not developed good parenting skills or have social support systems to help them deal with the stress of raising an infant. The risk of abuse or neglect increases.

Current programs to stop teen pregnancy are not having a major impact. For at least two decades, we have spent millions of taxpayer dollars on programs to delay the initiation of sexual activity, improve contraceptive use, and reduce or delay pregnancies. Yet to date there is little to no evidence that any of these programs actually work. In 1997 a study by Dr. Cynthia Franklin reported in the *Journal of Marriage in the Family* that only thirty-two pregnancy prevention programs conducted outcome research on their effectiveness. Of these thirty-two programs, *none* had a significant effect in reducing the sexual activity of teenagers.

Since we are not sure what works, I can only offer my opinion on some promising programs I have seen, tried, or read about. Many of these suggestions come from the teenagers themselves—the girls who have gotten pregnant or the boys who have had unprotected sex.

Strategy #1: Build Your Teen's Self-Esteem

Many pregnant teens say something like this:

> "We get pregnant for two reasons. We want to feel love from our boyfriends and have a child that we can call our own. We do this to fill in a missing hole of not feeling loved by our parents. We desperately want someone to love us. We are also too scared to say no to our boyfriends. We are afraid that they will get mad and reject us. Another reason is that we have nothing to look forward to in life: no goals, no skills, and no self-respect. We don't like ourselves enough to say no when a boy doesn't want to use protection."

These young women do not have strong enough self-esteem to say no either to sex in general or to unprotected sex in particular. According to research done at the National Campaign to Prevent Teen Pregnancy, pressure from partners not to use contraception is not uncommon. More than half of teens recently surveyed (51.7 percent) said one of the main reasons that teens do not use contraception is because their partner didn't want to. Here are some recommendations from our teenagers:

- **Sex education is not enough.**
  We want more than *The Miracle of Birth* film. In other words, please take things to the next level. For instance, we need to hear real stories from real people . . . like teen parents. We know that when it comes to talking about sex, there is a lot that schools can't do. But teaching from the heart and not the chalkboard will make a big difference. There should be teen mothers with kids who can speak from experience and get conversations going on the connection between saying no and self-esteem. Give us sex or abstinence education courses that are equal to DARE. Drugs are serious, but so is sex. We get DARE education twice a week, but sex education once a year or less.

■ **We need to feel good about ourselves.**
We need activities or opportunities to promote our self-esteem.
This could be anything from classes on getting a job to after-school activities like working in a nursing home. Unless we can respect ourselves and see a future, there is no reason to say no to sex. If we cannot love ourselves, we will look outside of ourselves and seek that love from others.

■ **We need love at home.**
We need for you to take the time to love us, listen to us, and tell us that you are proud. If we do not get love at home, we will find it in the streets. Sex feels good for the moment, and it feels like love. You want it more and more. But this is the lie. Sex and love are often two different things. We don't realize this until it is too late or when our boyfriends leave us as soon as we get pregnant.

These are hard truths. We can initiate all the programs we want, but in the end it comes back to this basic premise: When teens feel unloved and out of control, they turn to the one thing that they do have control over: their bodies. They can have sex and experience a false sense of love and intimacy.

To address some of these areas of concern, I recommend the strategies of volunteer work, special outings and praise, and educational or job success. There are obviously others, but these will get you started.

Volunteer Work

If you believe your teen is at high risk to have promiscuous or unprotected sex, you must find programs or ways to help raise his or her self-esteem. One successful method is volunteer work at elderly homes, homeless shelters, or animal shelters. Ask your teen to volunteer at one of these places. Offer to make it worth your teen's while. Perhaps you could excuse him or her from doing homework one day a week (unless there was a test or a major paper due the next day). Believe me, one day of missed homework will not do lasting harm and can be a great bargaining chip to jump-start the process. If you prefer, you can use other motivators like extra phone time, an extra hour of curfew, or money.

Once you get your teen to volunteer, amazing things will start to happen. By helping less fortunate people or animals, teens actually help themselves. Teens, especially teens who start out with low self-esteem, eventually look forward to going because it makes them feel better about themselves.

If your teen resists, make it mandatory. Your teen will be unable to see the payoff until much later. Until then you must take charge, as Gina's mother did in the following example.

Puppy Love

Sixteen-year-old Gina was in the high-risk category. She was shy and never looked you in the eye. Gina's parents both worked and had little time left over for her. This was one of the reasons she hit the streets. She felt ignored and unloved at home, and she tried to find this love in the arms of one boy after another.

Gina began having sex at thirteen and had had two abortions by the time she was sixteen. Her mother finally began to make the connection between low self-esteem and sexual promiscuity. To combat this problem, the mother cut a deal with her daughter. Gina would receive ten dollars a day for up to two days of volunteer work after school from the hours of 3:00 P.M. to 7:00 P.M. at the local animal shelter. Gina loved money, so she jumped at the chance.

One day something remarkable happened. A little Beagle puppy was brought in. The puppy had been hit by a car and was extremely malnourished. The puppy was not expected to live through the night. Gina called her mom and asked if she could stay with the puppy. Gina suddenly forgot her shyness and fed the puppy through an eye dropper. She prayed that the puppy would not die. She fell asleep but was awakened to the feel of the puppy licking her face. The puppy lived and Gina named her "Miracle."

From that moment on, people around Gina began to notice a change. She carried herself straighter, and she began to look you in the eye with confidence. Soon Gina was volunteering her weekends and donating her own money to the shelter. She even began a program called "Adopt a Puppy or a Kitten for a day" in which people could take the animal home and return it. Gina knew that once you felt the animal's love, the puppy or kitten would likely be adopted permanently. Most important of all, Gina stopped sleeping around. On the rare occasions that she did have sex, Gina made the boy wear a condom. She told her mother, "I don't deserve to be treated badly by anyone!"

Special Outings and Praise

Your teen craves your attention, praise, and appreciation. These three things will definitely raise your teen's self-esteem, which in turn can lead to a lower risk of unprotected sex and teen pregnancy. Step 7 presents a detailed discussion of special outings.

Catching teenagers doing something right helps them feel good about themselves. A girl who feels good will not need acceptance from a boy who refuses to wear a condom. A boy is less likely to have unprotected sex.

You also have to make the time to go on special outings with your teen once a week. Otherwise, your at-risk teen may turn to the street for this love and attention. Teens tell me all the time that it is easier to talk about difficult topics like sex in relaxed settings, such as McDonald's or the park. You also can use these special outings as a time to praise your teen

Such outings will backfire, however, if you are inconsistent. If you start making time for special outings once a week and then stop, your teen will get the message loud and clear: "You are not worth my time and effort." Inconsistency will lower your teen's self-esteem even more. If you are going to use this strategy, please do not start special outings and then stop them.

Remember one important factor: You and your teen may be out of practice in doing things together. Therefore, you should be prepared to have a lousy time, at least for the first two weeks. You have to get used to one another again.

Once you and your teen have begun to warm up to each other, you can gradually bring up the topic of sex, using the tips and resources in Strategy #2 to do so without scaring your teenager away.

Educational and/or Job Success

A 1999 review by the Department of Health and Human Services suggests that adolescents engage in risky sexual behaviors because they believe that they have little to lose. Teenagers who experience educational and job success and see positive future opportunities will likely have a stronger motivation to avoid pregnancy and parenthood.

Jobs are one of the best remedies available to raise your teen's self-esteem. A job is a rite of passage into becoming an adult. Unfortunately, though, teens who have low self-esteem often drag their feet or refuse to look for a job because they're afraid of rejection. Here's how you can help:

- **Preparation training**
  Conduct a mock job hunting training session with your teen from beginning to end. Start by showing how to search through want ads and develop a résumé. (If your teen has no job experience, help him or her type out a short biography.) Bring home a blank job application and demonstrate how to fill it out. Finally, conduct mock job interviews in which you pretend to be the potential employee as well as the employer.

- **Pose as a customer**
  Many entry-level jobs for teens are in stores, food service establishments, and movie theaters, where the interviews are conducted in the open. If your teen is interviewing for such a job, go with him or her to the first couple of interviews. Pretend you are a customer while your teen is talking to the manager. This not only allows you to get things going by taking your teen to the first couple of interviews, but it gives you a chance to observe and give your teen pointers.

■ **At least three job applications per day**
Require your teen to come home from each job search with copies of at least three application forms and/or the names of any manager who interviewed him or her. Randomly call these places to spot check that these interviews took place. Your teenager will try to come up with all kinds of excuses as to why this is unfair. You must be firm and say that there is no negotiation. Make sure to specify the consequences of noncompliance—such as grounding or loss of telephone or TV privileges—up front, and then carry out those consequences if necessary.

■ **Following up on applications**
Make sure your teen logs in the job applied for, the date of the contact, and the manager's name and number. Add a column in their log that contains the date and time of the callback. Show your teenager how to follow up on a job application. Specify in advance that if your teen gets the job but quits or is fired, the whole three-applications-a-day process will be repeated.

Each of these activities is an indirect way to attack the problem of risky sexual behavior by raising your child's self-esteem. Strategy #2 will help you confront the problem head-on.

Strategy #2: Talk to Your Teen About Sex

One of the most promising strategies to stop teen pregnancy seems to be the simplest: Talk to your teen directly about sex. The National Campaign to Prevent Teen Pregnancy revealed the following ten things that teens want their parents to talk to them about when it comes to sex. Please visit their Web site at *www.teenpregnancy.org*, which is one of the best resources that I have ever come across. It is reprinted here with their permission.

1. Show us why teen pregnancy is such a bad idea. For instance, let us hear directly from teen mothers and fathers about how hard it has been for them. Even though most of us don't want to get pregnant, sometimes we need real-life examples to help motivate us.

2. Talk to us honestly about love, sex, and relationships. Just because we're young doesn't mean that we can't fall in love or be deeply interested in sex. These feelings are very real and powerful to us. Help us to handle the feelings in a safe way—without getting hurt or hurting others.

3. Telling us not to have sex is not enough. Explain why you feel that way, and ask us what we think. Tell us how you felt as a teen. Listen to us and take our opinions seriously. And no lectures, please.

4. Whether we're having sex or not, we need to be prepared. We need to know how to avoid pregnancy and sexually transmitted diseases.

5. If we ask you about sex or birth control, don't assume we are already having sex. We may just be curious, or we may just want to talk with someone we trust. And don't think giving us information about sex and birth control will encourage us to have sex.

6. Pay attention to us before we get into trouble. Programs for teen moms and teen fathers are great, but we all need encouragement, attention, and support. Reward us for doing the right thing—even when it seems like no big thing.

7. Sometimes all it takes not to have sex is not having the opportunity. If you can't be home with us after school, make sure we have something to do that we really like, where there are other kids and some adults who are comfortable with kids our age. Often we have sex because there's not much else to do. Don't leave us alone so much.

8. We really care what you think, even if we don't always act like it. When we don't end up doing exactly what you tell us to, don't think that you've failed to reach us.

9. Show us what good, responsible relationships look like. We're as influenced by what you do as by what you say. If you demonstrate sharing, communication, and responsibility in your own relationships, we will be more likely to follow your example.

10. We hate "the talk" as much as you do. Instead, start talking with us about sex and responsibility when we're young, and keep the conversation going as we grow older.

Common Questions on Sex

The National Campaign to Prevent Teen Pregnancy asked teens specifically what they wanted to learn from their parents about sex, love, and relationships. If you don't talk to your teen and answer the following questions, your teen will get the answers on the street—answers that will be filled with misinformation. As the next page's cartoon illustrates, talking to your teen about sex is difficult. But would you rather do the talking or have your teen's friends fill her head with lies or half-truths?

Common Unanswered Sex Questions

- When is it okay to have sex?

- Does my partner really love me? How do you know when you're in love?

- How do I know when I'm ready?

- Why do so many girls get pregnant when there is plenty of birth control information available?

- Where can I find out about birth control?

- Can you get pregnant the first time you have sex?

- How can you tell if you might be pregnant?

- How well does the withdrawal method work?

- How far is too far for my age?

- How do I say no without making my boy/girlfriend feel bad and without feeling pressured?

- Why do teens feel they have to have sex before marriage? Is it to feel cool?

- How can I ask my parents about sex or tell them I'm ready to have sex without them having a heart attack?

- Why don't parents and other adults stress abstinence as a a way to avoid pregnancy?

- Can you get pregnant while having your period?

- What is the difference between intimacy and sex?

Source: www.teenpregnancy.org

Copy these questions and hand them directly to your teen. Ask which questions interest him or her. If your teen seems disinterested in the topic, say you would like to go through the questions anyway. This will allow your teenager to save face while opening the lines of communication.

In addition to talking to your teen about sex in general, you should use the books and resources available at *www.teenpregnancy. org* to have an open and frank discussion about the risks of AIDS and other sexually transmitted diseases. You will be surprised at how uninformed your teen may be about these subjects and how much inaccurate information there is out there.

If you don't know the answer to a question, use it as an opportunity to investigate the answer with your teen. You can even turn it into a game with your teen by initiating a competition that offers a reward to the first person who finds the information.

Reprinted with special permission of King Feature Syndicate.

Common Barriers

Parents tell me that one of their biggest barriers to talking about sex is the fear that by doing so they are actually encouraging their teens to have premarital sex. The most consistent research finding from the National Campaign to Prevent Teen Pregnancy, however, is that sex education does *not* cause teens to initiate sex when they would not otherwise have done so. Talking about sex does not make your teen more sexually active and may in fact have the opposite effect. If you talk about sex, it is not such a taboo subject—which may make it easier for your teen to talk to you if he or she is confused or feels peer pressure. In the end, an open dialogue is likely to decrease the risk of sex or teen pregnancy.

Strategy #3: Closely Monitor Internet Use and Abuse

Internet use will become more and more of an issue with the advances in computer technology. Teens on the Internet are already having cybersex—simulated sexual encounters— in chat rooms and setting up real-life sexual encounters. (If you don't believe me, check out some of the profiles of the teenagers online—and make sure to check your own teen's profile!)

Many of you are not as computer savvy as your teenager; you may barely know how to turn on the computer, let alone monitor e-mail or chat rooms. This can become a serious liability. There are more and more sexual predators online—older men or teens who will use any means necessary to meet and seduce your teenage son or daughter in person.

Sex is more likely to occur when your teen is left unsupervised and has too much time on his or her hands. The Internet maximizes their opportunity to find random sex partners. For example, your teen can go to "member profile" on almost any Internet service provider and type in the phrase "I want sex." Dozens of other teens—or predators pretending to be teens—in their area who fit this profile will pop up. Your teen can then chat with them online and perhaps arrange to meet them in person. Your teen also has access to pornographic sites.

I strongly encourage you to place the computer in the family room, where you can monitor your teen's online activity more closely. In addition, services like America Online or Earthlink have parental controls. Call up technical support and say you want to block access to chat rooms and your teen's ability to receive instant messages. You also can block your teen's access to pornographic sites and set it up so that they can only send or receive e-mail to and from certain friends. Ask them to take you through the process of looking through old e-mail. If your teenager does not agree with the parental controls, apply them anyway. There are too many sexual predators out there to take a risk.

If you do find sexually explicit e-mail, take the computer away or enable stricter parental controls. Your teen can use the computer for class projects and word processing without accessing e-mail or chat rooms. Some of the warning signs include

- Long hours on the computer in secret

- A sudden change in attitude

- Will not let you on the computer

- Staying out late

- Secret phone calls

Maggie's story demonstrates where these warning signs can lead.

Cybersex Turns Real

Fourteen-year-old Maggie was very naïve when it came to sex. The most she had ever done was kiss a boy at a dance. Then one day she went into a chat room by mistake. Several boys e-mailed and flirted with her. Maggie loved the attention and the next day could not wait to go home and get online.

Her computer was in her bedroom, and she had lots of privacy. Maggie's mom, who was as naïve about computers as her daughter was about sex, thought Maggie was online downloading articles for school. She never gave it a second thought. Besides, she had no idea how e-mail worked or that there was even such a thing as chat rooms.

One day Maggie met an eighteen-year-old online. He told her everything she wanted to hear, including that he loved her. Soon the conversations turned graphically sexual. He taught her how to masturbate and how to access pornographic sites. When Maggie told him that she felt guilty, he replied that it was only fantasy play. Soon Maggie was hooked and climbed out of her bedroom window to see him late at night.

Maggie's grades started to fall and she grew increasingly disrespectful to her mother. When Maggie's mom finally found out, she tried to pull the plug on the computer. Maggie went ballistic and told her mom that she would kill herself. The mother backed off and Maggie continued her relationship until she got pregnant. The mother wondered where the innocent Maggie she knew had gone.

Strategy #4: Contractual Contraception

If your teen has low self-esteem and is sexually active, you may have to buy time. It takes a while to help teens feel good about themselves again. In the meantime, they still may be having unprotected sex and risking pregnancy.

One option is to request that your teenage daughter get a birth control shot known as Depo-Provera. This contraceptive shot contains chemicals similar to those found in birth control pills. Shots are usually scheduled twelve weeks apart. Each shot costs between ten and forty dollars; some family planning clinics provide it for free or at a reduced cost. "Depo" is a very effective method of birth control. A user who receives her shots on time has about a 0.3 percent chance of getting pregnant. Go to the clinic with your daughter to make sure she gets the contraceptive shot. Doing this avoids the power struggles that will ensue if you make her take a birth control pill each day.

If your teenage daughter is at high risk for having unprotected sex, give her a choice: She can either receive the shot (or take the Pill in your presence every day), or she will not be allowed out without adult supervision. Some readers will think that this strategy is harsh or that it violates a teen's civil liberties. (Moreover, the strategy may seem unfairly directed toward girls; unfortunately, there are no equivalent shots or pills for boys.) Yet we place our teens in psychiatric hospitals every day against their will for things as minor as unruly behavior or as major as threatening suicide. I personally think that forced hospitalization is much worse than making your teen take birth control to prevent the birth of another unwanted child or the risk of abortion.

This is what happened to sixteen-year-old Paula.

The Shot or an Unborn Child

Paula had been in and out of foster care homes all her life. She felt unwanted and unloved. Even though she now had caring and committed foster parents, as soon as she started to get close to them, she would act out and misbehave.

Despite her foster parents' love, Paula still felt emotionally damaged. Years of scar tissue would not heal overnight. As a result, she still sought love through sex with older men that she met at the mall or online. Afraid of rejection, she didn't dare to say no if they didn't want to wear a condom.

When her foster parents found out, they were stunned. Paula seemed to be doing so much better. Why would she subject herself to being degraded by these men? Paula could not give them a good reason.

They explained to Paula that they did not approve of sex before marriage. Yet they could not be with her twenty-four hours a day. Therefore, as a precaution they would make the following mandatory rule: She either had to go with her foster mother every three months to receive a birth control shot, or she could not leave the house unsupervised. In the meantime, they would do everything in their power to help Paula feel stronger and better about herself. There was a local self-esteem group that she could enroll in and a volunteer job available at the animal shelter.

Paula reluctantly agreed to these terms. Privately she told me that she felt relieved. She could focus on getting stronger emotionally rather than on worrying about getting pregnant. Things were out in the open and not secret any more. Paula cut her sexual activity in half. As she said, "Now that my foster parents know and I have to go with my foster mom to the clinic, I don't want to disappoint them."

Strategy #5: Real Teens, Real Stories

It may be important for your teen to experience the harsh reality of teen pregnancy and parenthood. If your daughter or son is sexually active, I highly recommend this strategy as a preventive tactic.

The first step is for you to visit your local homeless shelter or halfway house. Do this first step without your teenager present. Tell the director your purpose and ask if you can speak with some of the teenage mothers. Tell the mothers your situation and ask them if they would be willing to talk to your son or daughter about the downside of teen pregnancy. Tell them that your goal is to prevent your daughter from getting pregnant before she becomes an adult or your son from engaging in unprotected sex. (It's important to speak with these moms ahead of time to see if they want to volunteer their time and if they share your same views. You don't want to visit the shelter with your teen cold and have a teen mom talk about all the benefits of a teen pregnancy.)

After you have laid the groundwork, ask your teen to go with you. If your child refuses, a bribe will be the best ten or twenty dollars that you ever spend. Your teen needs to see and hear the real-life consequences of unprotected sex and teen pregnancy. After the meeting, take your son or daughter out to lunch and try to discuss his or her thoughts and feelings openly. Talk about your reactions as well.

Go back with your teen for a visit every six months to take blankets, clothes, and food, especially around the holidays. In addition to being a Good Samaritan, you are keeping the consequence of unprotected sex fresh in your teen's mind.

The Real Deal

Fifteen-year-old Maria was currently having unprotected sex with several older high school boys. Her mother found out after openly talking about sex with her daughter over breakfast one

Sunday morning. Instead of lecturing or preaching, the mother decided to take a back-door approach to the problem.

The mother told Maria that she could not physically stop her from having sex. But as an alternative, she asked Maria to take next Saturday morning to visit teen moms who had newborn babies. The goal was to see what it would be like to have a child. Maria did not want to go but agreed after her mom offered her ten dollars for her time.

During the week, the mother visited the local shelter, where she found three teen moms who agreed to talk with Maria. Two of them said that they would do anything if it would stop someone from going through what they had to endure.

When Saturday arrived, Maria was shocked at the conditions at the shelter. The real shock came when she met the three women with their children. Each one told her own horror story; what stuck in Maria's mind was the way all the men had left these women high and dry and the fact that they no longer had any freedom to go out and have fun like ordinary teenagers. On the way home, Maria and her mom had a heart-to-heart discussion on what they had seen and heard. Soon after, Maria went on the Pill.

ACE #5: ALCOHOL OR DRUG ABUSE

One of the frightening realities of having an out-of-control teen is the high likelihood that he or she will experiment or abuse alcohol and/or drugs. When teens hang out with the wrong crowd, alcohol and drugs are usually part of the mix.

Substance abuse is one of the most difficult aces to stop. As soon as you think you've stopped the alcohol or drug use, your teen may relapse and you may feel as if you're back to square one. The risk of relapse gives your teen tremendous power to intimidate, frustrate, and scare you into backing down. Your teen knows the fear of an overdose is always in the back of your mind.

The Partnership for a Drug Free America has discovered an alarming trend. In 2000 a survey of 8,520 children and 822 parents across the United States revealed that "today's teens are less likely to consider drug use harmful and risky, more likely to believe that drug use is widespread and tolerated, and feel more pressure to try illegal drugs than teens did just two years ago." Overall, drug abuse by teenagers has risen dramatically since 1996, while overall drug use among adults has stayed the same or dropped, according to the Department of Health and Human Services.

A major reason for these trends is that teens almost never think that they have an alcohol or drug problem. Whereas adults who abuse drugs or alcohol usually have experienced the ill effects—including major disruptions in their lives such as blackouts, liver disease, relationship problems, money problems, or loss of jobs—the vast majority of teens have not.

Most often adults have spent a longer time abusing drugs or alcohol. They have progressed from experimental use, to abuse, to an addiction. Experimental use means that you simply dabble in alcohol or drugs once in a great while. Abuse means that you are getting high on drugs or getting drunk on a regular basis. Addiction means that you have an inability to control your use—it seems that regardless of what you decide beforehand, you frequently wind up drunk or high. You also begin to experience problems at work, school, or in your relationships.

Teens typically have had only one to five years of experimental use or abuse with alcohol or drugs. They usually have not had the time to experience the negative sides of a full-scale addiction. As a result, they only see the upside: the side that helps numb emotional pain, represents an act of rebellion, and simply feels good at the moment. They still think it's glamorous and sophisticated to use drugs or alcohol.

Why Traditional Twelve-Step Programs Often Fail with Teens

Because of these key differences, traditional twelve-step programs, such as Alcoholics or Narcotics Anonymous, can fall short. Teens cannot get past the very first step of admitting that they have a problem. They honestly don't see it. As one fifteen-year-old told me, "Yeah, we play the game if we are in drug centers or in detention. We work the program and tell counselors what they want to hear: 'Yes, we have a problem and yes, we will work through the twelve steps.' But it's all bulls**t. It's fun to get high and drink, so why stop?"

The twelve-step program itself isn't the problem; it is a wonderful program that has saved hundreds of thousands of lives. The problem is getting teens to recognize that they have a problem so that they are ready to take the program seriously.

"Should I Be a Parent or My Teen's Friend?"

Another reason why teens abuse alcohol and drugs is because they can. Parents are afraid to get tough lest it lead to their teens getting upset and using more alcohol or drugs. As one father told me, "I don't know if I should be my son's father or his best friend. If I come down too hard, he threatens me by saying that the pressure will drive him to drink and smoke more pot. My oldest son died of a drug overdose. I'm scared to get tough."

In fact, though, your teen has no reason to stop if you act like a best friend. Your teen has plenty of friends. What your teen needs is structure or someone to say "This is the last chance I get to play parent to you. I will not stand idly by and do nothing while you slowly kill yourself," or "I love you enough to earn your respect before I gain your friendship. I care enough to tell you to stop using."

Teens who are abusing alcohol or drugs cannot think clearly and make good choices. They need more structure and guidance than any other type of teenager. It isn't easy to take charge in this situation, but doing so could save your teen's life.

Hard Choices

Ultimately, you have two choices:

1. *Do nothing:*
   You can decide to wait until your teen grows out of it or gets deeper into using and hits bottom as he or she gets older. When your teen finally sees the seedy side of drug or alcohol use, he or she may recognize the problem and be ready for a twelve-step program or just decide to quit altogether.

2. *Raise Their Bottom:*
   You can use the strategies in this step to "raise their bottom." Adults often have to reach bottom, a point where everything they love and cherish is gone, before they give up the love of drugs or booze. You can speed up this process by helping your teen hit bottom sooner rather than later so that he or she can begin to recognize the downside of drug or alcohol abuse.

The problem with doing nothing is that your teen may die from a drug overdose or driving while intoxicated while you wait for reality to kick in. An excellent question to ask your teen is "Why do you want to stop using alcohol or drugs?" If he or she cannot come up with an answer from the heart, any promises to stop will be meaningless.

Caution

The following strategies can help your teen hit bottom. Before using these interventions, however, hire a competent counselor. Drug or alcohol use and abuse can cause death or serious injury. When you use these interventions, you will be unleashing a hurricane. Your teen will fight to hold onto the alcohol or drugs. You will need the guidance of a good counselor to help you stand firm through the initial hailstorm and not abandon hope.

Please read every strategy before selecting the one(s) that will work for you. Some of these strategies are very intense, but you may need this high drama to shock your teen back into reality. Your teen is not going to magically wake up one day and admit that he or she has an alcohol or drug problem. Only you can bring your teen to this point.

Strategy #1: Find Out How Often Your Teenager Is Using

This is a necessary first step regardless of the other strategies you use. You have to determine whether and how often your teen is using before you can intervene. Guessing will only bring about bitter conflicts and resentment. For example, many parents try to smell their teen's breath for alcohol, look for bloodshot eyes, or see sleepiness and low energy as a sign of being high. If you accuse your teen, he or she will simply deny it. A power struggle then begins, and you'll waste your time arguing instead of getting to the heart of the problem.

To avoid this, you must do two things: try to talk openly and honestly to your teen about his or her alcohol or drug use and use objective methods of testing. Today you can go to almost any pharmacy and purchase an inexpensive drug test or find a breath alcohol detection kit over the Internet.

Talk with Your Teen Directly

First, sit down with your teen and just ask if he or she is using alcohol or drugs.

Would it surprise you to know that most parents have no idea if their teen is using drugs or alcohol, how much, how frequently, and what kind? *In addition, most of them haven't even asked.* Many teens tell me that they would tell their parents at least part of the truth if they only asked. When I asked teens why they thought their parents didn't ask, they told me: "Because they don't want to know; they don't know how to ask; or they are too busy and they don't have the time." Unfortunately, drug dealers and negative peers will make the time.

A 1998 survey by the Partnership for a Drug Free America underscores this point. "While virtually all parents (98 percent) say they've talked with their teenagers about drugs at least once, fewer teens (65 percent) recall the same conversation." Finally, the survey found that teenagers were twice as likely to use marijuana if they had not learned about the risks from their parents.

Reprinted with special permission of King Feature Syndicate.

The following signs may indicate that your son or daughter is actively using alcohol and/or drugs.

☐ Giving up positive activities such as sports, homework, or hanging out with friends who don't use drugs or drink

☐ Looking rundown, hopeless, depressed, or even suicidal

☐ Sudden changes in moods and irritability

☐ Constantly walking around tired or sleeping in class on a regular basis

☐ A sudden drop in grades

☐ An abrupt change in personality—going from Dr. Jekyll to Mr. Hyde

☐ Avoiding you and others in order to get high or drunk

☐ Suspension from school for an alcohol- or drug-related incident

If you see these signs, choose a day and a time when your teen is in a good mood, and ask the following questions:

Is it OK if I ask you a difficult question? When was the last time you used alcohol or drugs?

Never ask your teen a "yes" or "no" question regarding drug use. If you ask, "Have you ever used alcohol or drugs?" the answer will most likely be no. Using the suggested format, you are respectfully treating your teen like an adult (teens love this) by asking permission to ask a difficult question. By asking *when* was the last time he or she used, lying becomes much more difficult. If teens do lie, their expression often will give them away.

I am not going to punish you for using alcohol or drugs until we have an agreement in place. I am asking because I care. How often have you used, and what are the types of alcohol or drugs that you have experimented with?

Your goal at this point is to establish trust and find out how deeply your teen is involved with drugs or alcohol. It is important not to punish your teen for being honest about past behavior; you are being honest in return by indicating that once a future contract has been struck, your teen will be held accountable.

If you yourself experimented with alcohol or drugs as a teen, you might want to tell your teen about this and how you wish that your parents had cared enough to ask. Modeling this kind of openness will make it easier for your teen to open up.

Monitor the Usage Objectively

If it appears that your teen is lying or actively using, monitor alcohol or drug intake carefully through drug kits or breath alcohol detection tests. If your teen refuses or states that he or she is only experimenting, say the following:

I appreciate your honesty and I want to keep the lines of communication open. To do this, I also have to be honest and straight up with you. If you are experimenting with alcohol, I definitely don't condone it. You are legally underage. However, I cannot watch you twenty-four hours, seven days a week. I want to trust you to do the right thing and tell me if you are getting in too deep so that we can work through the problem together.

I want you to know my position up front. If I find any drugs on these premises, on your person, or in your room, I will immediately call the police. If I don't, I could be held legally responsible. If I suspect anything, I will randomly search your room.

If you look drunk or stoned at any time, I will ask you to submit to a random drug or alcohol test. If you test clean, I will honestly apologize and my trust for you will grow stronger. If you test dirty or come up with any level of alcohol use, the consequences will be severe. They will be less severe if you tell me first or before I administer the test.

We know that teens will experiment. Many of us did. But the difference here is that you will be putting safeguards in place to prevent experimentation from turning into abuse or addiction. One of the main tasks parents face is to help keep their teens alive until they reach a level of maturity that will enable them to make better decisions.

Drug kits. Most local pharmacies sell kits that will test your teen's urine for drugs, for a price between ten and twenty dollars. You can also purchase these kits through the following Internet sites: *www.alcoholtesting.com* or *www.drugtestsuccess.com*. Aside from making the general notice in the statement above, do not give your teen advance warning about the test. He or she might try to contaminate the results through herbal vitamins, bleach, or special shakes. Goldenseal and vitamin B complex are used often by teens; they can be purchased at any vitamin store. If you see these herbs or vitamins, your teen is almost certainly using drugs. (The chances of seeing the labels go up if your teen is court-ordered to submit random drug tests.) Confiscate these items. The makers of drug tests have come out with a product called Tamper Test that will determine if your teen's urine has been altered. You can purchase this test for about ten dollars at *www.alcoholtesting.com*.

You must also physically watch your teen urinate in the cup, to be sure that he or she doesn't substitute someone else's clean urine. (Drug users even can buy clean urine off of the Internet; "it is guaranteed to give clean drug test results or your money back.")

If you suspect drug use, I recommend random testing about twice a month, or more often if your teen tests dirty. If your teen refuses to take the test, do not get into a power struggle. Tell your teen that he or she has five minutes to decide, then leave the room. If your teen refuses, simply remind him or her about the no-drug contract (see the next section), which states: "If you refuse to take the test, you are admitting guilt and are subject to the same consequence as if you tested dirty. This mirrors exactly what happens if were pulled over by the police for suspected drunk driving and you refused to take a breath alcohol test."

Breath alcohol tests. You can purchase a breath alcohol detector known as BreathScan through *www.alcoholtesting.com* at a current price of $15.95 for a packet of six. Unlike drug tests, breath alcohol tests cannot be administered randomly because alcohol does not stay in the body very long. Administer this test immediately after you smell alcohol on your teen's breath or you suspect that he or she is drunk.

A drunk teen may get angry or violent if you try to force him or her to blow into the BreathScan tube. Ask only once. If your teen refuses, do not spend time arguing. Do not remind your teen about the predetermined consequences for refusal. Simply exit and wait until your teen is sober.

If your teen has been drinking and driving, give him or her a BreathScan test. If your teen's blood alcohol level is above the legal limit (which in most states is .02 percent for youths under twenty-one years old) call the police. If your teen refuses to take the test and is obviously drunk, you should still call the police. (Do not tell your teen you are calling the cops or use the phone in front of him or her, as it could lead to violence.)

Tell the police officer that your son or daughter has committed an act of driving under the influence (DUI), and be sure to take down the officer's name. If the police refuse to come or don't show up, call back and ask to speak with the desk sergeant on duty. Tell the sergeant what happened and give the officer's name. Explain that you are counting on the police's help and that if no one comes a second time you will contact the local paper in the morning and give your story.

Choose from one of the following strategies as a consequence for drinking or drug use. Administer the consequences only after you have objectively established, either from a test or from the refusal to take one, that your teen is using drugs or alcohol. Once again, please use these strategies only under the guidance of a qualified counselor.

Strategy #2: The Prime Suspect

Call your local police department and ask to speak to a detective who specializes in juvenile crime. Many police departments have special departments devoted to teen drug and alcohol use. If there are no juvenile crime detectives, ask to speak to someone on duty.

Ask the detective to please come to your house. Tell the officer that you suspect your teen is drug trafficking from your home or using drugs or alcohol in general. You can say something like this:

I really need to scare my teen and I need your help. [Ask the detective if he or she is a parent.] As a parent, you know how we all need support sometimes. Could you come by unannounced on a time we agree upon when I know my son and some of his drug buddies will be here? If you can bring the K9 unit with the drug-sniffing dog, it would be even more dramatic. I will give you a picture of my son. You would then go up to him and say something like "I will take this picture so that I can be on the lookout for you and your friends. If I see you, I will shake you down or arrest you for suspected drug trafficking." Would you then search my son for drugs on his person and go with me to search his room? Your help will empower me as a parent and show my son that I mean business. Can we set up a specific date and time now?

Many detectives will be glad to help in this way. If the detective is hesitant, thank him or her for their time and hang up. Wait for the next shift to arrive and call to speak to another detective. Talk to as many officers as it takes until you find someone who will help. I once had to go through three detectives until I found the right one to help me with this intervention. The first two told me that they could not come out and search the teen for drugs, while the third one said that he would be happy to do so.

You also can use a camcorder, either secretly or openly, to tape your teen participating in illegal activities. One detective told me that she gets calls from parents all the time saying that their teens are using drugs, selling them, or drinking underage. However, once the detective gets to the house, the kids have left the scene or disposed of the physical evidence. Fooling the police becomes like a game to the teenagers, giving them the feeling that nothing can stop them. This is a very dangerous belief to have.

Parents who have bought, rented or borrowed camcorders have been extremely pleased with the results. When teens know that they can be taped at any time, they tend to keep the drugs or alcohol away from the house, which can make it more difficult for them to get drunk or stoned on a regular basis. This is exactly what you want to happen.

Pot, Lies, and Videotape

Fifteen-year-old Matt was extremely arrogant and felt that no one could touch him. He also had a bad attitude and was constantly disrespectful to his mother. He was so brazen that he walked around the home with bags of marijuana in his hand and began selling marijuana outside his ground-floor bedroom window, which quickly became a drive-through window for the entire neighborhood. Matt definitely did not think that he had a drug problem. There was no reason to stop; he was having too much fun.

Out of desperation, the mother borrowed a camcorder from a friend and secretly began to tape her son's dealings from behind some bushes, programming the date and time right on the tape. She then called the youth officer at the police department, explained that she had her son's drug trafficking on tape, and asked him to come by early in the morning before Matt got up. She asked if he could bring the K9 drug-sniffing dog because Matt would have his friends over as well. There would be plenty of pot on site.

The night before, the mom asked Matt if he wanted to have a sleepover with all of his friends. She even baked fresh chocolate chip cookies and served them with a smile. She suspected that everyone was smoking pot in Matt's bedroom and getting high. However, she said nothing.

Imagine everyone's surprise when they woke up to see four detectives with a K9 drug-sniffing dog sitting by their side and drug-trafficking movies playing on the big-screen television. Matt's friends' parents were also there; they had been called that morning. The detectives then searched Matt's room with the dog and found marijuana plants, bongs, and a one-pound bag of marijuana.

This intervention quickly ended the mom's nightmare. Under this intense supervision and accountability, Matt's arrogance began to crumble. He became like a leper among his drug friends, who were afraid of hanging around for fear of getting busted or videotaped. Suddenly drug use and dealing weren't much fun anymore. Matt began to hit bottom and see things differently. He ultimately completed a twelve-step program with an open mind.

These interventions are not for the faint of heart. It takes guts and plenty of preparation so that everything will go smoothly. Remember that every battle is won before the first shot is ever fired. Matt's mom masterfully thought two steps ahead by videotaping, calling the police, arranging the sleepover, and calling the neighborhood parents in the morning.

It basically came down to a choice for this mom. Should she let Matt run wild, sell drugs, and make her a prisoner in her own house, or take a risk and create a crisis to jolt Matt back into reality? With the support of her counselor, she decided to take the second path. No one else was going to care enough to stop Matt. She was Matt's last hope.

Strategy #3: Underage Posters and Shadowing

This intervention came from a desperate father. His sixteen-year-old daughter, Nicole, was dressing like a prostitute and going out to local bars to drink. Nothing her single-parent father did could keep her out of the bars. He tried calling the police, but they didn't want to be bothered. He tried to ground Nicole, but she simply climbed out of her bedroom window when he went to sleep.

The idea came to him at the post office, where he saw drawings and photos of missing children. He decided to create a poster that would include Nicole's picture and the fact that she was underage, as well as his cell phone number and the offer of a small reward for information leading to the bars she frequented.

The father went to the local bar owners and asked if he could put up posters. He told the owners that it would be good publicity for them, showing both the public and the police that they took underage drinking seriously. The bars also would not be duped into serving Nicole, a minor, by mistake. The father used the same argument at the convenience and liquor stores. Most of them agreed to put up this poster.

The father knew that some of the bars and liquor stores were serving his daughter, but the owners would have denied it if confronted. Instead, he knew that sleazy establishments often become cooperative if you draw attention to them, just as roaches will scatter for the darkness if you turn on a bright light.

WANTED: UNDERAGE DRINKER

Answers to "Nikki" or "Nik"
Height 5'3" / Weight 109
Birthmark on chin
Sleeps with her teddy bear.

This is My Daughter Nicole.

She is Only 16 Years Old!
You See Her Drinking or Using Drugs,
Call her Father @ 444-1111 for Reward.

You May Save a Life.

Teens like Nicole want to look cool at all times. This intervention mortified her. Strangers started to make fun of her. Her drinking buddies, who were also underage, did not want to be seen with her for fear of getting caught. Bars, convenience stores, and liquor stores stopped serving her. Nicole tried to rip the posters up, but each establishment had plenty of extras, or her dad would go by and replace them.

Next Nicole tried to disguise herself and go into bowling alley bars. This worked for a while, but her dad upped the ante. He began to follow her or just show up unannounced. He shadowed her wherever she went.

He dressed up in trench coats and pretended to be Columbo, passing out posters and informing the bowling alley bartenders that she was underage. Nicole was again mortified and begged him to stop. She began to "see this drinking thing as a real problem." It was cramping her lifestyle and she was rapidly losing friends.

The father now had the leverage he needed. He agreed to take down the posters and stop following her on three conditions:

1. She would obey curfew and not leave the house without permission. She had to call from wherever she was, and her dad had to verify it.
2. She would submit to random breath alcohol or drug tests when she returned home. This could not be past curfew, which might give her time to sober up.
3. If she tested positive for having alcohol or drugs in her system, she would attend three twelve-step Alcoholics Anonymous meetings per week and allow Dad to take her to make sure she attended. One additional meeting plus shadowing would be added per week for each future offense.

If any of these conditions were violated, the father would go back to the posters and the shadowing. Nicole did not want this to happen, nor did she want her father to tell the world that she slept with Max, her teddy bear.

Strategy #4: Fines and Misdemeanors

All teens like money and material things. When push comes to shove, they may value money or material items more than alcohol or drugs. The following example will show you how this strategy works.

"It Will Cost Me More to Keep Smoking Pot"

Fourteen-year-old Lee loved to smoke pot. He also liked to hang out with kids who were much older. He could see no reason to give up pot smoking. It was part of his lifestyle. If Lee gave it up, he might have to give up his friends as well.

Lee was also in a bitter power struggle with his parents over church. His family, who were Mormons, firmly believed that he must attend church. Lee's older brother had nearly overdosed on cocaine, and his parents were certain that the only thing that had saved him was prayer. They were convinced that going to church and learning moral values would save Lee from drugs, too. The more they pushed, however, the more Lee rebelled. Nevertheless, his parents forced him to go to church twice a week.

Lee was also on probation for grand theft auto. He had recently gotten high on marijuana, then stolen a neighbor's car and led the police on a high-speed chase across two counties before he was caught. One of the terms of his probation required testing clean on all drug tests.

With my guidance, the parents decided to take charge of the situation. They convinced the probation officer to let them administer the drug screening at home, arguing that the probation officer might not always be in Lee's life. Therefore, they had better start doing the job themselves. The parents drew up the following contract.

Lee's No-Pot Contract

Rule #1: You will be required to submit to at least three random urine drug tests per month. I (your father) will administer these tests. If we (your parents) or your probation officer suspect pot use, we can immediately require a urine drug test in addition to your three random ones. I will go into the bathroom with you and watch you to ensure that the test is accurate. You will not know when you will be asked to submit to a test. If you refuse to submit to a drug test, test dirty, or get caught trying to skew the test through herbal supplements or other means, Consequence A will occur. If you test clean on your drug test, Consequence B will occur.

Consequence A:

You will immediately be subjected to a $50 fine if you refuse to take the drug test, test dirty, or are caught trying to skew the test. You will have two weeks to pay back the fine through your own personal savings, selling your personal items at a pawn shop, or through extra chores at $5 per hour. A chore list will be posted on the refrigerator. You will hand over the $50 fine as a charitable contribution to the bishop of our church for missionary work. You will also have to use your personal money to purchase the next drug testing kit. If the total amount is not paid by

5:00 P.M. on the 14th day, we will immediately notify your probation officer and you will be placed in detention. Each time you
test dirty, the same process will repeat itself.

Consequence B:
You will receive the following reward that you picked out to celebrate a clean test—one day off from having to go to church
each week as long as you remain drug free. You also will receive
what is called a "sobriety chip" each time you test clean. Each
chip is worth $10, up to a possible $30 a month. This money is
yours to keep. But remember, you may have to use it to pay off
future fines.

Lee really liked the fact that there were rewards for staying
drug free and that his parents used his ideas in the contract. He
was not happy, however, about the fines and the fact that the
money would be going to a church he didn't like.

At first, Lee used the money from the sobriety chips to pay
for his pot. However, this got old quickly. When he tested dirty,
Lee had to pay the money back in sweat labor. He went from
gaining $30 to losing $50.

Lee also tried to throw a few curve balls along the way. His
parents, however, had done some troubleshooting and were
more than ready. He bought some herbal supplements at the vitamin store—spending even more of his cherished money. But
since he never knew when he was going to be tested, he couldn't
use the supplements effectively.

Lee also tried to hide his personal property and refused to do
his chores. He was shocked when he saw that there was a sleeping bag and a pillow where his bed used to be. His parents actually sold his bed to cover the $50 fine!

Underlying Family Issues

This intervention only placed a Band-Aid on the problem, stopping
the drug use long enough to address underlying family issues. In

Lee's family, the father was an overly strict and punitive parent. He preached about the evils of drugs and then secretly went to bars after work to drink. Drinking was against the church teachings.

Everyone in the family knew about dad's double life. Lee thought that his dad was a hypocrite, telling Lee to stop using pot, while he secretly drank. These underlying issues needed to be dealt with if there was to be any hope that Lee would not relapse and use drugs again.

Strategy #5: Invade Your Teen's Privacy

This strategy will take your teen completely by surprise. Alcohol and drug abuse often take place in private. How often have you seen a colleague openly snort cocaine at his desk in the office? In the same way, your teen's alcohol and drug use can thrive in an environment of secrecy.

This plan may sound crazy, but isn't alcohol and drug abuse crazy on some level? To counter crazy behavior, sometimes you must act just as crazy.

Take the next few months and move in with your teenager. Set up a cot and sleep in the same room. Make sure that you bring your stuff so your teen knows you are serious. Explain that you're doing this to get to know your teen better and because you are worried about his or her alcohol or drug use. Make your teen an offer he or she can't refuse: If your teen tests clean for a month, you will move out. You will move back in the room only if he or she tests dirty or refuses to take the test.

Your teen either will vehemently object or will play possum and pretend not to care. He or she also may try to keep you up or snore. If this happens, you can be disrespectful too. You can leave banana peels around or remove your teen's stereo from the room. If your teen abandons his or her room to sleep on the couch, either follow the teen there or place a padlock on the door to his or her room, with you having the only key. Stay the course and don't get flustered.

An aunt or a grandmother may make an even more effective "roommate" for your teen in these circumstances. One parent went so far as to recruit an army private to stay in the room rent free! These people will disrupt your teen's normal routine and make it more difficult for him or her to use drugs or alcohol in secret or at all.

You're in the Army Now

Seventeen-year-old Tony liked to hide away in his room with the door locked and the shades pulled down. He always wore Gothic-looking clothes; his room was painted black; and he would spend long hours there secretly taking his favorite drug, Ecstacy. His mother knew that something was going on, but she had no idea on how to stop it. Tony had no positive male role models. He seemed to be slipping further and further away.

There was a local army base nearby. The mother decided to place the following ad in the army base newsletter and post it in the army dormitories:

Are You Homesick and Want Free Rent?

I am the single-parent mom of a wonderful 17-year-old son.
I also make the best home-cooked meals in the South.
My fried chicken will melt in your mouth.
If you are willing to share the costs of the food,
I will absorb the cost of rent and utilities.
There is only one small stipulation.
Please call to find out.
Call Maria Jensen @ 555-1234 for more information.

Ms. Jensen's phone started ringing off the hook. When the army privates called, she told them that the stipulation was that they would have to share a room with her son, Tony. Tony would not like the idea, but he needed a good role model. She also explained that Tony was using drugs and was less likely to use if there was less privacy.

Even with these stipulations, twelve applicants applied. She interviewed them while Tony was at school. Imagine Tony's surprise when he walked into his room and saw an army private lying on a cot reading a magazine.

At first Tony started to yell at his mom. Mom and Neil, the army private, had troubleshooted this what-will-I-do-if scenario ahead of time. When Neil heard the yelling, he stood next to the mom and stared at Tony. Tony quieted down but threatened to run away.

The mom and private had also planned for this contingency. Neil sat down at the end of his bed and said:

"Tony, I really would appreciate it if you got to know me first. My family is clear across the country. I have no one, I'm homesick, and I need a place to stay. There may be other rooms in the house, but I have made the choice to stay with you. It is nonnegotiable. If you go to sleep in another room, I will follow. Maybe we can be friends and maybe we can't. That's up to you. Just know one thing. As a member of the U.S. Army, I took an oath to uphold the law. If I see any drugs or drug paraphernalia like vapor rubs, pacifiers, or glow sticks, I will dispose of it myself or call the police. It is nothing personal. By law I must uphold my oath. Your mom says that if you submit to a random drug test and it comes up clean for an entire month, you can have your room back. I will then move into the spare bedroom. I will come back in only if you test dirty or refuse to take the test."

Tony carried out his threat of running away. His mother had told him ahead of time that if he ran, he was always welcome back but under these same rules. She could also not guarantee that the army private would not touch his things. The mother also used the techniques under Ace #3, "Running Away," to let the parents of Tony's safe houses know that she wanted her son home. Tony returned in two weeks, tired of not having clean clothes and plenty of food.

From that moment on, he resigned himself to the fact that he had to live with Neil. He could no longer enjoy his long, private sessions with Ecstacy in the comfort of his own room; he could use the drug only in clubs or outside in the cold. It was beginning to lose its appeal. Besides, what would Neil think? Slowly but surely, Tony began to look up to and respect Neil.

Strategy #6: Relapse Is Normal; Prepare for It

A 1998 study by the Department of Health and Human Services revealed that 75 percent of all addicts who stop using alcohol or drugs will relapse at least once during the first year. While it's a mistake to expect a quick fix to the problem, it's also a mistake to believe that we are back to square one if your teen gets sober and then starts using again.

Instead, embrace the idea that relapses are a normal part of the healing process. Your aim is to help make the relapses fewer and farther between, until they no longer exist. For example, when you first get started, your teen may relapse once a week. As things progress, relapses may occur only once every two weeks, then once a month, and so on.

When your teen stops using, congratulate and praise him or her. Openly discuss the topic of relapse. *Talking about relapse does not mean you are condoning it;* relapses are inevitable whether you talk about them or not. When your teen is sober and in a good mood, tell him or her something like:

[Teen's name], research shows that 75 percent of all people who use alcohol or drugs may relapse. Therefore, you and I must produce a backup plan to get you back on track as quickly as possible if you do relapse. There will still be consequences if you relapse, but together we can slow these relapses down or make them less likely to occur if we plan ahead. Here are the questions that we have to answer:

■ *What are the triggers or the signs that tell you that you are headed for a relapse?*

■ *If those signs occur, what can we do or say as parents to help you through the danger zone and prevent a relapse?*

■ *If you do relapse, what do you need to do personally to get back on track as quickly as possible?*

■ *What do you need us to do or not to do to help you get back on track as quickly as possible?*

Write down the answers to these questions and use the troubleshooting strategies in Step 3 to create a set of backup plans around relapse. Here are several what-will-I-do-if examples to get you started.

- **What will I do if** one of my son's signs of relapse is feeling down or isolation:
  a. Do not allow him to sit in his room alone and vegetate for a long time.
  b. Talk about what he is feeling inside or keep him moving by doing something like volunteering at a nursing home or joining the local Boys Club. Do not take no for an answer.

- **What will I do if** my daughter relapses and tests dirty for drugs or is drunk?
  a. Do not take it personally. Relapse is normal and common.
  b. Tell your teen that you will help her get back on track as quickly as possible.
  c. Administer your predetermined consequence.

- **What will I do** to prevent myself from getting discouraged and taking my teen's relapse as a personal slap in the face?
  a. Energize yourself. This is draining work; you need to recharge your batteries by getting out of the house and treating yourself to a movie or a dinner.
  b. Talk to a friend and vent your frustration. You can realize that relapse is normal, but you don't have to feel good about it.

Under no circumstances should you take a relapse of drug abuse or drinking as a failure. It becomes a failure only if you don't hold your teen accountable.

Strategy #7: Spiritual Anchors and Nurturance

Whatever your personal beliefs may be about God, the fact remains that spiritual anchors help many teens and adults overcome drug or alcohol abuse. Those anchors may be found in conventional religion or in other ways. For example, one mother took her daughter to a meditation class, while a father took his son to an acupuncturist. Both parents saw tremendous changes in their teens. The daughter told me that meditation got her in touch with the poisons with which she was polluting her body. The son told me that acupuncture took away his anger and stress in the same way drinking had, only better.

We know that adolescence is a time of rebellion, and turning away from spiritual teachings is often part of that rebellion. Without spirituality or nurturance, however, your teen may feel empty inside and may have nowhere to turn except to a quick fix: a false high on alcohol or drugs. To stop the drug or alcohol use permanently, you will have to help replace your teen's emptiness with something better.

If you read the twelve-step program of Alcoholics Anonymous, a central piece is to let go and allow a power "greater than ourselves" to take over. This philosophy has helped so many people get sober that it must be on to something.

The Problem with Preaching

Sixteen-year-old Payton's dad was a recovering alcoholic who became sober as soon as he gave his life to Christ. As a result, he preached morning, noon, and night about the evils of alcohol and drugs. When he found out that Payton was coming home drunk every evening, it just about killed him. As a result, he preached even more.

Unfortunately, the more Dad preached, the farther Payton pulled back. They eventually became strangers under the same roof. To reverse this trend, I asked the father to avoid preaching. Instead, he was to pray, study, and meditate on the strategies within Step 7 to restore nurturance.

The father changed his tactics and stopped preaching altogether. Instead, he began to take Payton on one special outing every week. He convinced Payton to go by promising not to talk about his drinking or preach about his own sobriety. If he fell into old habits, Payton was permitted to remind him to "stop preaching." The goal was to get reacquainted with one another as father and son. They never really knew one another.

As the weeks went by, things began to change. Payton would even start to remind his father about their special outings during the week. Each week it was something new. One of Payton's favorite outings was the time his dad took him to yoga class, which seemed out of character yet fun. Soon they began to take the classes together.

Dad noticed something else: Payton's drinking started to drop as his father preached less and they spent time getting to know one another. The only stipulation during this whole time was that Payton could not drink and drive.

If Payton refused to take a breath alcohol test when he came home or had any alcohol in his system, his car would be impounded for thirty days or more depending on the level of alcohol. The distributor cap would be removed and the keys taken. There would be an impound fee of $5 per day. This would have to be paid off through cash or extra chores. If the money was not paid back, the car would be sold.

The father was successful for two important reasons. First, he helped replace Payton's emptiness with nurturance through special outings. He also stopped preaching and showed his Christian beliefs through actions, *not* words. The yoga classes were a nice touch and indirectly made Payton think about how he wanted to treat his body and the poisons that he was putting into it. Second, the father still held Payton accountable for his drinking.

I realize that this strategy may be difficult for you. I even hesitated to include it in the book. While the connection between spirituality, nurturance, and alcohol or drugs may make sense to you, it is hard to feel nurturing or spiritual when your teen is using drugs and putting you through the ringer.

All I can say is that it definitely works. Nurturance and spirituality are an antivenin to drug use. If your teen feels loved and secure, the risk of alcohol or drug abuse drastically decreases. He or she may continue to experiment, but is much less likely to cross the line and become addicted. Therefore, take your teens to church or synagogue, enroll them in a yoga class, praise them, give them hugs, or take them on special outings on a consistent basis. Try to find activities that have meaning for both of you. If you do, you will begin to see changes in your teen's substance abuse as you help build them up from the inside out.

Strategy #8: It Takes a Village to Help a Drug Addict

If you have a difficult time being tough, do not go it alone. An alcohol- or drug-using teen will sense your lack of confidence and eat you alive. The answer is to bring in reinforcements. Calling friends, neighbors, or extended family members to become "your village" will help you play parent instead of friend. These reinforcements will also give you the backbone and strength you need to make a change.

The idea for this strategy came to me from my work with fourteen-year-old Shawn and his family. At that first meeting, I learned that Shawn was using marijuana, stealing money from his mom's purse, ditching school, and leaving home without permission.

When I told the mother that she had to get tough, she replied, "Shawn is my baby, my youngest. I can't come down hard. He will smoke more pot and he will hate me. He's all I've got. His father ran out on me years ago."

The next week I rented the movie *Trainspotting,* and Shawn's mother and I watched parts of it together. I told her that even though these kids used heroin and Shawn used marijuana, he was heading in the same direction. When I brought in and read obituary columns of teens tragically dying of drug overdoses, the mom turned to me and said, "Enough already, I see your point. What do I need to do?"

I asked the mother to list all her extended family members and friends on the chalkboard. Together we called each person on the list and invited them to a meeting about Shawn's problem. The mother was amazed at how many of her sisters, brothers, and uncles agreed to come and help.

At the meeting, we openly discussed the mother's dilemma of being a friend or a parent. Shawn was not there; he had left home without permission that night to be with his friends. The family asked the mom what she needed from them to get a stronger backbone. She answered with one word: "Support."

I told everyone that support was an action word. The mother needed help with such concrete actions as searching Shawn's room and calling the police if she found drugs or drug paraphernalia. Her family could help her design consequences and stand next to her when she demanded that Shawn take a drug test. Ideally, someone could move in temporarily and support the mother if Shawn tried to retaliate.

No one was able to move in, but we pulled together a "sleepover" list of rotating dates so that Mom was never left alone. Each person agreed to spend one to two nights in Shawn's bedroom. Next, everyone helped the mother to search Shawn's room. She found a bag of pot and two bongs. Mom picked up the phone to call the police and then put it down twice. After her village spent forty-five minutes convincing her that it was now or never, she finally made the call. The police arrived just as Shawn was coming home. He was shocked to see so many people. As the cuffs went on, he told his mom that he hated her.

The storm had been unleashed. When Shawn returned home, he started swearing at his mother. This quickly stopped when his uncle came in and told him to shut up and that he and other relatives were going to stay in his bedroom until he cleaned up his act. Shawn then started running away. That behavior ended when posters turned up everywhere saying that Shawn's possessions were going to be sold at a neighborhood auction.

Shawn came home on the agreement that his stuff would not be sold. For every week he stayed clean and sober and did not run away, he would earn one item back. (Everything was safely locked in storage.) The first item was his bed. If he left again, half of his stuff would be sold automatically.

There were plenty of ups and downs along the way, but with the support of her village, Shawn's mother remained firm. Shawn slowly began to respect his mother and open up. Afterward the mother told me, "Not only do I have to be accountable to you, Dr. Sells, but now I also have to be accountable to my whole neighborhood. It is definitely giving me the confidence I need and the backbone I lacked to stand firm."

You can find a more detailed discussion of mobilizing support from family and friends in "The Nonviolent Town Meeting," under Ace #6, "Threats or Acts of Violence."

Strategy #9: Address Any Underlying Family Issues

Family stress is often a central contributing factor to alcohol or drug use. Of course, your teen still has a choice of whether to use or not and still is accountable for that choice. Nevertheless, family problems will definitely aggravate the situation. Here is how it works:

- Someone inside your family experiences problems. It could be anything from marital fighting, domestic violence, depression, a sudden illness, or even a parent who also abuses drugs or alcohol.

- Tension begins to grow as these problems play themselves out.

- Your teen feels and experiences this tension, which remains unresolved and buried in the family closet somewhere where all the other unresolved problems go.

- Your teen copes with the pain by self-medicating or burying his or her feelings inside a beer bottle or at the end of a joint.

- Your teen then becomes sober, but not for long. The pain is still there and flares up as soon as the next bout of family tension erupts. The cycle of self-medicating begins all over again.

- The longer this cycle continues, the more likely it is that your teen's heart will become hardened inside. He or she will be unable to cope with pain and loss the way you or I do. Instead, your teen will learn how to cope only through alcohol or drugs.

This cycle does not happen automatically in all families. Your teen may just enjoy getting drunk or high. The important thing is to ask yourself this tough question: "Do we have problems in our family and does this cycle mirror what happens to us?"

If the answer is yes, please employ the services of a competent family counselor who can see the connection between your teen's drug or alcohol use and unresolved family problems. It will give your teenager the best possible chance not only to get clean and sober but to stay that way.

ACE #6: THREATS OR ACTS OF VIOLENCE

When your teen threatens you with violence through words ("I'm going to hurt you bad"; "I'm going to punch the wall"; "I'm gonna kill you") or actions (kicking holes in the wall, breaking glass, picking up a knife), violence becomes a safety issue. (Harming someone can lead to serious injury or even death.)

Your out-of-control teenager may use this ace often because of its power to scare and intimidate others. In turn, this intimidation gets you to back down quickly. Unlike most adults, teens work off the pleasure principle when it comes to violence. They are impulsive and do not tend to think about the long-term consequences before they commit a violent act.

In addition, your teen may not possess the tools necessary to control his or her anger. For example, when you get cut off in traffic, you may get very angry, but you probably use tools like taking a deep breath or telling yourself to "chill out" to stop your anger from turning into road rage. Teenagers, however, may not have these same tools. Even if they do, they may see no reason to stop themselves; they enjoy being drunk with power through violence.

If you are expecting your teen to wake up one morning and voluntarily renounce the ace of violence, you will be waiting a very long time. Your teen will need your guidance in order to stop. If your teen could have done it alone, he or she would have done so by now.

I strongly recommend that you try these strategies only under the supervision and guidance of a competent counselor. The ace of violence will definitely push your hot buttons.

See Counselor for Direction!

Violence can also beget violence. If your teen is in your face yelling, screaming, and swearing, it's hard not to become equally upset and react in kind. We are all only human. If this happens, you or your teen may start throwing punches and injuring one another.

In addition, there is a risk that your teenager may call child protective services or the police to claim abuse. They know that these agencies are sensitive to words like "hitting," "punching," "slapping," or "pushing." A qualified counselor can guide you through the process and be your advocate to let these agencies know that your teen is playing an elaborate game.

Why Teen Violence Occurs

With the increase in school shootings, many theories have developed as to why kids become violent. I will present my top six reasons, then give you specific strategies to address them.

Many of these ideas were generated from reading Dr. James Garbarino's book, *The Lost Boys,* in which he interviewed hundreds of violent teenagers to get their insights into their own behavior. I highly recommend this book if your teen shows signs of violence.

1. A violence-saturated society

According to the Centers for Disease Control and Prevention, children see over 200,000 violent acts on TV before they turn eighteen. The Columbine High School teenagers who pulled the trigger were completely immersed in violence. They watched violent television, listened to violent music, and played a graphically violent game called "Doom" every waking moment. After a while, teens can get so desensitized to violence that it becomes romanticized. They play out the violence in their heads and lose all sense of reality. The person being shot or beaten up does not have feelings or emotions but is merely an object, a video game, or a movie character.

2. The soul is wounded

Troubled teens who lack spiritual anchors or positive relationships in their lives are particularly vulnerable to the violence around them. Such teens may seek out images of evil and become addicted to them as a way of responding to the emptiness they feel inside. Over time their soul or spiritual core, which helps distinguish between good and evil, becomes wounded by being saturated in the violence they find in negative friends, television, and video games. Violence then becomes an outward expression of acts that the teens have already committed in their imagination over and over again.

3. **Being left out is dangerous**
Peer rejection and teasing can send teens toward the dark side, where they may immerse themselves in violence. If your teen is picked on relentlessly or teased, a red flag should go up. If your son becomes part of a clique or group the mainstream views as different or odd, monitor your teen closely. If he gets picked on, his anger can slowly turn to rage, which can turn to violence.

4. **A violent code of honor**
Violent teens often have a distorted view of morality, with a code of honor that says that if someone hurts you, you must retaliate with double the force. Otherwise, the code maintains, you will be seen as weak or soft and become an easy target. Coupled with a lack of empathy, or caring for others, and an inability to trust, this code makes a virtue out of violence.

5. **Loss of emotional bonds**
Teen violence can result from the absence of a caring and resourceful parent. Foster care kids who get bounced around from family to family are almost always in this category. This loss of attachment leads to a lack of trust and a low self-esteem. These kids have trouble making emotional connections or feeling remorse for any pain they inflict on others. Without emotional connections, teens begin to feel numb inside. When this happens, their risk of retaliating with violence if someone hurts them is extremely high.

6. **Weapons of violence have increased in intensity**
In the past, children and teens had access only to fists, sticks, or knives. Today's kids have access to guns and automatic weapons. This shift has made violence more deadly. In 1997 the Centers for Disease Control revealed that 28 percent of adolescent boys carried a weapon (gun, knife, or club) to school, and two-thirds of all

teens surveyed reported that they could get a gun within an hour. Violence has always been around, it is just that the means to carry it out has become deadlier.

The Risk Factors for Violence

If any of the preceding descriptions reminds you of your teenager, it doesn't necessarily mean that your child will become violent or take a gun tomorrow and shoot someone. It often takes several factors working together to create a violent teen. According to Dr. Garbarino's research, chances of committing an act of violence are twice as high if a teen:

- Comes from a family with a history of criminal violence
- Has a history of being abused
- Belongs to the outsider group that gets picked on.
- Belongs to a gang
- Abuses drugs or alcohol

These odds triple when a teen:

- Uses a weapon
- Has been arrested
- Has a neurological problem that impairs thinking or feeling
- Has difficulty at school and attendance problems

How Teen Violence Works

When you get into a heated argument or disagreement, you and your teen often go through what I call Five Levels of Teen Aggression. Your teen gives you opportunities to pour cold water on the fire *before* it rages out of control. If you don't recognize the signs, the argument can quickly escalate to threats or even acts of violence.

Out-of-control teens operate differently from typical teens. Typical teens push their parents only so far. Although they may whine, complain, or even stubbornly refuse to do something, once they receive "the look" (the glaring facial expression) or "the tone" (firm tone of voice) from their parents, they know that it is time to back down. Out-of-control teens, however, like to win at all costs. If nonviolent methods don't work, they may up the ante and threaten violence.

In the movie *War Games,* made during the Cold War in the early 1980s, both the Soviet Union and the United States refused to back down from deploying nuclear weapons and began to escalate on what was called the "Defcon ladder," beginning with Defcon 5 and counting backward to Defcon 1. By the end, both countries had gone all the way to Defcon 1, where they were ready to release their nuclear missiles and annihilate one another. In the same way, your teenager may go all the way up to Defcon 5 if you refuse to back down. Here is the difference between an argument with a typical teen and one with an out-of-control teen.

AN ARGUMENT WITH A TYPICAL TEEN	ARGUMENT WITH OUT-OF-CONTROL TEEN
Level 1	If Evan were an out-of-control teen, he would escalate up Levels 1, 2, and 3 in the same way. However, he might not stop at Level 3. Instead, he might take the argument up to a Level 4, Threats of Violence, or go as high as a Level 5, Acts of Violence.
MOM: Evan, its time to clean your room *(A simple request)*	
EVAN: Do I have to? I'm really busy. *(Whiny and complaining voice to annoy his mother and get her to back down.)*	
Level 2	MOM: That's it—you're grounded. I am leaving now. I will not be talked to in that manner. You need to apologize later. The room still has to be clean. I will see you later. Good bye.
MOM: Yes, you have to right now. *(Does not back down.)*	
EVAN: I will after I finish watching this show. *(Counters by stubbornly refusing in an effort to win)*	

AN ARGUMENT WITH A TYPICAL TEEN

MOM: I will not play this game. Either you move off of the couch by the time I count to 3 or you are grounded tomorrow. *(The parent does not waver)*

Typical teens usually stop here. Some teens may push it to Level 3.

EVAN: This is bullsh*t. You never let me do what I f**king want. *(Evan ups the ante through swearing in an effort to push his mom's buttons and make her lose control of her emotions.)*

MOM: That's it—you're grounded. I am leaving now. I will not be talked to in that manner. You need to apologize later.. The room still has to be clean. I will see you later. Good-bye. *(Mom does an excellent job to control both the mood and direction of the discussion. She exits calmly from the room)*

ARGUMENT WITH OUT-OF-CONTROL TEEN

EVAN: Don't you dare walk away from me. *(He follows her and gets in her face.)* You'd better not ground me or you'll be very sorry. *(Evan is using intimidating behavior and verbally threatening violence.)*

It is now a high-risk situation. Both parent and teen have entered a lose/lose scenario. If the mom backs down, Evan will have successfully committed an act of parent abuse and gained more power. If the mom stands her ground, Evan may go up to a Level 5 and hurt her physically or destroy property. In both cases, everyone loses.

Five Levels of Teen Aggression

Like a Corvette, aggressive teens can go from 0 to 60 mph in 3.5 seconds. Shut them down at Levels 1 or 2 if you can.

Level 1: Whining and Complaining

Description: Teenagers often begin to whine or complain when asked to do something like pick up their clothes or do household chores. Teens do this to annoy you and get you to back down. If you are tired or overstressed, you may give in rather than continue to listen to the whining.

Solutions: Remember when you were a teen, and you too would moan, groan, and complain about everything your parents asked you to do? The best solution is to ignore the whining. Instead, calmly remind your teen about the rule and do not let your buttons get pushed. You can use the strategy of "reflectors" from Step 4 to keep from being sidetracked: "*Nevertheless*, the rule still stands," or "*Regardless*, you must clean your room." You can also become playful and whine right back to make your teenager laugh and defuse the tension. Avoid getting into a power struggle by invoking harsh consequences too

Reprinted with special permission of King Feature Syndicate.

early in the game. Your teen is probably just testing the waters. If you remain firm yet calm, more often than not your teen will follow the rule.

Level 2: Stubborn Refusal

Description: At this level, teens stubbornly refuse to follow directions or listen to authority. They will say that they are too busy or will do it later. Many teens will try to globalize the situation by exaggerating the way you are "always" on their case. The purpose of this is to get you off the subject and make you so angry and defensive that your judgment is clouded and you are likely to back down.

Solutions: Use the strategy of staying "short and to the point" in Step 4 to repeat back both the rule *and* the consequence. Your teen will try to change the subject or push your buttons. Control the mood by maintaining your calm. It is time to add the consequence portion of the contract. Your teen has gone beyond just whining and complaining and is now actively refusing to comply with your requests. Remind him or her of what the consequence will be if the teen continues to refuse.

Level 3: Verbal Abuse and Personal Attacks

Description: At this level, your teen senses your fear and lack of confidence in your own authority. You may still be holding firm at this level, but your legs are getting shaky. Your teenager senses your potential weakness and begins to swear and call you names. In most cases, your teen is just trying to intimidate you and push your buttons. Still, this level may become dangerous. By now teenagers often are becoming agitated and/or angry. If this continues, they may work themselves into an emotional frenzy. They desperately need you to take charge and stop them.

Solutions: Follow the strategy of "exiting and waiting" in Step 4. The longer you stay and allow your teen to abuse you, the more likely it is that you will become verbally abusive as well. While there should be consequences for the verbal abuse, make sure you administer them on your terms and when you are calmed down. *Never administer a consequence when you are angry or frustrated, or in the middle of a heated argument.* Sometimes it works to tell your teen in a stern voice to "cut it out" or "stop it." Playfulness also can work to change the mood of the argument and throw your teen off balance.

Level 4: Threats of Violence

Description: If you successfully implement the above solutions, you probably will not ever see your teen reach this level again. If your teen does enter this level, however, you must act quickly before threats escalate into actual violence. Even though teens may threaten to kill or injure their parents, another sibling, animals, property, or another person, they usually have no intention of following through on these threats. They want to scare you into submission. For many teenagers, threats have become the "big guns" they use if the previous three levels have failed to get you to back down.

Solution: At this level, the temptation is high for you to get aggressive, lecture, and lose control. If you lose your cool, however, you will be pouring gasoline on an open fire. It is critical to exit and wait until the teenager calms down. No explanation or reasoning will work at this point. It will only serve to agitate your teenager further. Pick out some of the strategies listed in the next section to call the police, be playful, or collaborate with your teen ahead of time and create a nonviolence contract together.

Level 5: Acts of Violence

Description: At this level, out-of-control teenagers actively attack objects or people. They may punch holes in walls, throw and break valuable objects, or smash windows. Teens may even attack another family member or attempt to hurt themselves in a fit of rage and frustration.

Solution: At this point, there is no more talk. You must take action quickly and decisively to ensure the safety of you, your teenager, and those around you. You must exit as quickly as possible and implement one or more of the following antiviolence strategies in the next section.

You also must call the police to file assault and battery charges. Otherwise, you send a dangerous message to your teenager: "You can physically hurt me and I will not hold you accountable," or "In the real world, you can physically hurt people and get away with it." (Please note that I do not recommend calling the local psychiatric hospital if your teen is violent. Doing so sends the message that your teen is crazy and not responsible for his or her actions. If your teen is violent, call the police.)

The Dance of Anger

Even with the recent outbreak of teen violence, the majority of our teens do not become violent. In fact, according to a 1997 study by Dodge in Development Psychopathology only 35 percent of abused kids with negative and aggressive social maps became violent. Why is it that 65 percent of these kids do not become violent?

My theory is that 65 percent or more of our teens stop short of aggression when the parent or another adult controls the mood and direction of the argument. Parents can control the mood or direction through a cold stare and a confident "No" or a soft hug or funny face to break the tension and anger in the air. It tells the teenager, "I'm in charge here"; "I will not back down"; "I do not fear your anger"; and "I control the tension and stress of this discussion, not you."

When you take a firm position, your teen begins to feel the security of your leadership. Wolves and other animals that live in packs act aggressively and out of control until a clear leader emerges and confidently takes charge. The rest of the pack then feels secure and immediately calms down. Similarly, if you show fear when you approach a strange dog, it's likely to show its teeth and attack you. In the same way, your teen will become aggressive unless you take a firm position and control the mood and direction of the conflict.

"My Bark Is Worse than My Bite"

Fifteen-year-old Malcolm was big for his age. When he got in your face, he could scare and intimidate anyone. Malcolm would tell you privately that he sensed his mom's fear when he yelled in her face. This dance of anger started when he was thirteen.

If Mom tried to be firm, Malcolm would go to a Level 3 and start swearing at her. Mom would get scared and immediately back down. It worked every time, so why stop?

The mom mistakenly believed that the only way to stop Malcolm was through physical restraint. Since Malcolm was bigger and stronger, he automatically won.

At first, the mother thought that my parallels between strange dogs and violent teens were pure hogwash. I asked her to secretly bring a high-powered squirt gun to our next meeting.

Together, the mother and I worked out the following experiment. We would intentionally make Malcolm angry by saying that he could not go to an unsupervised party Saturday night. If he started to get aggressive or get in the mom's face, she would do the following.

- **As soon as Malcolm started to get agitated at level 1 and 2, Mom would not get scared and back down as she normally did.**

- **Instead, she would playfully whip out a squirt gun and cool him down with a high-powered burst of water. She would duck behind the chairs and shoot him harder. If Malcolm moved forward, she would squirt him some more.**

The mother laughed and thought that this was the craziest idea she had ever heard. But she gave it a try. When Malcolm was told that he could not go to the party, he did exactly as we predicted. He started to growl and bark at his mother. In turn, the mother playfully started to squirt him, and moved behind my desk and doused him some more.

The mood in my office instantly changed from anger and tension to one of lighthearted playfulness. Malcolm was stunned and started rolling on the ground laughing. When everyone calmed down, the mother restated her position on no unsupervised parties. Further, if Malcolm retaliated with more intimidation, the squirt gun would come out again. If there was any violence in the form of pushing, shoving, or destroying property, the police would be called and charges filed.

For the first time since he could remember, Mom was taking a firm position and controlling the mood of their bitter arguments through her squirt gun. Malcolm said, "It's hard to get mad when your mom is acting like such a nut case!"

Many parents mistakenly feel that they must counter their teen's aggressive style with more of the same. In addition, they often believe that they have to be bigger and stronger than their teens to stop them. This is simply not true. More often than not, you can control your teen's violence by understanding the dance of anger and how to control the mood and direction of the argument. The following cartoon illustrates this process nicely.

Reprinted with special permission of King Feature Syndicate.

If your teen has reached a Level 4 or a Level 5 of aggression, choose from one or more of the followings strategies to stop the ace of violence.

Strategy #1: The Nonviolent Town Meeting

Violence survives and thrives in secrecy. Therefore, the mere presence of strangers in the house like the army private who helped Tony's mother stop his drug use can turn the tide. Here is how it works.

Mobilize Your Troops

Make a list of all your extended family members and trusted friends or neighbors. Call and ask if they could come to a town meeting at your house. Here is what you can say:

I know this may be a strange request, but I really need your help with my teenager. You don't probably know this, but [son or daughter's name] has threatened to harm me physically. [Add any examples of acts of violence here.] I believe that it will only get worse. I want to prevent this from happening in the future. I am calling you because I believe that it takes a village to raise a child. You are part of my village, and I need your insight and ideas. I am calling other people in my village as well. I know that you are busy. But will you come? I will even provide refreshments. You can volunteer to help once you see what it entails or just come and give me your ideas as we brainstorm together. Two or more heads are always better than one.

Very few people will decline such a request. Most of them also have kids and can understand the village concept and the seriousness of threats or acts of violence.

The hardest part for you will be that first phone call. You may feel ashamed or embarrassed that your teen is violent. You also may feel that you would be imposing on your friends and family, even though you would do the same if they asked you for help. But please make the calls. You will be surprised at how many people want to help. In addition, trying to stop the violence on your own without backup can be difficult if not impossible.

Your teen should not be present at the beginning of the town meeting, as he or she is likely to become disruptive or argumentative. Bring your teen into the meeting only after you have brainstormed with your village and have a written antiviolence contract in place. Normally, it is important to have your teen be the co-owner of any plan. But when it comes to safety issues like violence, you have to take charge.

Set the Agenda

Type or write an agenda and pass it out. Everyone's time is valuable, so you want the meeting to remain focused. On your agenda, include the following:

1. Introductions
2. The Problems
3. Brainstorm Solutions
4. Prioritize Solutions
5. Writing a Contract and Clarifying Roles
6. Dress Rehearsal
7. The Delivery

The Meeting

After everyone has introduced themselves and described their relationship with your teen, it is important for you to reveal each one of the violent encounters with your teen. Do not keep secrets. When you tell everyone, you will be surprised by how many people already knew. Even if others are shocked, explaining what has been going on will help you. It takes a lot of energy to keep secrets bottled up.

Brainstorming is the next step. Six, ten, fifteen, or twenty heads are always better than one in generating creative and effective consequences. Be sure to pass around a copy of the top ten consequences that teens care about, highlighting the ones that matter most to your child. Write down every idea on a big poster that everyone can see.

Rank each idea. You have the ultimate veto power, but prioritize the group's ideas. For example, during one meeting, the mother stated that her situation was hopeless. She could not get her fifteen-year-old son to go to school. When she tried, he would threaten to beat her up. One of the neighbors, who had a good friend who was a police officer, brainstormed the idea of "police intervention." This idea was immediately placed as number 1 on the list.

After the group agrees on the consequences, it is time to clarify everyone's role—who will do what, when, where, how, and under what circumstances—and write it into the contract, as in the following example.

Stan's Nonviolence Contract

Rule #1 (Problem from list: Son threatens to punch parent and sister.) Stan's behavior will be considered violent if he does one or more of the following.

- Verbally threatens to push, shove, beat, or punch Mom or younger sister. I (your mom) will determine if this rule has been broken, not Stan.

Consequence A (Positive)

For every week this Rule #1 is not broken, you will have the opportunity to go to karate class the next week and receive one hour of extra phone time per day.

Consequence B (Negative)

If this rule is broken, I [Mom] will immediately exit from the situation along with your younger sister, go to my room, and lock the bedroom down. I will call and activate my neighborhood phone tree. My mom friends will then come over, applying lipstick on the way. These neighbors will kiss you all over your face until you get beet red. They will then issue you the consequence on a piece of paper: If you get physically violent at any time, the police will be called and charges will be filed. My village will be my witnesses.

Mom's Role:

1. If Stan goes a week without violence or threats of violence, I will give him one extra hour of phone time and transport him to karate.
2. If Stan threatens violence, I will exit and wait in my bedroom and immediately activate the phone tree.
3. I will call the police and file charges if any items are missing or any acts of violence occur.

My Village's Role

1. We will come over as soon as we are able.
2. We will apply red lipstick to our lips and kiss Stan all over his face.
3. We will give Stan the pawn ticket.
4. We will bear witness and support Mom if a police report has to be filed for stolen property or acts of violence committed by Stan.

This was a creative use of both positive and negative consequences. First, the single-parent mom could not stop the violence on her own, especially since Stan was stronger than she was. Getting the reinforcement and ideas from the other moms led to the turnaround. Teens also like their violent acts to be secret. Inviting the neighborhood to come violated this secrecy rule.

Lipstick kisses all over his face might embarrass Stan, but it could also change the mood in the house from one of darkness to one of lighthearted playfulness, making it difficult for Stan to stay violent.

The Delivery

It is now time to invite your teen back into the room. Ask him or her not to speak until you have had a chance to finish. Go around the room and ask everyone in your village to tell your son or daughter that they know about the violence and why it is wrong. Ask them to recount any of their own personal experiences with violence and how it made them feel. These are powerful statements that your teen will remember, even if he or she pretends to be indifferent.

After everyone is finished, ask the teenager to tell everyone why he or she thinks violence is wrong. If your teen begins to open up, ask for any suggestions as to how he or she can personally prevent future acts of violence. The chances of the teen's cooperation will increase if he or she helps create the action plan.

If your teen refuses to speak or tries to derail the conversation— for instance, by saying the violence is all your fault—quickly move forward. Your teen does not have to like or agree with your plan in order for it to be implemented, especially since you have the support of your village.

Finally, ask your villagers to clarify their role to your teenager. Have them tell your teen what they are going to be doing and exactly how they will support you as the parent.

Strategy #2: The Old MacDonald Consequence

This strategy was inspired by the work of Dr. Neil Schiff and his work with a violent teenage girl. In this two-parent family, the sixteen-year-old daughter had complete control of the household. She was a terrorist in her own home. If the mother told her something that she didn't like, the girl went into a violent rage and pulled her mother's hair out. Both parents were afraid to call the police.

The mood in the household was filled with fear and anxiety. To stop the violence, Dr. Schiff struck upon an ingenious idea. Instead of imposing harsh consequences, such as grounding or physical restraints, which would make the daughter more violent, he concentrated on changing the mood in the household.

Dr. Schiff brought in a tape player with the song to "Old MacDonald Had a Farm." While the daughter waited in the waiting room, Dr. Schiff had the parents practice this strategy. Dr. Schiff played the part of the daughter and pretended that he was at Level 3, Verbal Abuse and Personal Attacks. The parents immediately started to play "Old MacDonald" and sing and dance around the table.

When the parents felt confident with the technique, the daughter came back into the room. She started to get angry and upset. As soon as she did, the parents played "Old MacDonald" and danced around the table, just as they'd practiced. The daughter stopped dead in her tracks. She started to crack up, and the tension immediately dropped. She could not get angry no matter how hard she tried.

At home, the parents continued to play "Old MacDonald" whenever the daughter started to throw a temper tantrum. Friends and neighbors were also invited. Violence is greatly disrupted when it is no longer secret and you invite friends or neighbors over to the house. Within weeks, the violence disappeared.

After watching this intervention, I began to suggest similar interventions with my parents and their violent teens. Some of these include:

- **The Wig and the Dance**   Parents have purchased wigs of the opposite sex. When they put these on and dance in front of their teenager, their teen's shock quickly turned into laughter.

- **Mr. Magoo**   In the 1970s, there was a cartoon character known as Mr. Magoo, who had thick glasses and bumped into everything. One parent got ahold of some thick glasses at Goodwill. He would put these on and run into things in front of his daughter's teenage friends if she had threatened violence the night before. The teen was so mortified that she begged her dad to stop.

- **Dueling Squirt Guns**   Several parents have purchased squirt guns. When the argument gets too heated, the parent has the option of calling for a duel. The parent and the teen will go out into the backyard. With their backs to one another, they will walk ten paces turn around and fire. Whoever drenches the other one the most wins.

Each of these interventions accomplishes the same goal: making the environment less toxic through playfulness, thereby decreasing the risk of violence. Have you ever tried to yell and laugh at the same time? You can't.

I am not saying that this strategy will work with every teenager, but it's worth a try to see if it will work with yours. Just be sure to use it before your teen gets to Level 5, Acts of Violence.

AN OLD CHINESE PROVERB:
THE ONE WHO IS THE MOST PLAYFUL, WINS.

Created by Brandon Paige.

Strategy #3: A Cowritten Antiviolence Contract

There was a time when I thought that all action plans had to be produced and directed only by the parent in charge. I figured that the teen was too young and immature. My viewpoint has changed as I have gotten older. The change was confirmed when I saw a friend of mine cowrite an antiviolence contract with a very violent, angry teen at a psychiatric hospital. This teen had been raped repeatedly by different foster parents and his own father. As he grew bigger and stronger, he had become increasingly violent and had been placed in eight hospitals. Each hospital tried the same thing—physical restraints in a time-out room—which only made the boy more violent.

My friend who was a counselor at the hospital, took a different approach. He brought the boy into his office and said:

I would like your help. Every adult it seems has tried to control your anger and frustration without asking for your input. This is ridiculous because you are the expert. You know what works with you and what doesn't. I am sorry on behalf of all the other adults who have done this. I cannot change the past, but together maybe we can change the future. I would like to propose that we put our heads together to come up with an antiviolence contract. We will then sign it and distribute it to all the staff on the unit. We will use physical restraint only as a last resort and if everything on our contract has been tried and failed. How does this sound?

The young man was astounded. He had lots of ideas, but no one had ever bothered to ask. In fact, part of his anger came from the fact that he had never been taken seriously and had been treated like a mental patient for so many years. Here are his suggestions:

- When you see me getting agitated (swearing, refusing to comply, mumbling under my breath), ask me if I need "to chill."

- If I say yes, ask me in a gentle but firm way to go to my room. Check on me every five minutes to see if I am ready to come out.

- Afterward, take the time to debrief with me. Ask me what pushed my buttons and how I might have handled it differently. If I do something right with some improvement, tell me about it and give me some encouragement.

- If I start destroying property or push or shove someone, immediately move back and tell me to "chill" in my room. Talk to me softly and with a gentle voice.

- If I continue to get worse and destroy property, then and only then physically restrain me as a last resort.

After this plan was implemented, the number of physical restraints dropped by 80 percent. The teen told the counselor that he was starting to feel in control for the first time in his life.

Since this experience, I have tried to coach parents to establish an antiviolence contract with their teenager. The results have been nothing short of miraculous. Teens have told me that they crave to be treated like adults and respected. Notice that I did not say "wish" or "desire." Teens "crave" it and will respond very favorably if you deliver.

Make sure that you initiate this strategy when your teenager is in a good mood. Have a sheet of paper handy to translate your teen's ideas into a contract format. Here are some questions to get you started:

- What are the top two things that I can do or say in the future that will decrease the chance that you will threaten any type of violence with me or with anyone else?

- What will you be doing or saying differently if you are on track to shutting down your temper starting tomorrow? What will be the first concrete signs that I should look for?

- What words of appreciation can I give you when you are on track toward conquering your temper?

- Take me step-by-step through what I should do to cool you down when you start to lose it.

If you take the trouble to ask them, it's surprising how often teens can and will provide you with a custom set of tools to stop their dance of anger.

Strategy #4: Monitor Your Teen Closely

If your child or teenager is threatening suicide, you don't leave a bottle of pills, a rope, and a razor on the dresser. You lock up or remove any items that children might use to harm themselves.

In the same way, if your teen is violent, don't leave a gun in the house even if the ammunition is hidden away. (It is easy for anyone who has a gun to buy ammunition.) If you are a hunter, move your guns to a friend's house until your teen shows consistent improvement.

Conduct random searches of your teen's room if he or she is prone to violence. For drugs and alcohol searches, I suggest that your teen be present. If the problem is violence, however, you should search while your teen is out of the house. If you find a gun or a knife and your teen explodes in anger, the weapon could be used in a violent struggle. If you find any illegal weapons, call the police and immediately press charges.

The kids who were gunned down in Columbine High School could have been saved if the gunmen's parents had looked in their bedrooms and garages, where both teens had explosives and automatic weapons.

Finally, you may elect to enroll your teen in a tai chi or karate class. In most teens' lives there comes a time when they cannot simply walk away and may have to defend themselves. A good martial arts instructor can show your teen how to channel and control anger. Most violent teens actually will become much less violent after taking these classes. It is also better to use fists than automatic weapons.

Strategy #5: Accountability and the Police

If your teenager reaches a Level 5 and pushes, shoves, slaps, or hits you or anyone else, it is time to contact the police and file criminal charges. Exit from the scene as quickly as possible and lock yourself in the bedroom or leave the house. Dial 911 and tell the operator that you or another person has been physically assaulted. Once the police arrive, file assault charges and request that your teenager be booked.

The police officers may tell you that once your teen has been booked, the station will immediately call you to come and take him or her home. If you do not answer the phone, however, the police will have to hold the teenager overnight. This can send a powerful message, and make your teen think twice before committing another act of violence.

Many of you will say that you cannot possibly have your son or daughter arrested. You love your child too much—and part of you is afraid that the arrest will make him or her even angrier and more violent toward you.

In the real world, though, people get arrested for assault or property damage. If you do not mirror the real world now, the chances are high that your teen will continue to be violent toward you, toward a future spouse, or toward others—possibly toward your future grandchild.

If your teen commits an act of property damage, it may be more difficult to get the police involved. Many police departments will tell you that property damage is not their problem and refuse to arrest teens. At this point, you can ask to speak to the desk sergeant. Keep going up the line until you find someone who will book your teenager.

It may be more effective to handle the property damage in the house by making your teenager work off the damage through sweat labor (extra chores) or a paying job. This remedy also mirrors the real world and can be more dependable than police involvement.

Strategy #6: Nurturance—The Antivenin of Violence

Teens often turn angry and violent when there are no role models to show them unconditional love. One common theme emerged from the hundreds of young men Dr. Garbarino interviewed for *The Lost Boys:* They would not have become violent if just one adult in their lives had showed them nurturance and softness. It did not even have to be a parent; it could have been a schoolteacher or a neighbor.

These findings have far-reaching implications. Teens need both limits *and* love. First, they need a healthy dose of parental presence. They need you to provide structure and discipline and also to stick around when they rebel and their behavior gets worse. When they pull out an ace like violence, these kids are testing to see if you are going to leave them physically or emotionally.

Second, they need you to use the strategies in Step 7 of this book to restore lost nurturance. They need hugs and special outings even if they act as if they could care less. Without an adult in their life to be a constant and to restore a lost emotional connection, they will take their anger out on the rest of the world.

ACE #7: THREATS OF SUICIDE

In my opinion, suicide is the most serious and deadly of all the aces. When teens are violent, they may hurt someone but live to face another day. When a teen successfully implements the ace of suicide, there are no second chances.

Unfortunately, this ace seems to be on the rise with teens. The latest figures from Centers for Disease Control report that suicide is the third leading cause of death among those fifteen to twenty-five years of age and the sixth leading cause of death among those five to fourteen years of age.

Your teen's threats of suicide may be emotionally based or based solely on manipulation. Emotional suicide threats mean that your teen is severely depressed and finds no reason to live. Manipulative suicide threats are a ploy to get you to back down. Your teen has no real desire to die. The scary part is that even if the suicide attempt is manipulative, teens still may kill themselves by accident. You must treat any suicidal gesture or comment with equal seriousness.

Suicide threats can give your teen a tremendous amount of power. A suicidal teen is not expected to do homework or even to go to school. A suicidal kid is not expected to clean his room or stay off the phone. If your daughter goes to the hospital, some of the kids there may personally show her how to take a razor blade and make small cuts all over her arms and stomach: not enough to do harm, but just enough to freak everyone out.

Recently one of the kids I worked with went into the hospital for trying to burn her house down and came out with a 101 crash course on how to get your way by threatening to kill yourself. Anytime her parents tried to ground her or hold her accountable, she started to cut herself. Her parents would get scared and back down, which served to reinforce the suicidal behavior.

By saying the words "I'm going to hurt or kill myself," teens learn that they can get everyone off their case. The problem is that if you call their bluff, they may feel backed into a corner and actually try to harm themselves.

For example, sixteen-year-old Mindy had problems with ditching school. During the course of counseling, Mindy's parents stopped this problem by attending school with her and sitting on either side of her in class. Mindy hated this consequence with a passion. She was the talk of the school.

One night at dinner, Mindy rose out of her chair and told her parents that they had better cease and desist immediately. Otherwise, they would be sorry. The father said that they would not stop. Mindy got angry, went to the kitchen, and picked up a large butcher knife. She said, "If you don't stop going to school, I'm going to kill myself."

This was the first time Mindy ever made this kind of statement. She had never been suicidal and was basically a very happy kid. Because of these facts, the parents thought Mindy was joking. The father said, "Mindy, put the knife down and stop. Your little drama-queen routine won't work. Come back to dinner."

It went back and forth like this several times until Mindy took the knife and sliced through all the tendons in her wrist. When asked later what she was thinking about, she replied: "I honestly had no intention of hurting myself. A girl in my class told me about how to use suicide to get your way. I thought my parents would get scared, back down, and that would be the end of it. I had no idea they wouldn't take me seriously. They called my bluff. I felt backed in a corner. I could not let them win, so I cut myself. I am sorry I did. I had no idea how bad it would hurt or that I could really die."

Teens often act without thinking and are afraid of losing face. This combination can make suicide threats a deadly game of Russian roulette. You never really know if there is a bullet in the chamber.

The Risk of Suicide

Because of the risks involved, there are really only several possible strategies to stop the threat of suicide. To use these strategies successfully, you must work through your own issues, such as severe marital conflict, incompatible parenting styles, domestic violence, or drug or alcohol use. These antisuicide strategies must be carried out precisely. If you make a mistake, your teen may die and you will never get a second chance.

Even if you have worked out your issues, you *must* employ the services of an outside counselor. In dealing with other aces, I recommend or strongly recommend counseling. With suicide threats, counseling is not recommended, *it is required*.

If, after reading the following strategies, you have any doubts about keeping your child safe, you must place your teen in a hospital until the danger has passed. Your counselor can help you decide when and if hospitalization is necessary.

Each strategy works from two central premises. First, the goal is to keep teens alive whether their threats are manipulative suicide, emotional suicide, or both. (Later in the chapter I explain how to tell the difference and how to modify the strategies to fit the particular type of threat.)

Second, you must make the very thought of suicide so distasteful to your teen that he or she will think twice before threatening it again. These strategies are not easy, but they are well worth your effort. They will likely keep your teen from ever trying the ace of suicide again.

Strategy #1: A Twenty-four-hour Watch

A twenty-four-hour watch is exactly what it sounds like: You and your spouse or another adult are with your teenager continuously until the risk of suicide has passed. This means going to school, shadowing the teen wherever he or she goes, and sleeping in the same room. When the teen is not in school, you must take him or her to work with you or take time off from work to stay at home until the danger has past. The bottom line is that suicidal teens cannot be left alone under any circumstances. (This strategy has also been used effectively for the ace of running away.)

During the twenty-four-hour watch, your manipulative, suicidal teen loses all privileges—no television, no going out with friends, no talking on the telephone. The teen is not allowed any privacy. Someone has to watch the teen go to the bathroom and stand outside the shower. At home, especially if a teen's threats are manipulative, have the teen sit in a room and stare at the wall. If the teen refuses, say that the watch will be extended for each day he or she refuses. You can also add that you will sell off personal items to compensate you for extra days in lost wages.

The house itself also should be suicide-proofed. Throw out or place under lock and key all household chemicals, medications (including over-the-counter medicines like aspirin and Tylenol), guns, knives, and other possible weapons. This may sound extreme and serious, but that is exactly the kind of message you want to convey to your teen if their suicide is manipulative. You want the very idea of suicide to be so distasteful that your teen will never want to have to go through such an ordeal ever again.

If your teen is emotionally suicidal, they are still put on a twenty-four-hour watch but privileges like watching television or talking to friends are not restricted. You do not punish an emotionally suicidal teen but rather keep them safe and buy time until they can work through their problems. A manipulative teenager, however, should have all their privileges removed to help stop this kind of suicidal behavior.

"I Can't Do This"

Many parents' reaction to this strategy is that it is too difficult and time-consuming. Consider the following:

■ You can pay thousands of dollars to have your teen placed in the hospital, or you can do the same thing that the hospitals do: Place your teen on a twenty-four-hour watch. If hospital staff perform this job, your teen may have no reason not to try these same threats once he or she is released, especially because the staff did all the work of keeping the teen safe, *not* you. Your insurance may stop paying for private hospitals, and state hospitals are not a place you want to send your teen.

■   Your teen may pick up worse habits at the hospital. Other kids in the hospital who are seriously ill may teach your teen how to cut him- or herself, ditch school, defy authority, and run away. Most kids I have worked with go into the hospital with one set of behavior problems and emerge with more creative and serious ways to manipulate their parents.

■   Your teen may come to like the hospital and want to stay there. As crazy as it may sound, some private hospitals are better than summer camp. Teens often get to swim, go on special outings, watch movies, and make crafts. More than one teen has told me that the hospital is a safe and fun place to go. The kids have no responsibilities, and the hospitals serve great food.

■   Parents and teens don't realize this, but once teens are labeled "mentally ill," a psychiatrist may control their freedom. If the psychiatrist considers that your home is unsafe, he or she has the power to recommend removal and the placement of your teen in a state hospital.

■   The twenty-four-hour watch usually lasts only four to seven days. If it is done right, your teen will get sick of the watch and will beg to be released after only the second or third day. On the other hand, if you do not nip this problem in the bud quickly, it can get worse and keep you living in terror for years to come.

■   What may start off as a manipulative game may become real over time. More than one teen I know started off in a manipulative suicide mode and ended up becoming emotionally suicidal over time. When you practice something long enough, it can become second nature.

Organize Backup

Going through a twenty-four-hour watch takes a lot of time and preparation. You also will need backup in the form of family, friends, or neighbors who can watch your teen while you take a nap or reenergize yourself. Otherwise, you will burn out. Use the same procedures in the town meeting strategy under the ace of violence to set up the village meeting of extended family and friends.

At this meeting, organize shifts as they do at the hospital. For example, at night, you can stay up from 6:00 P.M. to 10:00 P.M. and then have someone else relieve you from 10:00 P.M. to 1:00 A.M. and so on. Doing this will communicate to your teen how serious you consider the threat.

(If you leave someone else with your teen, you should wear a pager or be available by cell phone. If something goes wrong or your teen does try to hurt him- or herself, you and the counselor have to call the shots; you cannot let your neighbor, friend, or aunt or uncle take on this kind of responsibility.)

If Necessary, Go to the Emergency Room

If your teen takes pills or cuts or hurts him or herself in any way while on the twenty-four-hour watch or at any other time, rush the teen immediately to the emergency room. Avoid the psychiatric hospital unless your teen is emotionally suicidal. If your teen is using suicide as a form of manipulation, you do not want to communicate that they are crazy or mentally ill. Instead, you want to hold the teen accountable and keep him or her safe.

A good method to achieve this goal is stomach pumping, which is one of the most unpleasant experiences ever invented. Tell your teen that it is better to be safe than sorry. Stomach pumping will not physically hurt your teenager—but it may sour him or her on the idea of ever committing any more threats or acts of suicide. The only downside is that your insurance may not cover the costs and stomach pumping can be very expensive.

A great alternative to stomach pumping is over the counter medicines that safely induce vomiting or a suppository that will act as a laxative. The rationale you give your teen is that you cannot take any chances. You must clean out your teen's system of any poisons. Say that you take all threats of suicide seriously. If your teen tries to argue that it was an empty threat or that he or she did not take anything, tell your teen that you have to be sure. The idea of a suppository or taking medicine to induce vomiting has cured many suicidal and manipulative teenagers.

If your teen has to go to a psychiatric hospital, try to ensure that it is not an enjoyable experience. Have your counselor communicate this goal to the doctors and nurses on the unit. Suggest that all day passes be voided and support any restrictions the hospital comes up with, so that your teen won't ever want to return.

Troubleshoot Potential Problems

Backup Plan

The stakes are so high that you must design a contingency plan for every what-will-I-do-if scenario that you can possibly think of. Here is a sample.

Backup Plans for Twenty-four-hour Watch

What will I do if

. . . I place my teen on a twenty-four-hour watch and she still verbally threatens to hurt herself?

A. I will take any threat seriously. I will see if she has a plan to kill herself or if she is just trying to manipulate me. In either case, I will watch her even more closely.

B. If she still continues, I will ask my counselor what to do.

What will I do if

. . . I place my teen on a twenty-four-hour watch and he still tries to hurt himself?

A. I will immediately take him to the emergency room and try to get his stomach pumped as a precaution.

B. I will consult with my counselor to determine the next step.

What will I do if

. . . I place my teen on a twenty-four-hour watch and she runs away?

A. When I find her, I will place her in her room and bolt the windows shut. I will remain in the house and get my neighbors and friends to relieve me. The lock on her bedroom door will be reversed so that it can be locked from the outside. She will eat all of her meals in her bedroom and stay there until the watch is over.

B. If problems persist I will consult with my counselor to determine the next step.

What will I do if

. . . I cannot take the time off necessary to place my teen on a twenty-four-hour watch?

A. I will call a town meeting and see if I can get the support I need to take time off.

B. If I cannot take time off, I will have no choice but to place my teen in the hospital.

The Twenty-four-hour Watch in Action

Returning to Mindy's case, let me tell you what happened after she was released from the emergency room. At first, both parents were ready to play right into Mindy's hands. They were scared that if they pushed too hard, she might try to hurt herself again. This is exactly what Mindy wanted. The only preventive step they could imagine was to place her in a six-month residential treatment facility.

I convinced the parents to try the twenty-four-hour watch based on the following rationale:

■ Mindy's suicide attempt was not a cry for help. It was purely manipulative, as evidenced by the fact that she had made no previous threats and her suicidal act occurred only after her parents refused to give in.

■ The parents could place her in a residential program and pay thousands of dollars to have someone else do the job for them. When Mindy returned home, however, she probably would start the threats over again.

■ If Mindy went to the residential hospital, she could meet kids with serious mental problems, and her own behavior and attitude could deteriorate still further.

I told Mindy's parents that if we worked together, we could have this problem licked in a week. If all went well, Mindy would be sick of this kind of intensity after only two days. By the end of seven days, she would never want to hear the word "suicide" again.

The father and mother asked me to write a letter to their bosses explaining the necessity of this intervention, with a follow-up phone call. Both bosses were very understanding. They had kids of their own.

The parents agreed that, for safety reasons, they could not end the watch on their own. The final approval to terminate the watch had to come from me in collaboration with them.

Next, they had to suicide-proof their house by removing all razors, sharp objects, medicines, and chemicals. They stocked the house with food so they would not have to leave home.

Since Mindy was a flight risk, she would not attend school during the twenty-four-hour watch. Instead, the father would go to Mindy's teachers and get all of her homework. The teachers would not need to know why Mindy was out, just that she was "ill" and would return to school soon.

Mindy would be confined to her room all day, and the windows would be screwed shut to prevent escape. All televisions, games, and stereo equipment were removed. The parents would sit outside the door with the door open or removed from its hinges. The parents would not engage Mindy in conversation. She would be allowed to do homework or read books only. She could not see her friends or use the phone until the risk of suicide had passed.

Since Mindy might run away at night, she was required to sleep in a sleeping bag on the floor of her parents' room. The parents' dresser was placed in front of their door to prevent escape.

Finally, I would be on call twenty-four hours a day if any problems occurred. If Mindy wanted to renegotiate her terms and be taken off the watch after the second day, I would be called to the home to act as a mediator between the parents and Mindy. The terms and conditions would have to be good for both parties, or the watch would continue until further notice.

Mindy threatened to run away once, but the parents were ready with a contingency plan. They calmly told her that they would have to extend the watch and get her stomach pumped as a precaution when she returned home. That quickly ended this threat.

By the end of the third day, Mindy was going stir crazy and begging her parents to end "this baby watch." Mindy promised that she would go to school, be good, and never threaten to hurt herself ever again. The parents could not remember the last time Mindy was so respectful and compliant. This was a lot of work, but nothing compared to the thousands of dollars they would have had to pay to send Mindy to a hospital.

Special Circumstances: Emotional Suicide

If your teen is depressed and emotionally suicidal, you still need a twenty-four-hour watch. However, you must include intensive individual and family therapy at least two times a week. You must get to the core problems quickly, since your teen will be much more serious in trying to kill him- or herself.

If you are not strong enough to watch your teen and are unable to commit to three or four therapy sessions per week, you should place him or her in a hospital, where the teen can receive intensive therapy and possible medications to combat depression.

Since you may be too close to the situation to give an accurate assessment, ask your counselor to help you determine if your teen's suicide threats are emotional or manipulative. They also could be both. If you do not agree with your counselor's assessment, however, please get a second opinion. Your gut instincts are often correct. Finally, ask your counselor to construct an antisuicide contract.

Strategy #2: An Antisuicide Contract

If your son or daughter is emotionally suicidal, you must get the teen to sign an antisuicide contract, which you might want to call a safety agreement. There are no guarantees that the agreement will work; it may only slow down your teen and buy you more time. But even one day may make the difference between life and death.

If you suspect that your teen is emotionally suicidal, make an appointment to see a counselor for an evaluation that same day or the next day. Tell the secretary that you think that your teen is suicidal and that you need to see someone immediately. Some of the signs to look for are:

- A sudden loss of interest in something your teen loves
- A change in school habits, like a sudden indifference to grades
- Sleeping way too much or not nearly enough
- Frequent crying and expressions of hopelessness
- A preoccupation with death
- Giving away treasured possessions
- Chronic panic or anxiety
- Becoming more isolated—pulling away from normal social activities
- Saying that life is not worth living
- Talking about how they are going to kill themselves

After the evaluation, you must decide if you are going to implement the twenty-four-hour watch yourself or have professionals do the job for you. In either case, I recommend that you put together a safety agreement similar to the one below.

"I Don't Want to Go on Living"

Fifteen-year-old Danny showed many of the classic signs of emotional suicide. After his girlfriend died in a car accident, he became more and more isolated and withdrawn. He began to say that life was not worth living and to sleep all the time. The counselor who saw Danny confirmed the parents' suspicions. Danny was actively suicidal and had a detailed plan to kill himself that involved an overdose of sleeping pills.

By the end of the discussion, Danny at least agreed to talk to the counselor or his parents before killing himself. He also understood that he would need to be under constant observation by at least one parent or another adult. He could still go to school, but someone would be there to take him and pick him up. Danny refused to go to a psychiatric hospital but understood that he had to comply with the safety agreement or he would have no choice. The following contract was written and signed by all parties.

Danny's Safety Agreement

I, Danny Roberts, agree to the following conditions to prevent harm to myself. If I violate any of these conditions, I agree to be placed in a hospital for safety reasons:

1. Before I cause harm to myself in any way, shape, or form, I will talk to my counselor and to at least one parent. If they are not available, I will wait until I can talk to them.
2. I agree to be under constant supervision by a parent or teacher until I am no longer depressed or suicidal. I agree to be taken to school and picked up at the appointed time.
3. I agree that the house will be suicide-proofed with all medications, knives, and guns safety locked away so that I will not be tempted until the danger has passed.

4. I agree to attend grief groups at least twice a week and one individual or family session per week.
5. If I am blue or suicidal, I agree to talk with one of my parents and not stuff it inside.

| _____ | _____ | _____ |
| Danny Roberts | Mr. and Mrs. Roberts | Counselor |

This agreement bought Danny the time he needed to recover from the loss of his girlfriend. Later he told me that the intense structure gave him the security blanket he needed to heal, with the help of the grief and the family sessions. Danny told me that without the clear parameters and the twenty-four-hour watch, he would have never made it another week.

When it comes to suicide, judges, probation officers, police, and parents tend to assume the cause is mental illness rather than a manipulative ploy by teens to get what they want or desire. The first line of treatment for suicide threats is hospitals, drugs, and therapy. This is appropriate for emotional suicide but often counterproductive if it is manipulation.

Again, you must consult with your counselor and watch your teen closely to make sure that he or she isn't emotionally suicidal. But if your teen is using the threats to manipulate you, you may be able to stop the threats forever by making the consequences sufficiently unpleasant.

Step 6

THERE IS STRENGTH IN NUMBERS

How to Mobilize Outside Helpers
Like Friends, Neighbors, and Police Officers

Instead of turning to their own "village"—a natural support system of extended family, friends, neighbors, and/or ministers—more and more parents are abdicating their authority to outsiders like schools, police, judges, lawyers, hospitals, boot camps, medications, or probation officers.

The results can be disastrous. When outsiders take over your role, your parental authority can be undermined and your teen can become even more out of control. Daisy Scott, an elder spokesperson from an inner-city community in Savannah, Georgia, describes how this happens:

> When I was a child, if you got into trouble, your whole neighborhood knew about it and helped your parents raise you proper. One time I skipped school and it was like a telegraph

wire went up throughout my entire neighborhood. As I walked home, I was scolded by my neighbor, my minister, and someone I didn't even know. My mother knew what happened even before I walked through the door. That was the last time I skipped school.

Nowadays it's completely different. Instead of getting help from your neighborhood or village, parents call the police or put their children on drugs or inside hospitals. When this happens, the child has no more respect for their parents when they leave home than they do when they come back. These outsiders make the child change, not the parents. Our children know this and go right on disrespecting their parents.

As this mother of eight children and grandmother of twenty-three knows, artificial helpers can take away your authority and your confidence in your parenting abilities.

"I Lost Confidence and the Flood Gates Opened"

Nancy, the mother of fifteen-year-old Jamal, called Jamal's probation officer whenever her son threatened to push or shove his younger brother. At first this worked. Jamal was scared of the probation officer and did not want to go back into detention. Over time, however, these quick fixes made the mother second-guess her own parenting abilities. She lost confidence and started calling the probation officer each time Jamal became even slightly unruly.

Eventually the probation officer became irritated by the mother's constant phone calls and stopped helping her. But by this time the damage had been done. Having lost the habit of taking charge, the mother had become helpless. As Jamal watched this happen, he grew even more disrespectful.

By the time Jamal was taken off probation, the mother was left with no resources of her own, and the floodgates opened. Jamal started running away and hurting his younger brother. He knew that his mother had given away all her power to stop him.

I will show you how to address these problems by either mobilizing your natural village or getting an artificial support system to provide backup without taking away your authority as the parent. Even if you do not have a support system, I'll show you how to create one or revitalize an existing one. I also will show you how to try to mobilize the support of your teenager's friends or begin to limit their negative influence.

Strategy #1: Know the Playing Field

A helper road map can help you identify the people in your life who are helping—or might help—and those who are hurting your cause. For example, Jackson, a single-parent construction worker whose fifteen-year-old son, Cal, kept running away instead of going to school, realized that his boss, who was a good friend, might be a potential helper.

Jackson worked outdoors in 102-degree heat. Cal might think twice about running away if Jackson's boss let him bring him to work, and he had to sit on a woodpile all day sweating. To Jackson's surprise, the boss not only agreed to help but even came over in the morning to drag Cal out of bed. After a couple of days, Cal was begging to go back to school and into the air-conditioning! Please follow these procedures to create your own personalized helper road map.

Know the Players

For most of us, the list of potential helpers centers around one or more of the following six areas:

1. **Church, friends, or extended family**
   Many of us do not see these people or institutions as a place of support or backup. In the old days, it was common to have a grandparent, a neighbor, or a minister to help you hold your child accountable. Nowadays parents mistakenly believe that these people are too busy or do not want to be bothered. This is usually not the case. There is strength in numbers.

2. Peers: Your teenager's second family

Economic pressures, technology, moving from place to place, and divorce have disintegrated the influence of the family. As a result, the peer group exerts a greater effect on the heart and soul of your teenager than ever before. You can often enlist their help through some of the creative strategies listed in this chapter.

3. Child protective services (CPS) and police officers

When you start to take away your teen's power, they will sometimes retaliate by calling CPS or the police to falsely claim that you are abusing them. This is done to scare or frustrate you into backing down. Most CPS workers and police are beginning to catch onto this game. You must learn how to arm yourself beforehand in the case they are contacted by your teen.

4. Other counselors, probation officers, or psychiatrists

These helpers can either empower your position as a parent or unintentionally take away your authority to create "learned helplessness." The goal is to use the strategies in this chapter to organize these people in such a way that they will back you up without taking away your voice as the one in charge.

5. School: Your teenager's backyard

Behavior problems that occur at home often occur within your teen's school environment. For example, when your teen is disrespectful to you they are often disrespectful to their teacher as well. Therefore, teachers and parents must work together to solve the teen's school problems.

6. Co-workers, bosses, and your job

When your teenager has extreme problems, it can effect your work. For example, you are called away from work when your teen is suspended or expelled from school or they run away. Therefore, you must often gain the help or understanding of your boss to stop your teenager.

Create a Laundry List

To identify the helpers in your own life, make three columns on a sheet of paper. Label the left column "Currently Supportive People or Institutions," the middle column "Potentially Supportive People or Institutions," and the right column "Nonsupportive People or Institutions." Ask yourself the following questions to help you fill in each column:

- **Currently Supportive People or Institutions:** Who in my life currently helps me stop my teen's misbehavior (my neighbor, my best friend, my spouse, etc.)? What institutions presently help me stop my teen (my teen's probation officer, the counselor, the judge, etc.)?

- **Potentially Supportive People or Institutions:** Who in my life might potentially help me stop my teen's misbehavior if I picked up the phone and asked them (would my ex-husband or wife help, would my boss help, would my teen's friends help, etc.)? What institutions might help me stop my teen (the police department, my work, the runaway shelter, etc.)?

- **Nonsupportive People or Institutions:** Who in my life potentially or currently undermines my power to take charge of my own household (my ex, my teen's friends, my mother)? What institutions potentially or currently destroy my confidence to stop my teen's problems? (Would calling the police or the probation officer all the time undermine my ability?)

Janice's Laundry List

For example, Janice was a single mother who was feeling overwhelmed and hopeless. Her son, Malcolm, was sixteen years old and much bigger than she was. For the past year, it had been next to impossible to get Malcolm to school in the morning. He stayed up all night to watch television and was so tired the next day that he was late for school or didn't go at all.

When Janice tried to get him up, Malcolm either rolled over and ignored her or threatened to punch her if she did not leave the room. Malcolm had also learned how easy it was to get himself suspended from school by having a fight or cussing out the teacher. This "punishment" was like a reward to Malcolm, giving him an unassailable, ready-made excuse to miss school.

Janice had tried everything to stop these problems on her own—putting Malcolm on medication for ADHD, taking away his phone, grounding him, and calling his father. Nothing worked. The school also called at least every week and made it sound as if she were to blame. Janice came up with the following list of the people who were involved in her life and Malcolm's:

Currently Supportive People or Institutions

- My mother
  (Janice currently had only one helper. Janice's mother sometimes took Malcolm when Janice could no longer handle him. This provided temporary relief.)

Potentially Supportive People or Institutions

- My minister or church
  (Until we completed this list, neither Janice nor I thought about involving the church. The minister had offered to help, but Janice had never given it serious consideration.)
- My boss at work
  (Janice's boss was a dear friend who liked Malcolm and wanted him to succeed.)
- My neighbors
  (Janice knew two other single-parent moms who were also having problems with their sons.)
- The police department
  (There was a law regarding chronic truancy. Janice could press charges on her son but was hesitant.)

Nonsupportive People or Institutions

- My ex-husband
  (Malcolm's father would not support her and contradicted the rules she put in place.)
- *Malcolm's school*
  (Malcolm's teacher and school counselor seemed to blame the mother and offered little support.)
- *His medication*
  (Malcolm was given the label of ADHD and prescribed Ritalin. Whenever Malcolm did not want to do his homework, he told his mother that it was because he had ADHD or had forgotten to take his pill.)
- Malcolm's friends
  (Malcolm had an eighteen-year-old friend who constantly encouraged him to ditch school.)

Draw Your Road Map

Once you have made your list, you can create a road map that will help you pinpoint the trouble spots you need to fix and the people or institutions who will help you get there.

The road map begins with all the people who live under your roof. For example, in Malcolm's family, using squares to represent males and circles to represent females, we would place both Malcolm and Janice in the center of the "family or household" circle. Janice is placed at the top to symbolize that, as the parent, she is in charge of the household.

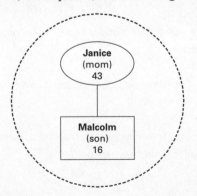

Since Malcolm is an only child and the mother is a single parent without a boyfriend or spouse, they are the only ones drawn inside the household circle.

Please fill in the names and ages of the family members, friends, or relatives who currently live under your roof.

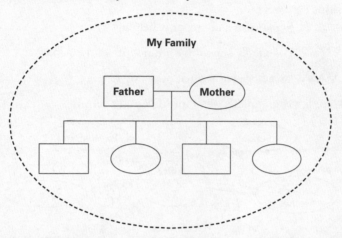

Helpers and Nonhelpers Outside Your Family. After you fill in your household circle, locate all the helpers and nonhelpers outside your immediate family. In Malcolm's family, the map would look like this:

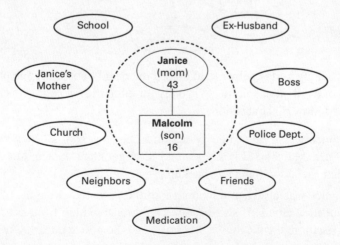

Draw up a similar map for your own family, taking the names from your list of helpers and nonhelpers.

Your Relationship With Each Helper. Use the symbols in the following map key to draw the appropriate lines indicating your (or your teen's) relationship with the person or institution. These relationships can be:

===== Supportive and presently helping

?????? Potentially supportive but not presently helping

WWW Unsupportive and not presently helping

Here is the completed map for Malcolm's family:

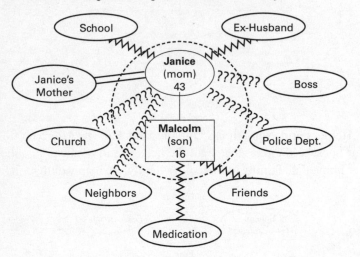

Looking at this helper road map, Janice and I could see the problems and potential solutions virtually jumping off the page. We came to the following conclusions:

- Janice was trying to get Malcolm to go to school all by herself. Since Malcolm was bigger and stronger than Janice, she was defenseless without any backup.

- Janice was clearly not tapping into the potential strengths of her outside helpers. If she did, she could receive help from her congregation, the neighbors, her boss, and the police department.

- Janice could strengthen the existing bond between her and her mother by asking her to come over in the morning to help get Malcolm out of bed and take Malcolm twice a week to give her a chance to recharge her batteries.

- Janice's ex-husband undermined her authority by telling Malcolm that he disagreed with how his mother was handling the situation. Janice either had to pick up the phone and try to make him an ally or find a way to limit his contact with Malcolm.

- Janice needed backup, not criticism, from the school in order to get Malcolm to attend. It was time to use the strategies outlined under the truancy acc, in Step 5, to devise a written plan and collaborate with the school.

- Currently Malcolm's friends (especially the eighteen-year-old) made matters worse. Janice could try to talk to these friends and ask for their expert help and advice. If that didn't work, Janice would have to figure out a way to neutralize their negative influence.

- Malcolm was using the fact that he was taking Ritalin as an excuse to avoid taking responsibility for his own actions. The pros and cons of continuing on medication needed to be reevaluated in consultation with a medical doctor.

Mobilize Your Helpers for Battle

Once you've completed your road map, start mobilizing the troops for battle. Use the same procedures outlined earlier under the Nonviolent Town Meeting in Step 5 to organize your helpers. You will be pleasantly surprised at how often a potential helper will say something like "What took you so long to call? I knew there was a problem and that you were stressed out. I wanted to help, but I didn't know how. What do you want me to do?"

Also try to talk to your nonsupportive helpers. Sometimes the lack of support is due to a misunderstanding, a false set of assumptions, or a lack of clarity on their part on how to help. For example, one school was nonsupportive until we brought it a clear plan of action and showed how the teen was making up stories to play the parent against the teacher.

If you cannot smooth out the rough edges and get nonhelpers to help you, you may need to turn to a mediator or counselor who is not emotionally involved. A mediator can help you get unstuck and provide a win/win scenario for both parties.

Janice's Little Helpers

Realizing that six heads would be better than her one to solve Malcolm's problems, Janice forced herself to pick up the phone and call her neighbors and minister for help. She was amazed at how willing they were to lend a hand. For example, the minister offered the church office as the meeting place so that Malcolm would not find out. The minister also volunteered to bring two fathers who had overcome problems with their teens.

At the meeting, Janice felt a sense of relief and hope that she had not experienced in years. The minister took out a big flip chart and some markers. Everyone brainstormed solutions to Malcolm's problem. At first, there were the traditional consequences, such as grounding and taking away the phone. Then suddenly very creative suggestions started to emerge. One of the fathers said:

> "I know this may sound weird, but when my son overslept for school, I just got to the point where I ran out of answers. Talking did not help. It was time for immediate action. So one day, without saying a word, I got a big bucket of ice-cold water and poured it on his crotch. Boy, did he move! After that, no more problems."

Everyone at the meeting started to crack up. Janice laughed but then raised a serious concern that if she tried to use ice water, Malcolm would likely become angry and hit her. The minister and neighbors offered to prevent this by coming to the house in the morning and standing behind her as she administered the cold-water treatment. If Malcolm threatened violence, the minister would tell him firmly to get himself together by the count of 5, or he would call 911.

Janice protested that this plan would be too much trouble for everyone; they had their own lives to live. But when the minister asked if Janice would do the same thing for them. Janice said, "Of course." The minister said, "Then it's not too much trouble."

The group added that if Malcolm got suspended, cut a class, or ditched school, Janice should sell part of his CD collection and donate the money to the church. If the problem of suspensions continued, she would sell more of his things.

Janice also asked if someone could go with her to the school and help her present this plan of action. The minister volunteered. The teacher and principal loved the plan and went from criticizing Janice to offering their support.

The morning after the school meeting, the minister and two fathers arrived at the house, prepared the bucket of ice water, and went upstairs. Malcolm did not notice the other people behind his mom and said "F**k you" when Janice asked him to get up. When his mother proceeded as planned and dumped the cold water on him, he jumped up and threatened to hit her. When he saw the minister and the other two men, however, he stopped immediately, embarrassed by the wet spot between his legs. He then proceeded to get dressed and arrived at school on time. Janice was both shocked and relieved.

Malcolm was just as shocked when he cut a class and saw a note tacked to his door explaining that part of his CD collection had been sold and the money given to the church. The rest were safely locked away; it would be sold piece by piece if there were any more school problems; it would be returned intact if he attended school regularly for two months. It took about a month, but the tide finally turned and Malcolm's school attendance improved dramatically.

I firmly believe that the changes in Malcolm would not have occurred without the revitalization of Janice's village. Through her helper road map, the mother realized that there is strength in numbers. It was hard for Malcolm to get violent or disrespectful in the company of strangers.

Strategy #2: Mobilizing Friends or Neighbors

One of the biggest barriers to involving friends or neighbors is your own hesitation. It is not uncommon to think that people either are too busy or don't want to be involved. You also may believe that you are the only parent with such an angry and out-of-control teenager.

It's Not What You Say But How You Say it

How you come across on the phone is a key to receiving help. Here are two different approaches by different parents. After reading what the parents said, ask yourself which one you would want to help and which one would turn you off.

> PARENT A: Hey, I have a really bad kid who I don't know what to do with. He's a terror. Would you talk some sense into him? I am at my wit's end.

> PARENT B: Hi, I was wondering if I could ask you for help. My teen is going through some tough times right now, and I feel alone and isolated. There is strength in numbers. I know that with your help, ideas, and support I can get him back on track. I wanted to know if we could meet someplace where my teenage will not overhear us. I can then explain exactly how I could use your help. Your help would be time limited, maybe three or four weeks at the most. What do you think? Will you help?

Parent A's sell job fell on deaf ears. You can imagine what the neighbor or friend was thinking: "There is no way I want to help." "What would this kid do in my home?"

Parent B's statement worked wonders. He was clear as to why he needed help (lack of support) and promised that the helper's role would be clearly defined and limited in duration. This parent also made it convenient on the friend or neighbor to meet and help.

You can't always tell in advance who can and will help, as Marie's mother, Josephine, learned in the following example.

The Retired Grandmother

Sixteen-year-old Marie was having unprotected sex with many different guys in the neighborhood. She was also failing all of her courses, especially reading. You could see Marie's low opinion of herself from the way she had trouble looking people in the eye and thought guys would like her only if she had sex with them. Her mother, Josephine, tried the usual grounding and threats to stop Marie from having sex, but nothing worked.

Finally, in desperation, Josephine produced a list of every possible helper she could think of. When she first considered a retired and very gentle grandmother in the neighborhood, she was ready to dismiss the idea, but she finally made the call.

> "Ms. Martinez, I know you live by yourself and probably don't want any more stress in your life. But I'm desperate. My daughter, Marie, doesn't feel good about herself, and men take advantage of her. She won't look you in the eye and has trouble reading. Her grandparents are no longer living, and I don't have any family nearby. Do you think it would be possible for Marie to come by one day a week after school so you could talk with her and help her read?"

Josephine was floored when she heard the response:

> "Of course I would! It gets very lonely being by myself, and I would love some company. In fact, I'm a retired schoolteacher."

Marie and the grandmother/neighbor became friends, and Marie started to visit almost every day. Over time Josephine noticed a transformation as Marie began to look people in the eye and not stay out late with boys. When Josephine asked her neighbor about it, she said:

> "I think Marie is gaining confidence as her reading goes up. I read to her now as much as she does to me. I tell her about the old days, especially when I was her age. I know that she

is mistakenly using sex to get love. Therefore, I tell her stories of how boys need to treat you like a lady and how to be courted properly. I think she is getting the message."

The Value of Role Models

The influence that elders can have on our young people is amazing. When troubled teens are surrounded by good role models, their behavior improves.

It reminds me of the movie *Fried Green Tomatoes*. Like Marie, the main character, Evelyn Couch, who was played by Kathy Bates, had very low self-esteem. One day she happened to meet a remarkable elderly woman at the nursing home. Once a week Evelyn came to visit and listen to the lady's stories about her childhood and the obstacles she overcame. As she listened, Evelyn began to grow stronger emotionally and stopped allowing her husband to walk all over her. She gained strength from the elderly woman who, in turn, gained strength by helping.

When I have a troubled kid with low self-esteem, I try everything in my power to get him or her to volunteer at least three hours a week at a nursing home or a homeless shelter. The parents and I arrange the setting, the days, and times in consultation with the teen, although we don't give the teen any choice about whether to volunteer *somewhere*. We may even bribe the teen with small amounts of money on an hourly basis—just to get the teen's foot in the door. After that, the positive effects of helping others begin to take hold of the teen's heart.

When these kids help others, they begin to help themselves. The negative grip that peers and society have on them begins to weaken, and hidden gentleness and strengths suddenly break through the surface. Don't overlook any possible friends or neighbors who could give your teen this experience.

Strategy #3: Mobilizing Churches, Synagogues, and Extended Family

I group these potential helpers together because churches or synagogues are often like an extended family to which you can turn in times of need. The following are some creative ways to recruit ministers, rabbis, members of the congregation, or extended family members.

Mentors on Call

Go to your local church or synagogue and directly ask the members for help, especially if you currently have no helpers. These people may be strangers, but you will be pleasantly surprised at the kindness of strangers. You may plan to use their help only until things have calmed down, but often you will find that these mentors quickly become close friends. It happens all the time.

People in churches or synagogues often help even if you are not part of their congregation. Many people sit in services and think, "I wish I could put my religious principles into action"; they want to help, but no one ever approaches them with a clear road map as to how.

Contact the Minister or Rabbi

Make an appointment to meet with your local pastor, priest, minister, rabbi, or community leader in his or her office. Face to face is always better than over the phone. If you are a member of a church or synagogue, start there first. If you are not a member, pick a name randomly out of the phone book. You do not have to be religious for this work.

At the meeting, explain the mentor-on-call idea and how it works. I would be shocked if the person you approach did not respond with enthusiasm. Many will give you a list of potential volunteers right on the spot.

A Personal Testimony

Ask the minister or rabbi if you could come to a service and speak briefly to the congregation during announcements, or to give you a list of bible study groups that you could approach. If you absolutely can't bring yourself to speak in person, you can put your request in the church newsletter, but a personal testimony from the heart will always get better results.

Tell everyone you are there to recruit volunteers to provide support as you try to stop your son or daughter's problem. Ask for a commitment of once a week for several hours. Ask those interested to meet with you in the back of the church or synagogue for five minutes after the service for more information.

Clarify Roles

Clarify and troubleshoot everyone's role. For example, tell each volunteer how you will need his or her help (to brainstorm solutions, to come to the house and provide support, to help with homework, etc.), and when you will need that help (when your teen is swearing at you, running away, etc.). Write down everyone's job description in a contract format and give a copy to everyone. Ask all volunteer helpers to repeat back their understanding of their role so that there are no misunderstandings. Troubleshoot all the what-will-I-do-if scenarios before you deliver the contract to your teen.

Get together for lunch or dinner once a month with your helpers and review your progress. If there are any unanticipated glitches, use this time to solve them.

The Kindness of Strangers

Eileen was a single mother whose seventeen-year-old son, Hardin, would drink and drive. Hardin did not think his drinking was a problem. He constantly called his mother a "bitch" and walked out when she tried to stop him. Eileen was deathly afraid to call the police because he threatened to hurt her if she did.

Eileen had recently moved into town. She had no friends or extended family to help her out. She worked as a card dealer in Las Vegas. As a last resort, she called one of the larger Catholic churches and told the pastor about her dilemma.

The pastor was deeply moved and suggested that she come to their weekly Parents Without Partners group. She could meet new people and ask for some support. Eileen was hesitant but decided to give it a try.

At the group, she gave her testimony and was taken completely off guard by the outpouring of support. Many of the parents had kids of their own with behavior problems. For the first time, she did not feel alone.

Eileen went around the room and asked everyone for ideas. Two single dads had the best answers. They suggested the purchase of a breath alcohol test over the Internet. They also told Eileen how to disable Hardin's car by unscrewing and removing the distributor cap. These volunteers offered to come over and stand by her side as she required him to take the test. They would also remove the distributor cap if necessary.

Three important things happened to Eileen. First, she no longer felt alone. This gave her confidence to get tougher with Hardin and consistently follow through on consequences. Second, the volunteers brainstormed great solutions. Finally, now that she had the backup of two male volunteers, Hardin could no longer successfully bully and intimidate his mom. These mentors on call empowered the mother to regain control of her household.

Respite Care

Sometimes things get so out of hand that you need a rest or a breather to regroup. Ask your extended family or best friend to take in your children or teenager for a few weeks.

Put some time limits on the stay (no longer than a month if possible, preferably one or two weeks) so that your teen will not get too comfortable. In fact, during those weeks, it's a good idea to ask your friends to become wardens and make your teen's life as tough as possible. For example, they might feed your teen spinach or broccoli and cut off television privileges. Doing this can help your teen to appreciate home.

The exception to the usual time limit is if there is physical or sexual abuse in your home and you need the extra time. That time period should be decided with the help of a counselor. Hire a competent family counselor to conduct meetings with both you and your kids.

Otherwise, the same problems will be waiting for you when your teen comes back. Your window of opportunity is before your teen returns home, not after.

Strategy #4: Getting Help from Child Protective Services (CPS) or the Police

Child protective service (CPS) workers and police officers can be play a big part in either backing you up or taking away your authority. Some teens may try to regain control of their household by calling CPS or the police and falsely accusing their parents of abuse. Other teens may commit acts of violence on people or property. The police can support you by booking your teenager for assault and battery, or can undermine your authority by writing a police report that means nothing.

If Your Teenager Reports Abuse

If a teenager (or perhaps one of your teen's friends) reports abuse in your home, you must act quickly. By law, the CPS worker must investigate any report of abuse. Often the particular caseworker's training, experience, and treatment philosophy will determine if he or she will support or disarm your authority.

Fortunately, many CPS workers now seem to understand that some teenagers use the system to intimidate their parents into backing down. It has been my experience that most CPS workers are willing to look at this issue before charging a parent with abuse. But it's vital to prepare in advance by using one of these three options:

1. **Cooperate fully.** Let the CPS worker come into your home and even offer him or her coffee or a soda. Try to remember that the CPS worker is required by law to investigate any and all reports, and if even one report is accurate, it could save the life of a child. Usually, there must be hard evidence before a CPS worker will remove your teen or bring charges against you. Once the investigation has cleared you, ask the CPS worker

to back you up and tell the teenager in your presence that no more false claims will be tolerated. Usually this works to stop further calls.

2. **Arm yourself with an advocate.** Your teen is so good at this game that you may want to beat him or her to the punch by hiring your own counselor to work with you in the same way that you

would hire a lawyer if you were about to get a divorce. Just as it is better to go to court with a lawyer, it is better to have your own counselor when dealing with CPS or the police. A CPS worker or police officer is more apt to believe you if you are seeing a professional counselor or psychiatrist, and will find it reassuring to know that a third party is closely monitoring the problems.

Give the CPS worker or police officer your counselor's business card and ask that they call. If you do not have a counselor, the next best thing is to give the CPS worker or police officer the name and number of your best character witness, perhaps your minister or family doctor.

3. **Be proactive.** This option will take your teen completely by surprise. If you suspect that your teen will call or have a friend call CPS or the police, fax or mail a copy of the following letter to the supervisor of your local Child Protective Service agency and your local police chief. After you send this information, follow up with a phone call to make sure they received your letter. (If they have further questions, try sending them a copy of this chapter.)

Both CPS and the police will be expecting your teen's call. Workers still might have to go through the motions of coming to your house as required by the law, but imagine your teen's surprise when they show up with this letter! (Keep a copy of the letter to give the CPS worker or police officer at your home, in case the worker doesn't bring it along.)

[Date]

[Name of CPS Supervisor or Police Chief Here]
[Agency or Police Department name]
Address
City, Zip

Dear _____:
Our names are _____, and we are the concerned parents of a _____-year-old son/daughter, _____. We are writing you because we expect that our teen may call you or get another person to call to say that we are abusing him/her. This will be a false accusation.

Dr. Scott Sells's book, entitled *Parenting Your Out-of-Control Teenager: Seven Steps to Reestablish Authority and Reclaim Love*, states that teens sometimes claim abuse to prevent their parents from setting limits on misbehavior. These teens hope that you will believe their claims and take away our power as parents. They want us to get scared and back down so that they will be free to start their self-destructive cycle all over again.

We realize that by law you must investigate every report. There is no abuse in our household; we are following the treatment procedures outlined in Dr. Sells's book to turn our teen's behavior around. The treatment has been working, which is why our teen may make a last-ditch attempt to undermine it by filing a claim of abuse. If this claim is accepted at face value, it will not only diminish our ability to be good parents but also send a powerful message to our teen and others that they don't have to listen to their parents if they turn around and accuse them of abuse.

Our hope is that you will work with us and make it clear to our teen that false claims will not be tolerated. If you have any questions, or if my teen or someone else contacts you, please call me at [leave the best phone number where you can be reached].

Sincerely,

The letter provides solid reasoning as to why your teen is claiming abuse. It can disarm his or her weapons even before they are fired.

Strategy #5: Mobilizing Counselors

Parents are more willing to shop around to get the best deal for a car than to shop around for the best counselor or psychiatrist. I'm astounded by the number of parents who have told me that they trust *any* counselor who has a degree at the end of his or her name. Having a degree, however, does not necessarily mean that the person is competent or is a good fit for your particular teenager.

Different counselors also have different theories on the "best" way to treat your teenager. For example, one counselor may tell you that your teen's violence is due to a chemical imbalance in the brain that can be controlled only with medication. Another counselor in the same office may say that your teen is stuck in a rut and needs stricter limits. Listening to so many different points of view can get very confusing and frustrating.

To combat this problem, you must shop around at least as much as you do for a new car. If the counselor seeks to work only with your teen and exclude you from the process, red flags should go up immediately. Like you, your teen does not live in a vacuum. The surrounding environment influences him or her. Therefore, while individual sessions are critical, your counselor also should incorporate your family or other helpers into the overall treatment plan. For detailed advice on finding the right counselor for you, please see the appendix or visit my Web site at *www.difficult.net*.

Strategy #6: Working with Institutions (Schools, Hospitals, Foster Care, and Probation Officers)

All teens are involved with at least one institution—school—but out-of-control teens and their parents may also have to deal with others. Behaviors like running away or violence often end up involving the courts, which assign the case to a probation officer. Teens who commit acts of drug or alcohol abuse or threaten suicide often end up in hospitals or long-term residential programs. Teens who ditch school or fail grades are in direct conflict with the schools they attend.

Ultimately, teens who exhibit these behaviors are at high risk of engaging in long-standing arguments with their parents. Over time, parents get burned out and stop caring. This may lead to neglect or violence that could lead to a teen's removal from the home and into foster care.

If you do not work collaboratively with these institutions, your teen may continue to have problems for the following reasons. First, you may hand over your parental authority to these institutions to fix or raise your child. You then run the risk that these people will fix your kid and not you. When your teen comes home, old problems will quickly return.

Second, there may be disagreement on the right way to solve your teen's problem. For example, fifteen-year-old Tiffany was in foster care. Her foster parents were finally setting firm limits when she started yelling, swearing, and becoming disrespectful. It was working until a foster care worker came to the house and told the parents, in front of Tiffany, that they were too tough on her. When Tiffany saw this disagreement, she quickly went back to her old disrespectful ways.

Here are some ways to work with institutions and professionals so that they can provide backup without taking over your role as a parent. If possible, I recommend hiring a counselor or consultant to accompany you to any meetings. The counselor will be able to speak the professional jargon of the institutions and may persuade them to be more responsive to your needs. It is like the difference between taking an accountant who understands the tax code to an IRS audit or going by yourself.

Meet Face to Face

The first step is to meet with these outsiders face to face. You can do it over the phone, but it will not be nearly as powerful. You probably will have to meet the school, hospital psychiatrist, or probation officer on their own turf. People are busy and they will appreciate it if you make the meeting convenient to their schedule. Appreciation usually leads to better cooperation.

Clarify Your Purpose and Gather Their Ideas

When you meet, it is critical that you immediately state the purpose and goals of that meeting. Helpers are pressed for time; usually they have between fifteen and thirty minutes to talk. Begin the meeting with the following statement and question:

Thank you for meeting with us. We called this meeting to accomplish two goals: first, to get your ideas and to brainstorm solutions to help solve our teen's problem of [name the specific problem]. Three or more heads are better than one. Second, we hope that by the end of the meeting we can clarify everyone's role. We want to be on the same page and present a united front so that our teen cannot divide and conquer us. I want to begin by getting your views and your suggested solutions.

Seek to understand before you seek to be understood. People are more cooperative when you listen and gather their ideas first. You also want to find out each helper's position before revealing your own.

Getting on the Same Page

If there are vast differences of opinion, begin by helping everyone understand what will happen if they continue to disagree:

It seems like we have some pretty different opinions about what we think my son's [or daughter's] problem is and how to solve it. I hope and pray that we can reach a consensus. If we cannot, can we agree to disagree for the moment and decide to try one of the plans presented? Let's try it for at least three or four weeks and see if there are any changes in my son [or daughter]. If there are, let's keep going forward. If not, let's try something different. The most important thing is that we walk out of this meeting on the same page and we bring [teen's name] in to go over the plan and speak as one voice. If we are in opposition to one another, [teen's name] will not improve but continue to divide and conquer us.

You do not have to obtain unanimous approval from everyone in the room to make your plan work. You just need everyone to agree to give the plan a chance to work without sabotaging it, even if there is disagreement. Ask for their permission to confront them in the future if you see that they are sabotaging the plan unintentionally. Examples of sabotage include not following through with promises or failing to back you up.

Strategy #7: Mobilizing Your Teen's Peer Group

It is often helpful to involve your teen's friends, and it's important to try, because peers exert such a powerful influence over your teen that they become like their second family.

You do not have to like your teen's friends or embrace their value system to work with them. Your goal is time-limited: to get your teen to stop his or her problems as quickly as possible, so that he or she can get on with the business of becoming a good citizen, getting a job, and moving out of your house.

To make this happen, you may have to be creative and recruit those individuals to whom your teen will listen and respond. For example, if your teen is partying all the time, whom do you think might make a bigger impact, a parent who lectures and says "You will never amount to anything if you keep on like that," or a friend who says "We both need to slow down and find other things to do besides partying"?

Making Friends the "Expert" Consultants

One possible approach is to ask your teen to invite friends over to the house. Say that you would like to ask their friends' opinions on how to solve the problem because they may know your teen better than you do.

If they refuse, try telling your teen that there is $10 in it for him or her. Call it a bribe, but sometimes you have to do whatever it takes to get results. Make sure you tell your teen up front that the bribe won't be given until after the friends leave. You also will not give money to their friends or if they tell the friends about the bribe.

Ask your teen to be present while you ask the friends' advice. Here are some sample questions:

- "I asked you here because I am stumped. Nothing I do or say has been good enough to make [teen's name] want to give up [insert problem behavior here]. What am I missing?"

- "You know [teen's name] as well or better than I do. Therefore, I need your expert advice. What suggestions do you have that would slow this problem down or stop it cold in its tracks so that everyone can get off [his or her] case?"

- "Is there anything you can do or say to [teen's name] in the future that will help [him or her] get over this problem—a pep talk, keeping him or her straight, and so on?"

In asking your teens' peers for their expert advice, you are treating them with the respect they crave, and you may be astonished at the results. Sometimes even your teen's worst friends will become helpful and cooperative if they feel valued and appreciated.

A Peer Helper Contract

Another great way to enlist the help of your teen's friends is to incorporate their role into a peer helper contract like the one in the following example. (Before doing this, give the parents of the potential teen helper a draft of the contract and ask their permission.)

Martin's Peer Helper Contract

Rule #1:
Martin agrees to raise his grades in each class to a C average or better. Progress will be monitored by a weekly progress report and random phone calls to Martin's teacher. If any subject falls below a 70 percent average on Martin's progress report or if he refuses to bring it home, Consequence A will occur. If Martin maintains a 70 percent average or better, Consequence B will occur.

Consequence A:
Martin will be grounded Saturday night. If he comes back with a below-average grade the next week, he will be grounded both Friday and Saturday night.

Consequence B:
Martin will be able to go out on weekends with Sam and Mike until a 10:00 P.M. curfew. He also will qualify for the weekly cash drawing for the person with the overall highest percentage increase for that week.

Mom's Role
1. Mom will administer both negative (Consequence A) and positive (Consequence B) consequences. She will ask Sam and Mike to bring their weekly progress reports when they come by to see Martin.
2. Mom will check the progress reports and issue the payoffs.

Mike and Sam's Role
1. Mike and Sam agree to complete their weekly progress reports and show them to Martin's mother on Friday.
2. Mike and Sam agree to give Martin their support to start doing better in school and not disown him if he starts doing better.
3. Mike and Sam will not tempt Martin to go out if he is grounded.

At this point, you may well be thinking: Why should Martin, Sam, and Mike get paid for something they should already be doing? But consider this: Do you get paid if you do your job well? Similarly, it can make sense to motivate teens to do well with financial incentives. In Martin's case, everything else that the mother tried had failed. It was time to try something creative: a competition between friends for doing well academically. It was not just the money but the competition that made the difference.

Limiting Peers' Negative Influence

What should you do if your teen's friends either refuse to help or exhibit such a negative influence that they must be stopped? At this point you have two options, the direct, straightforward approach or the indirect, backdoor one. You are not guaranteed success with either approach, but it's worth making the effort to try both of them.

The Freedom Not to Choose: A Direct Approach

Many parents feel that choosing their teens' friends somehow violates their civil rights. In addition, they commonly believe that if you try to take away your teens' friends, the kids will just want to see them that much more.

I agree with these positions up to a point. If your teen is not exhibiting extreme or out-of-control behavior and generally makes good and thoughtful decisions, then let your teen choose. In most cases, your teen will eventually drop or outgrow the negative friends on his or her own.

If your teen is out of control, however, he or she will likely only get worse with negative friends. Negative energy tends to feed off other negative energy. As one parent put it:

> "My son's bad behavior is manageable until he starts hanging around his thug friends. It is like he becomes a different person. He comes home mouthy, disrespectful, mean, and angry. I wish I had the power to choose his friends for him."

This is where this parent and others are mistaken. If your son or daughter is out of control and a friend is contributing to the problem, you have the right and responsibility to say "You are no longer allowed to see this friend while you are living under my roof."

To accomplish this goal, offer teenagers a choice. If they continue to see their friends, they will receive negative consequences. At first, there will be a power struggle. You must, however, outlast the struggle and stick to your guns long enough to see a change. It will definitely not happen overnight, but it can happen, as the following three examples demonstrate.

The A List

Fifteen-year-old Bryant told his father that kids who got As were "nerds." They would never like a kid like him, and besides he was not interested in meeting them. Bryant's friends were older drug dealers on the corner lot. At this point, the father took action. He went to the school and presented his dilemma to the principal. In turn, the principal presented the father with a list of names and numbers of all A students.

Bryant was then given a choice: Either call some kids on this list and make a date and time to meet one of them to go to a movie, or ride with Dad in the back of his police car instead. Faced with these options, it was amazing how quickly Bryant found someone on the list whom he was willing to see outside school. Before long Bryant actually started to form friendships with two of these kids. He told his drug buddies that he was forced to spend time with these "nerds." This allowed Bryant to save face with his friends.

Friends or Consequences

Sixteen-year-old Megan and her friends liked to stay out all night partying. When her mother told her to stop seeing this group of friends, Megan said "F**k you." As a result, Megan was presented with two choices: Either stop hanging out with these friends or suffer the consequences.

First, the mother personally went over to the parents of Megan's friends. Most of them were reasonable and agreed not to allow Megan to sleep over any more. The two parents who were not reasonable received a notarized letter stating that the mother would call the police if Megan did not come home. These parents did not want the police in their lives and complied.

Second, Megan's clothes and makeup were placed in lockup outside the house. For every day she went out with her friends, one article of clothing and item of makeup would be given away. Megan stomped, kicked, and screamed but slowly stopped partying with these friends.

Guardian Angels and Chocolate Chip Cookies

Thirteen-year-old Latrell hung out with a very rough street gang, and whenever he was around them, something bad happened. One time he was arrested for spray-painting a building; another time it was shoplifting.

His mother and several of her neighbors came up with a very creative idea. They told Latrell that they were worried about his safety. Therefore, he needed some guardian angels. Whenever he went out on the weekends, Latrell's mother and neighbor would shadow him. If he tried to run away, his mom and her friend would just hang out where his friends were to "get to know them." They brought these kids homemade chocolate chip cookies.

The friend's began to like Latrell's mom and her friend. In turn, out of appreciation and respect, they started to look out for Latrell. They stopped taking him on their stealing sprees and made him go home on time. Latrell's mom rewarded these efforts with more cookies and hugs for the street gang.

In each example, the consequences to the teens outweighed the pleasure of seeing their friends. It is not easy, but I especially like the last example because of its softness and creativity. It takes this kind of creativity to loosen the grip of negative teen influences.

An Indirect, Backdoor Approach

There's a clear connection between the softness in your parent-child relationship and the amount of influence the peer group can have on your teenager. In general, the less nurturance there is between parent and child, the greater the influence of the peer group. For example, one sixteen-year-old teen told me:

> "Dr. Sells, I know my boyfriend shouldn't beat me up and get me to snort coke, but at least I know he loves me. He tells me all the time. This is more than my dad does. All he does is lecture and tell me how I am throwing my life away."

A lack of nurturance between daughter and father contributed to the fact that this teen continued to stay with this boy, even after getting severely beaten. She still needed structure and discipline, but she also needed her father's tenderness.

Once the father understood the bigger picture and changed his tactics, the daughter dropped the boyfriend. The father changed three things: (1) He stopped saying negative things about the boyfriend; (2) he stopped lecturing and criticizing; and (3) he started hugging her without saying a word. Once the daughter felt the closeness of her father, she no longer had to seek it out in the arms of an abusive boyfriend.

Read the following scenario and decide for yourself the connection between nurturance and peer pressure:

> Imagine for a moment that your teenager has a choice between two families. In the first family there are rules, restrictions, and adults who always seem to point out the negative or lecture on what the teen is doing wrong. At the same time, there is a lack of special outings, good times, hugs, or trust. In the second family, the teenager feels accepted for who he or she is, maintains trust, experiences a lot of good times, and enjoys special outings. In addition, this family may not require the teenager to follow any rules or accept responsibility for his actions.

Now, do you realize who is competing for your teen's heart, mind, and soul? The peer group often is equipped with a better set of commercials and a marketing plan. Plus, its members spend more quality time with your teenager.

However, you have a secret weapon—your love. Your teen craves it more than you know, even though most teens won't talk about it because they're supposed to be too old for that mushy, baby stuff, especially in front of their friends.

Reprinted with special permission of King Feature Syndicate.

Without softness between you and your teen, he or she will turn to a second family of peers, gangs, or drugs. Unfortunately, this second family is often not mature and wise enough to handle the job.

Therefore, to reverse this trend, you must balance both love and limits. The previous steps have shown you how to set consistent limits. It is now time to turn to the final step, Step 7, to learn how to inject nurturance back into your parent-teen relationship. As my grandfather used to tell me, "If your own house is in order, there is no reason to look for trouble and guidance somewhere else."

From personal experience, I know that this statement is true. I hope you will hear my story and commit to going down a similar path with your teenager.

A Change of Heart

I was a difficult teenager, and my dad and I had years of long and bitter arguments. But I remember when he and I started playing tennis every Saturday morning. When I didn't want to go, he refused to take no for an answer, and we went anyway. At first I said nothing; I was still mad at him after the years of fighting. But he didn't press or lecture as he had in the past; he said nothing.

I began to think "What does he have up his sleeve? I'll show him. Two can play at that game." Weeks went by, and still no response or retaliation from Dad. It seemed as if the angrier I got, the more he stayed his present course. We still played tennis and had special outings together, regardless of how mean or bad I was that week. It was as if he were somehow separating my bad behavior from his love. It was very confusing.

Over the next several months, it became harder and harder for me to get angry with my dad. He still disciplined me but without personally attacking my character and telling me that I was a "loser." No matter what else happened, we played tennis together like clockwork every Saturday morning until it became a ritual.

Then something really weird happened. I started looking at my friends differently. They still wanted to party all the time and skip school, but I was changing. It didn't hold the same thrill as it once did. I also wanted to ask for my dad's advice and tell him how down I was feeling. My friends' answer of "get another beer; don't worry about it" was no longer working for me. I also started thinking, "Do they really care about me, or am I just another drinking buddy? Would they still be around if I stopped partying?" Deep down inside I knew the answer was no.

At out next tennis match, I started to pour out my heart to my dad, and he just listened. He didn't lecture, pass judgment, or bring up the past. He just listened. For the first time, I began to cry. He held me, and it got real quiet for a long time. Then my dad said, "I love you, son, and I am sorry for being so hard on you all these years. No matter what happens, I will stick by you and love you."

You know what happened next. We still had our problems, and I still had some rough times. But I started to think for myself, and my negative friends continued to lose their grip on my mind, my body, and my soul.

You can have the same effect on your son or daughter that my dad had on me. Life is a giant do-over, and my dad decided to do it over with me. Now it is your turn to step up to the plate and lessen the negative power that this world has on your teenager.

Step 7

RECLAIMING LOVE BETWEEN YOU AND YOUR TEENAGER

If you turn on the television or flip through the newspaper, you will see another politician, talk-show host, or child psychologist telling you that we need tougher laws, more prisons, and stricter punishments to stop out-of-control teenagers. I have just one question: If tough love is the miracle cure for the twenty-first century, why do the same teens keep having the same problems over and over again?

The answers come from the voices of our teenagers:

My dad ruled our house with an iron fist. I was so mad. He could never give me what I really needed: to say just once that he wasn't disappointed in me.

—Stephen, age 13

I never had parents. My foster parents thought I needed harsher and harsher punishments to set me straight. Don't get me wrong, I still needed the discipline. But where was the love? So, I started having sex with these guys because I wanted to feel loved. Instead, I ended up getting pregnant and having a child that I can't take care of.

—Tamara, age 17

My friends are my family now. My mom always tells me that if I don't get in trouble we will do something together. Well, I always screw up. So we never do anything. I choose my friends over my mom.

—Michael, age 16

As you read these stories, one common theme emerges. These parents demonstrated tough love through discipline but failed to show what I call "soft love" through special outings, warm hugs, or words of praise. A lack of structure allows teens to act out because they can, while a lack of nurturance causes teens to act out because they are angry and bitter inside. Over the years, this anger grows like a cancer and is taken out on you and the rest of the world.

This is why harsh consequences like prisons, pills, and boot camps usually do not yield long-term changes in your teenager. Without a balance between love and limits, your teen may have just as many emotional or behavioral problems.

Restoring Nurturance Is Challenging

Parents tell me that restoring nurturance is more challenging than all the other steps in this book combined. One mother summed it up this way:

"If my teen doesn't do his chores, I get angry, but I get over it pretty quickly. But if I try to hug my teen and he pushes me away, it is as if something dies inside. The emotional rejection is not so easy to get over."

It is difficult to hug someone or take him or her on an outing if they tell you to "f**k off" or refuse to do what you ask. You may still love the teen, but you find yourself not liking him or her any more.

Nevertheless, this step is the missing piece to stop your teen's anger and misbehavior for good. Tough love and structure will temporarily stop the bleeding and get your teen's problem under control. Soft love, on the other hand, will permanently heal the wound. One without the other will only lead to temporary changes.

The Fine Line Between Love and Hate

The evolution from warmth with your young child to the current deep freeze of coolness and distance with your teen did not happen overnight. The following time line illustrates how the chill factor developed in your parent-teen relationship.

Stages That Lead to a Loss of Nurturance

Stage 1: Behavior Problems
Your child becomes more and more rebellious as s/he gets older and experiences behavior problems on a consistent basis over a six-month period.

Stage 2: Negative Interaction
As your child becomes a teen, s/he fails to comply with your requests more often. Disrespect increases. As a result, lecturing and negative interaction jumps from only 20 to 40 percent to an unbelievable 90 to 100 percent of the time. There is now only 5 to 10 percent of the time left over for soft love.

Stage 3: Conditional Love
In a last-ditch effort to reconnect, parents tell their teen that outings or signs of affection will be based on how good his/her behavior was that week. Your teen mistakenly comes to believe that your love is no longer unconditional but conditional based on whether s/he displays good behavior.

Stage 4: Emotional Deprivation
Emotional deprivation sets in. This means that a deep freeze occurs. Both you and your teen stop hugs or special outings

because you and your teen feel so burned by previous rejections that you both shut down and stop trying.

Stage 5: Second Family Takes Over

If your teenager does not receive nurturance in your family, s/he will look to an adopted "second family" of peers, gangs, or drugs. This becomes a problem when these friends are a negative influence on your teen's heart, mind, and soul.

Stage 6: Parent and Teen Get Stuck In a Vicious Cycle

As you watch your teenager pull away to this second family, you start to lecture more and impose more rules. You are worried or afraid. Unfortunately, your teen does not understand this. Your efforts only push him/her farther away until both of you get stuck in a rut. Each of you are unable to make the first move to break down the walls of emotional deprivation.

Stage 7: Teen Becomes Hardened and Lacks Remorse/Empathy

As this rut continues, your teenager becomes more and more hardened inside. Over time, your teen develops an inability to show remorse or empathy. If this remains unchanged into adulthood, s/he may develop what is called an antisocial personality disorder. As adults, s/hc will pass these problems onto children where this time line may begin all over again.

A good example of this time line in action can be seen in my work with sixteen-year-old Bruce and his father. Bruce was a very angry young man. At fifteen, he beat up a student so badly that he had to be hospitalized. What disturbed the police the most was the fact that Bruce had stuffed a dead rat down the unconscious boy's throat.

Stage 1: Behavior Problems Began Early in Life

The father told me that he and Bruce were once "very tight." As a young child, Bruce was held, hugged, and cuddled often. Father and son were inseparable. They spent most of their time on the floor playing, reading stories, or watching television together.

About 90 to 100 percent of the time was spent in nurturing and soft interaction. As Bruce entered kindergarten, however, he became more and more irritable and difficult to discipline. His parents started getting calls almost daily to pick him up early because he was acting out and hitting the other kids.

The father did not know why this sudden change of behavior happened. The only thing he could think of was that he and Bruce's mother constantly disagreed about parenting. The dad would come down hard on him, but his then-wife would intervene and accuse him of being abusive. Bruce started to play one against the other.

Dad admitted that he started spending less and less soft time with his son. He seemed to be constantly putting out fires and trying to correct Bruce's problems both at home and school.

Reprinted with special permission of King Feature Syndicate.

Stage 2: Negative Interaction Becomes the Norm

Over time, the percentages of positive interaction between father and son decreased. By the time Bruce was ten, softness and nurturance dropped to 50 percent, by the time he was thirteen, the percentage was now at 30 percent. By the time Bruce was fifteen, things had gotten so tense that only 5 percent of the time was spent in soft communication. The rest of the time consisted of harsh discipline and limit setting.

At fifteen, Bruce was skipping school constantly, smoking pot, and running away if he did not like his father's rules. Around this time, there was also a bitter divorce in which the father gained custody. A bitter chill developed between Bruce and his dad. Each person waited for the other to make the first move and restore good feelings. It never happened.

Stage 3: Conditional Love

At this point, Dad decided to bargain with Bruce out of desperation. The father admitted telling Bruce something like

> "Bruce, if you can just hold it together for one week and not get into trouble, we will go on a special outing together as a reward. You can pick what we do."

Unfortunately, Bruce never held it together for one week at a time; therefore, Dad and Bruce never went on a special outing together. In fact, Dad took Bruce's defiance as a personal slap across the face and eventually removed this reward completely. At this point, something very dark began to grow inside Bruce. Dad's love was supposed to be unconditional, but now Bruce saw it as dependent on how good or bad his behavior was for that week.

Bruce began to think that nothing would ever be good enough to receive his dad's love, so why try? He then literally shut down and grew hardened inside. Bruce and his dad had now crossed the fine line between love and hate.

Stage 4: Emotional Deprivation Sets In

Things started to get very tense between Bruce and his dad. Arguments grew more bitter, and Dad began to shut down as well. Both Dad and Bruce lost hope that things would ever get better and began to protect themselves from getting hurt by building massive walls around their hearts. The pain of emotional rejection was becoming too much to bear. They stopped remembering the old days when things were soft and loving.

Bruce was so hurt and angry at his dad that he started taking out these feelings on the rest of the world. He started beating up other kids for no reason and was becoming more and more cruel. Strangers were easier to lash out at than his own father whom he both loved and hated all at the same time. This inner turmoil only led to more drug use to dull the pain he felt inside.

Stage 5: Bruce's Second Family Takes Over

When Bruce could not find the love he needed from his dad, he began to seek out love and acceptance from a "second family" outside the home. Unfortunately, this second family of friends had an extremely negative influence on Bruce.

Bruce and his new friends started to get high on marijuana all the time. He began to lose interest in school. Bruce was rapidly going down a path of total destruction; his friends saw his anger and violence toward other kids as "cool." This reaction only fueled his violence more to gain acceptance.

Stage 6: Bruce and His Dad Get Stuck in a Vicious Cycle

At this point, Bruce and his dad got caught up in a vicious cycle. Dad watched helplessly as Bruce's heart, mind, and soul was being guided and taken over by his second family. As this happened, fear and anxiety took over, and the father began to lecture more and attempt to impose stricter limits and rules.

Dad did this out of fear and concern. Unfortunately, Bruce could not see this. He only saw the fact that his dad was trying to limit his freedom and criticize his friends. As a result, Bruce wanted to spend even more time with his second family. In turn, Dad tried to limit Bruce's freedom to even a greater degree, which caused Bruce to resist even more.

Stage 7: Bruce Becomes Hardened and Lacks Empathy/Remorse

As this vicious cycle continued, Bruce became more hardened inside. He started to develop a clear inability to show remorse or empathy for others. If this pattern of behavior continued, Bruce would become a high-risk candidate for developing antisocial personality disorder as an adult. If this happened, Bruce's behavior problems and lack of caring would become a permanent part of his personality.

Bruce would then become untreatable and continue these behaviors for the rest of his life. Bruce also would have a very difficult time developing and maintaining a healthy marriage. He would likely drift from job to job and blame everyone else for his problems. As an adult, Bruce might ultimately pass these problems onto his children, where the cycle would begin all over again.

After we went over this time line, the father sat in my office in stunned silence. After three minutes had gone by he finally said:

> "I now see the bigger picture. Early on in Bruce's life, the tables turned. Over the years Bruce went from the sweetest child ever to a hardened criminal. But it didn't happen overnight. The softness in him got slowly sucked away. All that is left behind is anger, hurt, bitterness, and frustration. He took out this anger on that poor innocent kid. All this time, I have been waiting for the system to fix him. But the system cannot inject him with softness, only I can. The answer has been right in front of my eyes the whole time. What do I do now? How do I get started?"

Timing Is Everything

In Bruce's case, nurturance could be introduced only after we had stopped the bleeding through tough-love tactics. We had to defuse Bruce's time bomb of anger before he hurt someone else.

Over the next six months, we used contracting, troubleshooting, working with outsiders (the school), and creative consequences to stop the violence both at home and at school. Once the threat of violence was lifted, the father went to work on restoring soft love as well as tough love to the relationship.

To determine your own timing, please see which of these options best describes you and your teen.

Which Comes First: Soft Love or Tough Love?

Option #1: The Soft Side Before the Tough Side

The problem behaviors are very minimal. Negative interaction or arguments occur only 0 to 25 percent of the time. You are not burned out and do not feel bitterness toward your teen. Nurturance is needed to strictly strengthen an already solid relationship and prepare for any future problems. This option usually best works with a young child who is just starting to act out or a teen whose hormones are raging and is simply a little moody or blue. With out-of-control teens, this option is usually the exception, not the rule.

Option #2: Address Both Toughness and Softness at the Same Time

This option is possible when problems like disrespect or running away first begin. These behaviors have not persisted longer than six straight months, and arguments have not yet become a normal everyday routine. Negative interaction is about 26 to 49 percent of the time. The rest of the time you are still emotionally close. However, if the future remains unchanged and the behavior problems persist, you will enter into stages 2 (negative interaction), 3 (conditional love), and 4 (emotional deprivation) of the time line. In this option, you need an equal balance between activities to restore nurturance and an ironclad contract to maintain structure and discipline.

Option #3: Address the Tough Side First

This option is necessary when months or years of conflict have taken their toll on your parent-teenager relationship. Negative interaction and arguments with your teen now jump to 50 or 100 percent of the time. You are officially in stage 2 (negative interaction), 3 (conditional love), and 4 (emotional deprivation) of the time line. Therefore, nurturance cannot be addressed until the bleeding has stopped and you have neutralized or stopped your teen's seven aces of disrespect, running away, truancy, violence, suicide, teen pregnancy, and drug or alcohol abuse. This is the most common option if you have an out-of-control teenager.

Your timing should be based on three critical factors:

1. **How long has the misbehavior gone on?**
The longer the misbehavior continues, the harder it will be to restore nurturance. Think about it. The last thing you want to do is to be soft with someone who has treated you disrespectfully. If your teen is disrespectful through one of his or her seven aces for six months or more, you have entered Option 3. You have to stop your teen's misbehavior through structure and discipline *before* you can move into the nurturing process. Otherwise, you will be spending all your time and energy trying to put out fires.

2. **How serious are the problems?**
In addition to length of time, you must consider how serious the misbehavior is in and of itself. For example, you may get temporarily angry if your son won't clean up his room, but if he threatens your other children with a tire iron, you're likely to feel a far more lasting bitterness. In turn, this bitterness makes it more difficult to restore nurturance. If the misbehavior is serious, you will likely need to stop your teen's problems in Option 3 long enough to feel hope and risk another emotional rejection.

3. **What is your present-day burn-out factor and tolerance for rejection?**
Every parent has a different tolerance for burn-out or rejection. Some parents are able to separate the person from the behavior; they despise the misbehavior but don't take it personally. These parents can go into Option 2 even though by all accounts they should be in Option 3. This is true even if present-day conflict currently runs between 50 percent or higher and the behavior problems are long-standing and serious.

Emotional Warm-ups

A good middle ground to this dilemma is what I call "emotional warm-ups." In the gym, you must warm up the muscles through stretching before lifting heavy weights. In the same way, you can warm your teen up to the idea of restoring lost nurturance through small gestures, such as leaving small notes of appreciation or encouraging words.

Initially your teen will probably throw these warm-ups back in your face. This is normal. Your teen is not used to this nurturing stuff. You must stick with it long enough to see a change and expect nothing back in return. As soon as things in your household start to settle down to manageable levels, use the following warm-up gestures:

- Small notes
- Positive incident reports
- Brief hugs

Without saying a word, leave small notes around the house for your teen to find. You can place these notes on his or her pillow, taped to the bathroom mirror, or inside the cereal bowl (without milk, of course). The notes should contain only words of encouragement, compliments, or praise. *They must not include any criticisms.* Leave a note every day or every other day for at least four straight weeks.

This exercise costs you nothing but pays huge dividends toward restoring nurturance. Your teen may question you or ask you to stop, but keep writing these notes. Your teen is so out of practice at receiving positive attention that he or she will not realize that small notes are good medicine.

As outlined in Step 2, you can give your teenager a PIR certificate every time you see positive behavior or progress on the contract. Progress can be anything from helping a brother or sister to completing homework on time. Teens love these certificates and will respond accordingly.

Look for moments when things are not so tense and your teen is in a relatively good mood. When these moments appear, however brief, take the opportunity to give him or her a brief hug or a gentle pat on the back.

Please remember that your teen's body will go stiff, or he or she may initially push you away. This is normal because your teen is not used to

hugs and is out of practice. However, these tender moments will go far
to softening your teen's walls, as it did between Jane and her mother.

Small Notes and Brain Teasers

A bitter relationship existed between fourteen-year-old Jane and
her mother, Lynn. Jane had problems with obeying her mother.
Their arguments often turned into screaming matches, followed
by pushing and shoving.

As a result, Lynn was extremely skeptical about restoring
nurturance on any level. She felt extremely burned out. She fit
the criteria for Option 3. Lynn, however, agreed to use warm-up
gestures at the same time she was getting tougher at setting limits. She chose the small-notes exercise because it did not involve
a lot of emotional risk and it required no response from Jane.

At first, Jane had no reaction. Lynn would leave notes on
Jane's pillow that read:

> "Jane, I am proud of how hard you are trying in school."

> "Jane, remember when you were little and we walked the
> dog? I thought about that today and smiled."

Created by Brandon Paige.

Jane reacted by ripping up the notes and putting them on Lynn's
pillow. Luckily, I had prepared Lynn for this possibility as a nor-

mal reaction. You can imagine Jane's surprise when Lynn doubled her efforts the next day by leaving two notes! Jane could not believe it. Lynn began to add riddles to the end of her notes with small clues on how to solve them. Lynn offered Gap gift certificates for each riddle Jane solved. Before long, mother and daughter were no longer arguing. Instead, they got into more and more playful discussions about how to solve the riddles. The softness started to return.

Five Toxic Behaviors That Poison Your Relationship with Your Teen

You must identify and address these toxic behaviors in your relationship before you can restore nurturance, or they will poison any real chance of restoring softness in your relationship.

If you are engaging in any or all of the following behaviors, please follow the recommendations to remove this poison from your relationship with your son or daughter:

1. Bringing up the past
2. Attacking the person rather than the misbehavior
3. Making compliment sandwiches
4. Intimating that the teen must be good to earn your love
5. Offering no opportunities to regain trust

The first toxic behavior occurs when, during an argument with your teenager, you whip out an imaginary scorecard and bring up the past. You say you forgive, but you *never forget*. Many teens tell me that "bringing up the past" is their #1 button. Over time, they begin to think, "Why should I even try, if I always get reminded of my past?" This is very much like how an ex-convict feels when he or she gets out of jail. It becomes almost impossible to find an honest paying job. Every potential employer looks at the past criminal record and refuses to hire the person. The convict who is unable to get a fresh start quickly returns to a life of crime.

Recommendations: Go cold turkey and stop today! No good will come of bringing up your teen's past misbehaviors. Old habits die hard, and you may want to put a helpful reminder in place before your next argument or heated discussion. Some parents have tied a string around their finger the first month. Others have had their teens or another family member make a cutting motion across the neck. Once in a while you may need to bring up the past in order to make an important point. However, use these criticisms extremely sparingly.

The second toxic behavior, attacking the person rather than the misbehavior, happens when you fail to separate your teen's misbehavior from his or her personality or character. For example, if your teenager fails to complete chores, do you currently react with Statement 1 or Statement 2?

1. Mitch, you did not take out the garbage for the second time this week. You are worthless and lazy. I don't know why I bother to ever care anymore.
2. Mitch, you didn't take out the garbage today. Our written contract says that if the kitchen garbage is not taken out by 5:00 P.M. you lose all phone privileges tonight.

If you chose 1, you are attacking your teen's misbehavior as well as his or her character. If you chose 2, you are simply dealing with the bad behavior itself.

Recommendations: Many parents don't realize that they are doing this; it is like a knee-jerk reaction that was role modeled to them by their parents. Please remember two key things before you start to criticize:

1. *Do not criticize your teen's character or personality.* Never say things like "You are manipulative," "You are a no-good liar," or "You can never be trusted." These things may be true, but you are not going to stop them through criticism.
2. *Deal with only the problem at hand.* Stick with what your iron-clad contract states. Hold your teen accountable for his or her misbehavior (late for curfew, disrespectful, steals, lies, runs

away, etc.) without adding statements about personality or character flaws.

The third toxic behavior occurs when a parent puts a "but" in between a compliment and a past criticism. For example, "Thank you for coming in on time, *but* you are still not doing the chores right," or "I am proud that you pulled your grades up, *but* I see that you still have that D in English." As you can see, "sandwiching" can cause bad feelings between you and your teen. When your teen hears a compliment followed by the word "but," your good intentions get buried beneath the criticism.

Recommendations: To break this habit, ask a friend, spouse, or another child to whisper in your ear when you are "sandwiching." It may take some time before you are able to break this habit. Many parents tell me that it helps to imagine a giant period at the end of each compliment. Other parents physically write down their list of compliments for the day and practice delivering them to their teen. This is known as an end-of-the-day wrap-up. Right before bed, tell your teen everything that he or she has done well that day. It usually takes only five minutes, but it works wonders to build your teen's self-esteem and soften your relationship.

The fourth toxic behavior concerns being good to earn your love. When your teenager has behavior problems, there is a high risk that you will make special outings, hugs, or other signs of softness contingent upon good behavior. You don't do this on purpose; you just get so frustrated that you run out of answers. It is also tough to show softness when your teen is swearing at you or stealing your property. Since your teen works on the pleasure principle, he or she probably will misbehave at least once a week. Therefore, you have a hard choice to make: Do you still show softness regardless of how good or bad your teen's behavior was that week?

Recommendations: Make an agreement with yourself under which you will punish your teen for any misbehavior but you will still go on special outings and provide signs of affection like hugs.

The final toxic behavior is offering no opportunities to regain your trust. Teenagers tell me that a lack of parental trust is one of the biggest reasons why they shut down and stop trying. As one teenager told me: "At any given time, I only have 10 percent trust. I have messed up so many times that I have lost it all. Without trust, there is no reason to try. They don't trust me anyway so it's not like I am working toward something better." Trust is the cornerstone of any good marriage, and it is also the cornerstone of a good parent-teen relationship. Without trust, the relationship becomes severely damaged. You become jailers in your own home. You cannot leave the house or let your guard down. A sense of hopelessness sets in and with it deep resentments.

Recommendations: To combat this problem, you must strike a balance between giving away trust too quickly and not giving it back at all. I discuss this further in conjunction with the "Three Levels of Supervision" chart on page 320.

Six Strategies to Reclaim Love Between You and Your Teenager

I have showed you why nurturance and tenderness are currently damaged between you and your teenager, not in a spirit of blame but in one of understanding. As the nurturance time line pointed out, you and your teen unknowingly both played a part in creating the distance between you.

It's time to forgive yourself and your teen and move to the next step. I must warn you, though, that fostering lost nurturance may be the most difficult thing you have ever done. Your teen may spit on you, call you every name in the book, and fail to appreciate your love or kindness. Like you, most out-of-control teenagers have layers of scar tissue around their hearts. To cut through these layers, you must give your son or daughter the greatest gift a parent can give: unconditional love.

Select the strategies that you think will best fit your particular child, and consult a counselor if you are having particular difficulties in implementing them or if they don't seem to be having a positive impact after several weeks or months.

Strategy #1: Special Outings

Besides hugs, soft talk, and consistent praise, no other nurturing strategy will have a bigger impact on your son or daughter than special outings. Many teens will not openly admit that they want to spend time with you. They have this image to protect that says "I don't need anybody." But that's all that it is—an image. Your teen still needs an emotional connection with you throughout the difficult period of adolescence. In fact, no matter how old we get, we all want our parents to be proud of us and show us tenderness. But with hormones racing through their bodies, teenagers are less aware of this—or willing to admit it—than people at other points in their lives.

One or two hours with your teenager on a weekly basis will make all the difference in the world. The only stipulations are:

- Outings should be one on one and without the television on or at the movies. These distractions make good communication very difficult.

- Outings should ideally take you outside the house because most of the arguments take place at home. Try to go somewhere positive or at least neutral, without any bad or painful memories.

- Outings need to be consistent from week to week whenever possible. If not, you will keep starting from scratch. Rituals or routines your teenager can count on (working on the old car with dad every Saturday afternoon, going to the park on Sunday, etc.) are critical to achieve success.

Many parents with out-of-control teens cannot remember the last time they had a special outing together or one-on-one time without arguing. Here are the reasons why and the suggested solutions.

Years of conflict have taken their toll on your parent-teen relationship. I wish I could say that you will magically wake up one day and feel like taking your teen on special outings. Unfortunately, it does not work this way.

Your feelings of bitterness will soften only through action. For example, depressed people do not usually just start to feel better. They must force themselves out of bed and into an activity that will make them feel better. My own grandmother got depressed after my grandfather died. She stopped doing the things she enjoyed—being with friends, going shopping, and exercising. All this contributed to her depression.

My grandmother told me that she would have to start feeling better before she had the desire or strength to do fun things again. It was not until her neighbors forced her to go out and resume her normal routine that her depression lifted.

Similarly, instead of waiting for your feelings toward your teenager to change by themselves, you can start to change them through special outings. Please be patient, though; it took my grandmother at least eight weeks of going through the motions before she felt better, and every parent-child relationship mends in its own time. Here are the procedures you must go through.

Set a Date, Time, and Activity Ahead of Time

It is absolutely critical that you set a date and a time with your teenager in advance. You both have busy schedules, and things will come up if you do not plan in advance. Unless you agree on an activity ahead of time, you may spend your time arguing over where to go. (In the beginning, both of you also may be looking for excuses to abandon the outing.)

Take turns planning the outing within the parameters of a certain budget. For example, the first week might be your pick while the second week will be your son or daughter's pick. If your teen cannot decide, you must make the decision.

Please note that you do not have to physically leave the house or buy something for a special outing to take place. It can be just as special watching a video together, playing a board game, painting nails together, or just talking. The most important thing is that you make a date with your teen and stick to it.

Expect Resistance from Your Teenager

Also expect that your teen will be resistant or refuse to go. Please do not accept no for an answer. As the outing unfolds, your teen usually will end up having a decent time. If asked, your teen will deny it, for teens do not want to give parents the satisfaction of being right. This stubbornness is just part of being a teenager.

Troubleshooting

After you both set a date and time, use troubleshooting to anticipate everything that could go wrong ahead of time. For example, what is your backup plan if you have to cancel because you have a work-related emergency? It is critical to have a backup plan for each what-do-we-do-if scenario. Without such a plan, the special outing

will fail, the momentum may never catch on again, and you will be unable to restore nurturance with your teen. Review the following list of common what-do-we-do-if scenarios and backup plans. Use this list as a guide for your own troubleshooting efforts.

Potential Problem #1:
What do we do if we set a date and I have to cancel because I am called into work for an emergency?

Backup Plan:
We will go the next night or set a future date that same day.

Potential Problem #2:
What do we do if a friend calls me up the night we are supposed to go out and invites me to a party?

Backup Plan:
You will get two coupons that say "get out of one special outing free" every six months. You can use them to get out of a special outing for any reason. However, once these are gone, you agree to go no matter who calls or what the activity is.

Potential Problem #3:
What do we do if the person cannot decide where to go when it is his or her week to pick?

Backup Plan:
The other person has a chance to pick the place and the activity. If no one can decide, the ultimate decision will fall on the parent.

Potential Problem #4:
What do we do if one of us feels like not going or feels too tired?

Backup Plan:
We will both agree up front that unless one of the two coupons is used, the special outings are mandatory. Otherwise, we will not gain momentum and melt the blocks of ice between us.

Don't Expect to Enjoy the Outings Right Away

Expect to have a miserable time when you first start to go out. Both of you will be out of practice and not used to talking unless there is a problem. Understand that these feelings are normal and to be expected.

The more you go out together, the easier it will become and the better you will feel. There will be periods of awkward silence, and you will be tempted to go to the movies or watch television together to avoid talking. Please resist this temptation. Go somewhere like a restaurant or a park where you have to say something. You can also stay at home and do the same thing.

"But We Have Nothing in Common"

Going out together will allow you to discover what you have in common or at least get to know one another better. Your teen may not share your interests; still, special outings will help him or her understand you better. In turn, this will strengthen your emotional bond. Your teen is then more likely to come to you when he or she is in trouble or emotional pain.

For example, one father had no interest in his daughter Becca's fascination with body piercing. He had a strict house rule that no piercing was allowed. I told the father that a special outing to the local body-piercing shop simply meant that he was willing to explore Becca's world to understand her better. He could then understand her fascination for piercing and its appeal from Becca's point of view.

The father would visit the shop with Becca, but told her in advance that going there did not imply consent; she would not be allowed to get her body pierced under any circumstances. If Becca whined or complained, they would leave immediately.

The special outing was a success. It gave them a lot of material to talk about at dinner afterward. In the past, they usually sat at the table and said nothing. Now Becca could not stop talking. She became the expert who informed her father all about the world of body piercing. In turn, these conversations made Becca feel closer to her father.

Initially the father thought that these outings might encourage Becca to go behind his back and get her body pierced. However, the opposite occurred. When Becca felt as if her father listened and respected her opinions, her desire to go behind his back became less and less important. Soon she began to open up about other issues as well.

"I Just Don't Have the Time"

If you will not make the time for your teen, your teen's friends will. What if friends and movies, rather than you, end up shaping your teen's values and morals? Do you really want your teen to pass these values and morals on to your future grandchildren?

I apologize for the guilt trip. But now it is time for some good news. You have all heard the saying "It is not about quantity time, it is about *quality* time." Of course, it is always preferable if you have both. However, quality time can still work wonders.

"I Don't Have the Money"

One of the bonuses of this strategy is that I recommend that you *not* spend a lot of money. Otherwise, your teen may think that you are trying to "buy" his or her love.

For wealthy or middle-class parents, this recommendation may be very difficult to follow. If you customarily spend a lot of money on your teen, he or she may already feel a sense of entitlement—that you somehow owe it to him or her. If this is the case, no explanation you give will be good enough; you must simply start scaling back.

If you have not yet set this precedent, it will be easy. Simply take your teen out to inexpensive places like parks, museums, casual restaurants, and sporting events, and activities like miniature golf, bowling, fishing, playing catch, walking around the block, free concerts, hiking, skating, and bike riding. These activities promote good communication without the distractions caused by money. You have to make your own fun.

"We'll Go Out If My Teen Behaves This Week"

If a teen misbehaves, it's a normal reaction for parents to stop special outings or to make them contingent on good and respectful behavior. But doing this perpetuates the vicious cycle that has brought you and your teen to this point. As difficult as it may be, try to make a commitment that you will separate your teen's misbehavior from the love you give. For example, if your teenager is disrespectful, continue to hold him or her accountable with rules and consequences. *But also go on special outings whether your teen misbehaves or not.* Even if your teen is grounded for disrespect for the entire week, don't cancel the plan to take him or her out for ice cream or a bike ride in the park on Saturday morning. This may sound weird, but it is critical to make your teen feel loved no matter what.

It's also important to explain this plan to your teen in advance:

[Teenager's name], from this moment on we will do something different. In the past, I told you that we could not go on special outings together until you stopped misbehaving. I made a mistake and I'm sorry. In the future, I will still hold you accountable through our contract, but now we will go out together regardless of how good or bad your behavior is. For example, if you are grounded for not cleaning your room, you will still serve out your time, but we would take a break and go out somewhere, just you and me.

Initially, your teen will be extremely skeptical. He or she may say that someone put you up to this. (Secretly I may have, but don't say that!) Your teen has to see it to believe it. Therefore, do not be discouraged if he or she does not get excited or enthusiastic. If you prove that your teen can absolutely trust you to go through with the outings you've promised, that trust will ultimately spread to other aspects of your relationship.

Strategy #2: Accept Underlying Feelings

There is a direct connection between your teen's misbehavior and whether he or she feels understood. If you acknowledge your teen's underlying feelings, you will see improvement in your parent-child relationship and better behavior.

For example, if your teen comes to you and says that she is too tired to clean her room, you can respond in one of two ways. One response might be "You're not tired, quit giving me excuses. Clean your room or you're grounded." Another response might be "I bet you wish that you didn't have to clean your room because you're tired. But your room still has to be cleaned by 6:00 P.M. as we agreed upon."

In the first response, the parent discounts the teenager's feelings and moves right into a disciplinarian role. This only leads to anger and resentment. In the second response, the parent acknowledges the teen's underlying feelings of being tired but still holds her accountable. This second response creates an atmosphere of mutual respect because the parent takes the time to acknowledge the teen's feelings.

In my research, teens reported that "being heard" went a long way toward repairing their relationships with their parents. Parents also reported a difference once they learned that they could acknowledge their teens' feelings and still hold them accountable for their behavior. Follow these procedures to learn how to accept your teen's feelings and become emotionally closer.

Do You Currently Ignore Underlying Feelings?

The following list was adapted by permission from a book that I highly recommend, *How to Talk So Kids Will Listen and Listen So*

Kids Will Talk by Adele Faber and Elaine Mazlish. How many of these behaviors do you recognize in yourself? It can be helpful to try to imagine how teens feel inside when you ignore their feelings.

Six Ways to Ignore Underlying Feelings

1. *Denial of Feelings.* You may respond to your teen's statement of pain or anger by simply ignoring or minimizing the feelings altogether. This will lead to feelings of being discounted or misunderstood. Close your eyes for a moment. Imagine your reaction if your father or mother said: "There is no reason to be upset"; "You are probably just tired and blowing the whole thing out of whack as usual"; "It is foolish to feel that way"; "Big deal, I would not be mad if that happened to me."

2. *Cliché or Philosophical Answer.* You may respond to your teen with a standard cliché or a philosophical answer. Your teen will then feel that you do not care or that you are making light of the situation. Close your eyes for a moment. Imagine your reaction if your father or mother said: "You are still young, you have your whole life ahead of you"; "I told you so"; "You know, it's like my father always used to say . . ."; or "Rome was not built in a day."

3. *Pity.* No one likes to be pitied after finding the courage to express a painful event. Pity makes your teen feel angry and the pain much worse. In addition, a teenager whose problems are met with pity is less likely to risk coming back for your support a second time. Close your eyes for a moment. Imagine your reaction if your father or mother said: "Oh, you poor thing"; "I feel so sorry for you"; "My heart just breaks"; "I guess it was just meant to be"; "I feel so bad, I could just cry."

5. *The Trouble with You.* Sometimes parents use this phrase as a prelude to negative criticism. Teenagers who hear this statement often become angry and feel attacked. Close your eyes for a moment. Imagine your reaction if your father or mother said: "The trouble with you is you never listen";

"The trouble with you is that you're always putting your foot in your month." Please write down how you would feel.

6. *Instant Problem Solving.* When their teenager tells them a problem or concern, some parents will try to instantly problem solve instead of just listening. Teens tell me that they will ask their parents if they want their advice or solutions. Close your eyes for a moment. Imagine your reaction if your father or mother said: "Here is what you should do"; "I know just what you need and how to solve your problem"; "You are doing it all wrong. Here is what needs to be done." Please write down how you would feel. (Reprint permission by Rawson and Associates)

Using Emotional First Aid to Acknowledge Feelings

Currently you are likely to react to what your teen tells you in one of three ways:

1. **Agree with your teenager.** You approve and agree with your teen, saying things like "You're right, your sister did start the fight"; "Yes, you can stay out past curfew tonight to go to the party."
2. **Disagree with no discussion of feelings.** "Don't tell me your sister started the fight; I saw you push her"; "No, you can't stay out late tonight no matter who's giving the party."
3. **Discount your teen's feelings.** You ignore your teen's underlying feelings in one of the ways described earlier, for example, by saying "It's not such a big deal" or "You're probably just tired and blowing the whole thing out of proportion."

There is a fourth and often more effective way of reacting—the nonjudgmental response.

4. **Reply nonjudgmentally.** This response simply identifies what your teen might be feeling underneath the surface. For example, if your teen comes home tomorrow and says, "School sucks," you could respond by saying "It sounds as if you are pretty angry and frustrated. Is that close or way off?" You are not supporting his or her

statement that school sucks. You are simply trying to uncover what your teen feels inside and to administer emotional first aid. Your teenager feels heard rather than ignored or misunderstood. In turn, this leads to less misbehavior and a closer parent-teenager bond.

Most people need practice to react with a nonjudgmental response, which initially may seem mechanical and unnatural. The more you use the following techniques, the more comfortable they will get, and the more your teen will open up to you.

Listen with Full Attention

It is easier for teens to talk about their problems or concerns when you are *fully* listening. Most of us try to talk to our teens with the television on, while the other kids are around, or while we are talking on the phone. Under these circumstances, it is difficult, if not impossible, for your teenager to feel as if you care. You're also more likely to discount the teen's feelings if you're not paying full attention. You know how it feels when you try to talk to your spouse or your boss when he or she is not listening. You get frustrated and feel unimportant and ignored. Your teen feels the same way. Here's how to prevent this:

- Turn the television off and look your teen square in the eye so that it is clear that he or she has your full attention.

- Don't try to do two things at once. If you are on the phone or doing another activity, stop the activity or give your teen a specific time to come back when you are not busy. If your son or daughter doesn't come back on his or her own, seek the teen out.

- Make a date to talk. If you are busy, arrange a meeting time, date, and place.

- You do not have to do or say anything. Teens just need to know that you are listening without trying to fix the problem or give your opinion. Instead, just listen in silence and ask your teen if he or she wants your opinion.

Acknowledge Your Teen's Feelings with Words Like "Oh" and "Mmm"

By using these words, you avoid being judgmental or saying the wrong thing at the wrong time. For example, if the teenager comes home and says that the teacher is unfair, you can reply with a simple "mmm."

This gives your teenager an open door and more time to explain what he or she is thinking or feeling. You may even become a sounding board for your teenager to work out his or her own solutions. Here is an example of how this strategy works:

SHAWN: I get tired of having to do homework all the time.

MOM: Mmm. *(Mom is tempted to comment here but she holds her tongue. She uses this response to remain neutral and allow Shawn to vent some more. If she moved too quickly to agree or disagree, Shawn probably would have shut down and stopped talking.)*

SHAWN: It's sooo frustrating. I try, but I never seem to get caught up.

MOM: I see, please tell me more. *(It's working. Shawn is opening up instead of shutting down. Mom is being nonjudgmental.)*

SHAWN: I just don't know what to do.

MOM: Would you like my opinion, or do you want to try to figure out this problem on your own? I might have some good ideas. *(Mom can offer to help solve the problem, but she is doing it in a respectful way. She can do this because of her patience and nonjudgmental listening early on in the conversation.)*

SHAWN: Yeah, go ahead.

Give Feelings a Name

Naming feelings is your most effective tool to acknowledge your teen's feelings. The teenager who hears words that describe what he or she is experiencing will be deeply comforted. Even if you are totally off base, your teenager will correct you and describe how he or she is really feeling.

For example, start each statement with "It seems like or sounds as if . . ." You can also end each statement with "Am I close or way off?" This allows your teenager to agree or disagree with your interpretation of his or her underlying feelings. Initially this strategy will feel weird and unnatural. Your teen may accuse you of trying to become a therapist. Ask your teen to bear with you.

Say that you are learning how to listen better by practicing a new form of communication. This explanation will be good enough for most teenagers. If not, go forward anyway until your teen gets used to the idea. One parent even turned it into a playful game. Every time the parent would say "It seems like," or "Am I close or way off?" both of them cracked up. The chart below illustrates how this strategy works.

How to Give Feelings a Name		
Your Teenager says . . .	One word that describes what he she might be feeling	Use a statement that tells the teenager what you hear him or her saying
"School really sucks. All of my teachers are terrible."	Angry	"It seems like you are angry about school; is that close or way off?"
"I am just so tired of all the bullshit."	Frustrated	"It seems like you are frustrated; is that close or way off?"
"My friends are spreading rumors about me, and I don't know what to do."	Worried and unsure	"It seems like you are worried about the rumors and unsure about what to do. Is that close or way off?"

Commonly Asked Questions and Rules of Thumb

- *Should I always use these emotional first-aid strategies even when my kid is swearing at me or being disrespectful?*

If your teenager is disrespectful, swearing, or agitated, it is not the time to acknowledge the feelings. You should exit and wait until things have calmed down or punish your teen for disrespect. He or she should be encouraged to express feelings, but it must be done in a respectful and calm fashion. Otherwise, you are giving him or her the wrong message.

■ *When should these strategies be used and under what circumstances?*
You should use these strategies only when your son or daughter appears to be hurting, upset, frustrated, or angry. With the exception of listening with full attention, you do not need to use these strategies in casual conversations. It is the negative and painful emotions that really require our skill.

■ *If I acknowledge my kid's underlying feelings, am I telling him or her that I agree with his or her misbehavior?*
No, you are simply acknowledging his or her feelings. For example, you may not agree with your son's statement that he has terrible teachers. You are simply reflecting back an underlying feeling so that your son recognizes that you heard him. He may not like his teachers, but he is still responsible if he gets poor grades, ditches school, or acts out in the classroom.

Strategy #3: The Power of Hugs

In a famous research study from the 1930s, babies in an orphanage were divided into two groups. The babies in one group were given surrogate mothers to play with, talk to, and physically touch. The other babies did not have any surrogate mothers. Only their basic needs of food, clothing, and shelter were provided. The babies stayed in their cribs all day and received no human touch except diaper changes.

After two years, the first group of orphans thrived and grew up healthy. A twenty-year follow-up study showed that these children were married, self-supporting, and graduated from college. The second group of babies showed the opposite results. Many of these orphans grew sick and died. Others had immune systems that did not work properly. Most of these children did not progress past the third grade, had unhealthy marriages, or became institutionalized with mental problems.

The only difference between these two groups was that one received nurturance and human touch while the other did not. Many studies like this one have yielded similar results. Studies conducted by K. M. Fick in 1993 and cited in the *Journal of Occupational Therapy* (47) have shown that stress levels in the elderly immediately decreased when they hugged dogs and cats.

Hugs release a chemical in our brain called endorphins, which is the same chemical reaction we experience when we are in love or eat large amounts of chocolate. We need these chemicals to grow mentally and to feel good inside.

If hugs are so good for us, why is it that so many teenagers report that they cannot remember the last time they were hugged? I believe that there are two main reasons:

"My Teenager Is Too Old For Hugs"

The 1955 classic movie *Rebel Without a Cause,* starring Natalie Wood and James Dean, shows Natalie Wood going up to her father at the dinner table and trying to hug him. The father pushes her away and tells her that she's "too old for hugs." Natalie Wood tries to hug him a second time, at which point he slaps her. "This scene symbolizes what has happened in many households today; many parents grew up believing that hugs were only for young children.

"My Teenager Won't Let Me Hug Him"

Out-of-control teens are usually out of practice at both giving and receiving hugs. After all, as your child's problems grew, it became harder and harder for you to want to hug him or her. How many of you feel like hugging your teen after he or she swears at you or calls you names?

By this point your teenager is so unaccustomed to hugs that they feel weird and strange at first. It is quite normal for your teen to push you away initially and not respond. But you can overcome this reluctance with practice and patience.

© Lynn Johnston Productions, Inc.-Dist. by United Feature Syndicate, Inc.

Caution: Rule Out Sexual Abuse

Before you can initiate hugs, you must rule out sexual abuse issues. If there is ongoing sexual abuse, your teenager will misread hugs. Teens with an extraordinarily bad reaction to hugs (push away violently, go into a shell, get physically sick, etc.) might have been abused sexually.

Since sexual abuse occurs in secret, it is often difficult to pin down. At the same time, don't jump too quickly to assume abuse is the problem and go on a witch hunt. Your teenager might just be overreacting. If you honestly suspect sexual abuse, ask your teenager point blank and take him or her to a competent counselor to rule it out.

If you rule out sexual abuse and your teenager still has a bad reaction, you might want to pave the way by using special outings. For some teenagers, the scar tissue of past conflict may be too severe. At first, your teen may not let anyone physically come near. If this happens, you must move slowly and begin with a simple pat on the back or a series of special outings to warm the teen up to the idea of hugs.

Insulate Yourself from Rejection

Your teenager may be suspicious initially. When you hug him or her, your teen may think that you have an angle or want something in return. Your teen is out of practice when it comes to hugs and therefore skeptical. In turn, your teen's skepticism might make you feel rejected and cause you to quit prematurely.

You may find that giving hugs is harder on you than your teenager. You may be as out of practice in giving hugs as your teen is at accepting them. It is normal for hugs to feel awkward and mechanical at first. Just continue to fake it until it becomes a natural part of your daily routine.

Your teen's body will stiffen up when you initially try to hug him or her. Persevere and hug on a consistent basis even if your teen is unenthusiastic. In this way, you will be telling your teenager "I love you and I am not going anywhere," or "You can try to reject me, but I love you unconditionally. I will not stop the hugs." These are powerful messages that can break down even the thickest walls.

For example, fifteen-year-old Luis and his father rarely spoke to one another. Luis constantly got into fights both at home and school. On more than one occasion, Luis and his dad had punched one another.

To address this problem, the dad agreed to try this strategy for two weeks to see if it would help lessen Luis's anger. To insulate the father from rejection, I faxed him the following prescription that included a warning label:

Dad's Hug Prescription

Rχ

Please hug your son 2 times per day between 15 and 30 seconds. Do not hug Luis in front of his friends or his younger brother because he might get embarrassed. The recommended times for hugging will be in the morning when he gets up and in the evening before he goes to bed.

Warning!

Do not administer this hug medicine without understanding the following counterreactions: (1) At first, the hugs will be bitter tasting to your son. His body will stiffen or he will try to push you away. This is normal and to be expected. His hug muscles are out of practice. Hug him anyway; and (2) At first, you will also feel strange and weird. Hugging will seem unnatural and forced. This is normal because you are also out of practice. Therefore, until it seems more natural, "fake it until you make it." Be patient; this will take some time.

Luis came to my office the following week and demanded to see me. He wanted to know "what I had done with his real father." Luis said it felt weird to have his father "hugging him all the time." In addition, it made it harder for him to stay mad at his dad. I told Luis that "we were initiating hugs for his dad's sake." Luis replied by saying "I guess it's OK then."

From this point on, the relationship between father and son continued to soften. They still had their ups and downs, but Luis eventually allowed his dad to hug him. The deep freeze between father and son began to melt. As the dad stated, "It is hard to stay mad when you are hugging your son all the time."

Don't Make Hugs Dependent on Good Behavior

As with special outings, do not make hugs conditional on good behavior. No matter what your teenager does that week, you should continue to hug him or her.

When you start hugging your teen, please follow these guidelines:

- I recommend one to two hugs a day to start out with. Eventually work your way up to four or more hugs a day. Virginia Satir, a leading family therapist, recommends four hugs per day for survival, six hugs per day for maintenance, and eight hugs per day for growth.

- Do not hug your teenager in front of his or her friends. As I said earlier, he or she might get embarrassed. Often the best time to hug teens is in the morning when they get up and in the evening before they go to bed.

- Do not hug when your teen is upset or angry. Doing so will only aggravate the situation. Wait until the teen is calm or in a good mood.

- Continue to hug even if your teen's body stiffens or the teen pushes you away. (If the teen's physical reaction is extreme, you should consult a counselor.) You must help your teen work out the soreness in his or her hug muscles. This will not happen overnight. You must be consistent until you wear them down.

Strategy #4: Be the First to Restore Good Feelings

To understand the importance of this strategy, read the words of thir-teen-year-old Jerome as he describes what happens after a typical fight with his father: "Dr. Scott, I just don't understand. When Dad and I fight, he stops talking to me. I get the cold shoulder. He thinks that I should always be the one to say 'I'm sorry.' I don't know what to do. Even when I do say 'sorry,' he tells me I don't mean it. I just wish my dad would punish me and be done with it. All he does is carry a grudge and bring up the past. I'm ready to give up!"

What Jerome describes happens to many families. The process starts with a fight. It does not matter who started it; the result is the same. Both you and your teen walk away feeling hurt, rejected, or angry. In the best-case scenario, you or your teen approach each other when things calm down and restore good feelings through an apology, a hug, or discussing what happened.

In families with out-of-control teens, the opposite tends to hap-pen. Parent and teens fight, but neither party makes the first move to restore good feelings. As a result, nothing gets worked out. Instead, cold and bitter feelings replace soft and warm ones. Over time, the relationship becomes severely damaged. A deep freeze sets in between you and your teen.

The longer this deep freeze goes on, the greater the chance for emotional cancer to develop and spread. If left untreated, it will kill all softness and nurturance in your relationship. Emotional depriva-tion will set in and your teen will seek out lost softness from a second family of peers.

Parents Must Make the First Move

To stop this from happening, *you* have to make the first move, if things are stuck longer than a week. I know I am asking a lot, but your teen is not developmentally mature or wise enough to under-stand that life is too short to hold a grudge and argue over who should say "I'm sorry" first. No one will write on your tombstone that your life was happier and better because you could hold a grudge the longest. Instead, It will read that you stayed angry and bitter.

Your teen needs a role model to show love and compassion even when there is only anger and hatred in the air. That person is you.

Not a License to Misbehave

The fact that you will make the first move toward reconciliation does not, however, give your teen a license to misbehave or be disrespectful. You should still administer consequences for these actions. Just don't punish with a cold shoulder for weeks or months at a time. As soon as things calm down, say something like:

Life is too short to stay mad. Can I give you a hug to tell you that you are more important than a stupid argument?

-or-

I'm here to make the first move and say that I'm sorry about the mean things that were said in anger and frustration. I may not like or agree with how you act or what you say, but I still love you.

You can then hug your teen, agree to exit from the next argument before things get heated, make a peace offering, or simply apologize. It's worth it to restore good feelings and give your teen a role model for mature behavior.

Strategy #5: Give Your Teen Opportunities to Regain Trust

During focus group interviews, teens reported that hopelessness quickly set in when their parents stopped giving them opportunities to earn back trust. Teens stopped trying and completely shut down. Misbehaviors then escalated into a downward slide. Deep resentments and bitterness followed and day-to-day communication became increasingly tense or even violent.

Repairing lost trust is challenging. You may feel caught between a rock and a hard place: If you trust again, a common concern is that your teen will take advantage of your goodwill.

Reprinted with special permission of King Feature Syndicate.

There is a direct relationship between the level of trust and the emotional bond between you and your teenager. If your current trust level is out of sync with your level of supervision, your teen will become resentful and angry. In turn, this can weaken or destroy any softness in your relationship. The good news is that your emotional bond will strengthen when your level of trust equals the level of supervision needed. The following chart can help you determine how much trust you should give your teen.

Three Levels of Supervision

Level 1: Mandatory Supervision
A Level 1 teenager is not trustworthy. This teen completes tasks or follows rules less than 50 percent of the time. S/he obeys curfew less than 50 percent of the time or chronically runs away. S/he may have friends over when the parent is not at home or lies frequently. These teens require constant monitoring until they adhere to a contract of rules and consequences over 50 percent of the time and obey curfew at least 75 percent of the time. Until then, these teens should not be allowed out unless accompanied by the parent or another adult the parent trusts.

Level 2: Structured Supervision

Level 2 teenagers are semitrustworthy. They comply with tasks and follow rules at least 50 to 75 percent of the time. They obey curfew 75 to 90 percent of the time and do not run away or leave home without permission. They do not have friends over when the parent is not at home. These teens are required to check in at regular intervals when they go out and must be home at preestablished curfew times. Otherwise, they risk going back to Level 1, Mandatory Supervision.

Level 3: Limited Supervision

Level 3 teenagers are trustworthy. They can regularly be depended on to complete tasks and follow rules 80 to 100 percent of the time. These teens obey curfew 100 percent of the time. They are where they say they are going to be. These teens are dependable and not required to check in at regular intervals.

An Angelic Approach to Regaining Trust and Curfew

Fifteen-year-old Angel was functioning at Level 2, within a structured supervision status. She was semitrustworthy. Angel complied with rules and her parents' requests at least 50 percent of the time. She obeyed curfew 75 to 90 percent of the time and did not leave home without permission.

To regain trust, Angel was required to check in at regular intervals when she went out and be home at required times. Angel was told that if she did this consistently for three consecutive weeks, her parents would move her to Level 3, or limited supervision, for a tryout period. At this level, Angel would have to obey curfew 100 percent of the time. However, she would not be required to check in at regular intervals. Three weeks was chosen because any longer would seem like a lifetime to a teen who works on the pleasure principle.

Angel could stay at this level as long as she did not break curfew. However, Angel was told beforehand that what could be given could also be taken away. If she violated curfew, she would go back to Level 2 and have to maintain consistent curfew for another three straight weeks. This cycle would be repeated as many times as necessary until Angel had achieved trustworthiness on a long-term basis.

For the first time in her life, Angel could see a clear road map and had something to work toward. It also put the responsibility for earning trust squarely on her shoulders. She could track herself on the Supervision Level chart taped to the refrigerator door. Now she had opportunities to move toward less supervision and more trust.

As the weeks went by, Angel's behavior began to improve dramatically. As she told her parents, "It's in my hands." In turn, Angel became less bitter toward her parents. She saw that what they were trying to do was fair. Angel relapsed several times, but the supervision chart allowed her to get back on track quickly and regain lost trust. In the past, once trust was lost, it was lost forever. This difference helped turn things completely around.

Issue Trust Deposit and Withdrawal Bank Coupons

If the current level of supervision is at a Level 1 or 2, ask your teen this question to determine how he or she wants to regain trust:

Right now your bank account for trust is in the red or negative numbers. But together we can change that. You can fill your account up with trust deposit slip coupons that will be issued to regain your trust as quickly or as slowly as you want. To do this, I first need to set up a trust bank account in your name and include the areas in which you want to regain trust. Some teenagers want privileges like a longer curfew, extra phone time, or sleepovers. How do you want to regain trust?

Write down the answers to this question on a sheet of paper. Ask your teen to prioritize them into the top three. Please remember that you have full veto power as the parent. Most teenagers understand the idea that bank accounts contain both deposits and withdrawals. The idea of getting in the black through trust deposits appeals to most teenagers. Here is an example of a list that a teenager and his family agreed on.

Trust Bank Account

#1 Come Home on Time	To regain trust, you need to come home not one minute past the curfew time of 10:00 P.M. on weekends and 8:00 P.M. on school nights.
#2 Inform Us Better	To regain trust, I need to know who your friends are and meet their parents.
#3 Baby-sit Responsibly	You need to baby-sit your younger brother responsibly. This means no friends over, no leaving him unattended, and no fighting.

Once you finish your list, create deposit coupons with expiration dates on them. Base the coupons on your trust bank account list and your teen's level of supervision. The expiration dates are necessary to make your teen realize that regaining trust is time limited. Here are some of the deposit coupons that this family created based on their bank account.

"Come Home on Time" Bank Deposit Coupon

Good for one on-time return to the house either by 8:00 P.M. on school nights (Sunday through Thursday) or 10:00 P.M. on weekend nights. If you are one minute late by the kitchen clock, this coupon will be null and void.

Expiration Date: This Week

"Inform Us" Bank Deposit Coupon

Good for each time you inform us of who you are going out with and the names and numbers of the friends you are with. We will

have to call these numbers and check their accuracy for this coupon to be valid.
Expiration Date: This Week

"Baby-sit Responsibly" Bank Deposit Coupon
Good for each time you baby-sit your younger brother responsibly. This means no friends over. Do not leave him unattended and no fighting. We will ask your younger brother privately to confirm the accuracy of your report. Expiration Date: The next time you baby-sit.

After you create your coupon book, determine in advance how many bank deposit coupons your teen needs in each area to get the trust bank account out of the red. For example, if your teen is on mandatory supervision, his or her trust level is in the red. Therefore, you might want to require at least ten to twelve bank deposit coupons per area over a fourteen-day period before the privilege you pick out is given back.

Some teens need more positive reinforcement than others. If you are not sure how many deposit slips are needed in each area, ask your teen. He or she probably will give you a lower number. The actual number needed usually lies somewhere between what you need to feel more comfortable in giving back trust and what your teen wants.

Strategy #6: Creating Soft Talk

Soft talk takes place whenever your conversations are free of criticisms or attacks on your teen's character. Instead, you use one of the previous five strategies—special outings, acceptance of feelings, hugs, being first to restore good feelings, opportunities to regain trust—to initiate discussions or actions that are nurturing and soft instead of critical or harsh.

Stop Button-Pushing

Button-pushing poisons your ability to engage in soft talk with your teen. To avoid this problem, I suggest two options. First, reread Step 4, on button-pushing, and use one or more of the button-buster techniques from that step. Second, separate in your mind the difference between button-pushing and soft talk. If your teen is pushing your buttons, remind yourself that it is only a game. He or she is trying to control your emotions. Walk away or deal with the misbehavior right then and there.

Later, try soft talk again but exit and wait if button-pushing starts up again. Repeat these steps as often as needed until your teen gets the message. Review the following conversation closely. See if you can pick out the soft talk.

DAD: Hector, how was your day?

HECTOR: It sucked! *(Hector is grumpy and immediately tries to push his dad's buttons and change his mood so that he will also get grumpy.)*

DAD: Tell me what's going on. What was it about your day that made it suck? Are you frustrated? *(Dad stays calm, cool, and collected. He knows that Hector is button-pushing at this point, and he chooses not to play the same game. Instead, he uses the strategy of acknowledging underlying feelings.)*

HECTOR: I'm not frustrated; I'm pissed off. My girlfriend won't talk to me and I don't know why. Why am I talking to you? You would never understand. *(Hector initially opened up but then felt vulnerable and immediately tried to push Dad away with another button by saying "that he [dad] would never understand.")*

DAD: I may not understand, but I might be able to relate to some of the pain or anger inside. Women are strange sometimes. Did you know that your mom did the same thing to me when we were dating? She refused to talk to me for an entire week. *(Again, Dad does not let button-pushing kill his soft talk. Instead, he holds fast and shares a similar painful time in his life when he was also hurting.)*

HECTOR (LOOKS SURPRISED): What has gotten into you today? You never talk like this to me. You usually just get mad and leave. This is totally strange. *(Persistence pays off. Hector tried to end soft talk several times through button-pushing, but Dad did not budge.)*

In the next example, soft talk combines with the other strategies to restore lost nurturance between parent and teen. See if you can pick out the soft talk in this conversation.

CHRISTINA: Get away from me with those stupid hugs. You never cared before so don't try to start now. I will never forgive you if that's what you want. *(Christina is very scared. There has been a lack of softness for many years. She is not going to open up at Mom's first attempt. She has no reason to trust that it is either sincere or real. This reaction is normal.)*

MOTHER: I know I have to prove myself. A lot of water is under our bridge. But I won't give up. I can't change the past, but I want to change our future together. It seems like you don't trust me. Is that close or way off? *(Great job by Mom here. She did not take her daughter's buttons as a personal attack but a normal reaction. She uses emotional first aid and put a name to what Christina is feeling.)*

CHRISTINA: Whatever, Mom. I hate you and I don't want to talk about it! *(Christina is going for the jugular here with the I-hate-you line. This is her big gun to push Mom away emotionally.)*

MOTHER: Thanks for being so honest. I just want to say that I don't take it personally. I love you and I am sorry. Since love is an action word, I am going to show you by hugging you every day whether you push me away or not. *(Mom hugs her again and then walks away without saying a word. Christina is left with her mouth wide open.)*

Troubleshooting

This is one battle that you cannot afford to lose. The stakes have just gone up: You are no longer battling for whether your teen follows rules but for whether you or your teen can love one another again. Make sure you troubleshoot potential problems ahead of time.

Potential Problem #1:
What should I do if my son or daughter tries to poison my soft talk by pushing my buttons?

Backup Plan:

You have two choices. You can either exit and wait if things get too heated and try later or keep soft talking.

Potential Problem #2:

What should I do if my warm-up gestures seem to be backfiring: My teen is ignoring them or ripping my notes up?

Backup Plan:

Be patient! Don't give up too easily. This is a new way of communicating, and the teen is not used to it. Therefore, don't take it personally but maintain the course and outlast his or her stubbornness.

Potential Problem #3:

What should I do if my teen rejects my nurturance strategies? She will not let me hug her, she will not go out for special outings, and she thinks my praise is phony.

Backup Plan:

Try to stay the course for a while. Remember, there is a lot of scar tissue left over from the past. To heal these scars, you must be consistent.

As this cartoon shows, communication with teens is not always easy. They tend to like one-word answers and are moody at times.

Reprinted with special permission of King Feature Syndicate.

Please be patient and keep trying. Your teen is not used to soft talk but needs it to thrive. You will make mistakes, but keep trying anyway. Your teen is counting on you.

The Next Step

WHAT TO DO IF THESE STEPS FAIL OR YOU EXPERIENCE SPECIAL CIRCUMSTANCES

Single Parenthood, Divorce, Stepfamily, or Teen Emotional Problems

By this time, the steps in this book should have given you renewed energy, clear direction, and a better road map to follow. But what if the steps don't go as smoothly as planned? What happens if your buttons still get pushed, your contract fails, the consequences don't work, and restoring nurturance falls by the wayside?

Other parenting books provide great suggestions on paper but offer little backup if what you try fails. It's like going to a doctor for help and receiving no follow-up visits if the recommendations don't work.

If the steps in this book aren't working as planned, turn to the following support services for additional help and assistance.

Get Support on the Internet
and in Your Own Town

To give you additional help and support in implementing the steps in this book, I have set up a Web site called **www.difficult.net.** At this site, you can use several tools free of charge to interconnect with other parents, get help fast, or locate counselors in your area. I will also show you how to form your own parenting support groups in your hometown.

To access this support, simply type in **www.difficult.net** and click on the icon called "Parents Attic." You will then instantly be transported to the following menu of services:

Get Help Fast

When you have a problem with your teen, you want quick answers. If you click on the "get help fast" icon you will see the most common problems that parents face with suggested solutions to combat these problems. For example, one of these problems is called, "What to do if you try to ground your teen and they simply walk out the door without your permission." You would then be directed to a solution page to solve this particular problem.

Possible solutions might be to carefully examine a specific page and section in this book, additional suggestions by myself or another counselor, links to other resources on the Web, or a combination of all three. If the problem you need help with is not posted, you can e–mail us and we can add it to the list. Chances are that if you are having this problem, thousands of other parents around the country are also experiencing the same dilemma.

Video Examples of Key Principles and Workbooks

According to a recent study by the Xerox Corporation, people retain 10 percent of what they read and 50 percent of what they see! To address this issue, I have placed many of the rich case examples in this book on video or DVD that you can purchase through the difficult.net Web site. You can then pop in a video on "button push-ing" and see exactly how parents skillfully get their buttons pushed and why this is happening. You can then watch all six button busters or countermoves that you can choose to defeat button-pushing once and for all.

You can also purchase videos on such key steps as stopping the seven aces, restoring nurturance, why teens misbehave, and how to recruit outside helpers. Parents and teens have both told me that the videos make the book come alive and pull everything together.

The blank worksheets to complete the exercises throughout this book are also available for purchase. You will get a paperback workbook with additional examples and worksheets to better assist you in completing steps like contracting or locating your top three buttons.

Find a Counselor

One of the services I am most excited about is helping you access counselors in your immediate area who understand and embrace the ideas in this book. Parents who see my one-day seminars come up to me all the time and ask the same question, "Your approach speaks to me but who in my community does what you do?"

To address this problem, I am now conducting two-day intensive trainings in universities to teach other counselors the strategies and techniques in this book. To reach these counselors, you will simply click on the icon "Find a Counselor." You will be presented with a map of the United States and a list of cities with counselors who are certified in this approach.

These counselors will have a picture of themselves and a biographical sketch of their areas of expertise. You can then e-mail or phone them directly for help with your teenager. This service is completely confidential. No one including myself will have access to the private correspondence you send to a counselor except that counselor.

Parenting the Out-of-Control Teen Seminars

At the difficult.net home page, you will find a calendar of one-day parenting seminars that my colleagues or myself will give throughout the country. At these seminars, we will show video clips and conduct role plays to demonstrate all seven steps in this book. You will have a chance to ask questions and learn from other parents who are also struggling with their teenagers.

You will also find out about a new three-week Parenting the Out-of-Control Teenager parenting class that will be led by certified counselors in your area. This three-week class will be unlike anything else you have seen. Both you and your teen participate in this class together and graduate with your own ironclad contract, a clear understanding of all seven steps, and how to customize these steps to fit your family.

You can find information on how to become the parent leader in your community to start up a support group. The purpose of this group is to provide ongoing support to one another and brainstorm ideas if one parent is stuck or burnt out. This is a parents-only support group and complements the three-week parenting class.

Parent Discussion Boards

You can also link to a bulletin board to post questions for anyone to give you answers or suggestions. For example, one parent asked, "My teen is starting small fires in his room. Any suggestions on how to get him to stop?" About twenty people answered, some professionals and some parents.

In the end, this parent posted that she liked the suggestion of her son spending the day at the local fire station with the fire chief. I personally visit the parent discussion board often: both to read the discussions and to post questions when I am stuck with a particular family and am looking for advice from the experts.

Understanding the Complexities of Single Parenthood, Divorce, Stepfamilies, and Teenage Emotional Problems

Four areas seem to cause parents particular difficulty when it comes to out-of-control teenagers: You are already overloaded if you are a single parent, involved in a bitter divorce, part of a stepfamily, or have a teen with emotional problems. If you add out-of-control behavior to the mix, things really become difficult.

You do not have the time, energy, or patience to deal with out-of-control behaviors when you are already overloaded. Your teen senses this and may use it to become even more out of control. When the steps in this book don't work, you may need customized interventions that fit these special circumstances.

Single Parenthood

The single-parent family is emerging as the majority family unit in today's society. Most single-parent families are female-headed. Since women generally earn less than men, therefore, the probability of parenting overload increases as maintaining the household and caring for the children constitutes one job and supporting the family financially represents another. Doing both jobs alone can create parent burnout.

If you are a single parent, you often come home from work exhausted. The last thing you want to do is discipline. You're so overwhelmed, and have so little support, that being consistent can also be more difficult. You do not have the energy to fight with your teen, so you give in. Once this door is open, your teen may test your nerves again and again. Teens know that if they keep pushing, a worn-out parent eventually will back down.

Another problem may be that lower income levels force you to settle for less than suitable housing in a less than suitable neighborhood. Your teen's easy access to crime, gangs, and drugs will only make the task of parenting that much more difficult.

It is also harder to supervise your teen when there is only one of you. Without adult supervision, your teen's friends serve as supervisors. This supervision may come with values and a moral code that have a harmful effect on your teen.

To combat these special problems, I have used three strategies: (1) collaborative contracting, (2) coparenting with the oldest child, and (3) social networking. A central theme of each of these strategies is that a single parent *must* have the support of others. Without this support, you are vulnerable to task overload and you may shut down. If this happens, your teen may go from someone who has minor problems to an out-of-control teen.

Collaborative Contracting

Earlier I described the importance of incorporating your teen's input into the behavior contract. Doing so allows your teen to become a co-owner of the contract; shared ownership increases his or her cooperation.

It is important to use this strategy in two-parent families, but it is almost mandatory in a single-parent family. Meet with the other children in your family to come up with the top three problems in the household and then brainstorm solutions to each one. If you only have one child, meet with him or her and follow the same procedures.

Write down each possible solution, and prioritize its potential effectiveness. This exercise works best when each family member is part of the problem and works collaboratively to find a solution.

You still retain your authority as the parent through final approval or the veto power of any plan developed. However, this process shifts the focus off your teen and expands it to include other family members. When this happens, both you and your problem teen feel less overwhelmed. You now have the support and cooperation of other family members.

"I'm Not the Only Problem"

Severely depressed and overwhelmed, a single mother blamed her oldest child, Phil, for all her problems. Phil was in a gang, used drugs, and was constantly in trouble at school. The family's home environment was extremely disorganized with no rules or consequences.

Instead of focusing exclusively on Phil's problems, the counselor convinced the mother that she needed to be supported more by everyone in the family and called a meeting to brainstorm ways to make the household more efficient.

From this meeting, chores were divided up equally, bedtimes negotiated, mealtimes designated, and special outings with the mother planned. As the household became more organized and less chaotic, the mother felt less depressed. Phil was no longer seen as the sole problem. Over time, this made Phil see things as fair. He then offered to pitch in more and the relationship between him and his mother greatly improved.

When roles are clarified and everyone has his or her own rules and consequences, it is less likely that one child is singled out. This is an important concept because teens are particularly sensitive to the idea of "fairness." If they feel that other children are receiving preferential treatment, they grow resentful and rebel.

It is critical that all children have rules and consequences appropriate for their particular developmental level. These differences should be explained so teens understand why their brothers or sisters receive punishments tailored for their particular chronological age.

Coparenting with the Oldest Child

In two-parent families, there is no question that the mother and father should be the only ones in charge. However, a single-parent family brings about a different set of circumstances. You need the support of someone in the household. That someone is often your oldest child. If the oldest is your out-of-control teen, you may have to approach the next oldest child. This decision should be on a case-by-case basis. Sometimes your problem teen may become cooperative if he or she is given the special status of your "designated helper."

If you use this strategy, meet privately with the designated teen to determine rules and consequences without the other children present. This meeting acknowledges the special status and trust you are giving that teen.

For this plan to work, you must outline clear parameters of your teen's role as "substitute" parent. This includes when you expect your teen to function as a substitute parent (specific times and situations), when your teen is relieved of this burden, and a list of your teen's responsibilities in that role.

You must explain this substitute role to your other children, clearly stating that your teen is in charge when you are not home. If there are problems while you are at work, meet privately with your teen for a debriefing when you return home.

You should be the only one administering the consequences, not your teen. Your teen monitors the other children's behavior, but you administer punishments. Otherwise, resentment and bitterness will develop between your teen and the other children. Your teen easily could physically hurt the others in a heated argument.

Your teen's role is simply to inform the child that he or she is in violation of a certain predetermined rule (not cleaning his or her room, doing homework, taking out the trash, etc.). Your teen should then immediately exit the room to avoid a confrontation and write down the incident on a notepad. You should not be called at work except for an emergency.

The Substitute Parent

The mother reported that thirteen-year-old Nick refused to do chores and would terrorize the rest of the siblings by threatening violence when his mother left for work. The oldest daughter, Mandy, was the designated substitute parent but was ineffective at stopping her brother's behavior. However, using the just-described strategy, the mother told Nick that Mandy was in charge during her absence.

If Nick continued to refuse to do chores or threaten violence, Mandy would no longer try to stop him. Instead, she would write down what Nick did and debrief the mother privately when she returned from work. The mother would then administer the consequence and not his sister.

Nick would have to complete his chores under his mother's supervision and would lose the privilege of going out on the weekend. Since Nick valued his freedom, this was a harsh consequence. Nick's misbehavior stopped immediately.

In this example, the mother clarified the substitute teen's role to each of the other children. Doing so immediately took the pressure off Mandy and decreased the risk of resentment. Mandy was now there to monitor, while the mother backed her up. The end result was a household that ran more smoothly.

Social Networking

It is critical to build a support system. If you do not have one, please create your own, using the strategies in Step 6 for recruiting outside helpers. If you have a social network, you will not feel as over-whelmed. If you do not feel overwhelmed, you will be a better parent. It is that straightforward.

Having other people to rely on will also free up some time for you to get away and recharge your batteries. Everyone needs a mental-health day or evening once in a while. Go out with a friend or go to a movie by yourself. The problems will still be waiting for you when you return, but you must escape reality even for an hour.

Difficult Divorces

A difficult divorce occurs when both you and your ex-spouse cannot control your disputes and place the children in the middle of your heated arguments, unresolved conflicts, and hostilities. The children become pawns when one parent tells the children negative things about the other or tries to turn them against the other.

When out-of-control teens are involved, difficult divorces present several opportunities. If you are not communicating with your ex at all or only with hostility, you cannot exert joint authority and back one another up to stop our teen's misbehavior. For example, if your teen does not like the rules of one household, he or she often can move into the other household. This scenario can repeat itself over and over again until you as parents can communicate, work together, or agree on a plan of action.

If not, your teen never has to obey any rules or consequences he or she doesn't like. You may even stop enforcing consequences for fear that your teen might move away or form a special alliance with the other parent. As long as you and your ex continue to blame the other, neither has to take responsibility for solving your teen's prob-lem. Teens can then divide and conquer parents who are divided in anger and unable to stand united to conquer their problem.

Organize a Controlled Encounter

If these problems occur in your household, hire a counselor who is skilled in setting up what is called a "controlled encounter." A controlled encounter is a mediation meeting between two warring parents in which the counselor takes charge and negotiates concrete ways for you to reorganize your relationship with each other and your children.

The plan you develop could be anything from agreeing not to bad-mouth one another in front of the kids to setting up structured visitation. Your teen should not be at this meeting. Furthermore, the parents should talk to one another through the counselor rather than directly to each other because they are on such unfriendly terms.

If a controlled encounter is not possible, some parents turn to the person who can talk some sense into their ex-spouse—for example, an ex–father-in-law. Ask that person to be your mouthpiece and go-between.

Some parents will let their teen stay with the other parent on one condition: If the teen doesn't like it, he or she can come back *but only* if the teen signs a contract agreeing to obey the rules. If the teen leaves again, he or she cannot come back. Teens fantasize that the other parent's house is like Disney World. Sometimes your teen needs to figure out for him- or herself just how good things are in your household.

Stepfamily Issues

Stepfamilies blend the traditions of two different families together. For example, your old family may have celebrated Easter each year. However, the new stepmom is Jewish and does not celebrate this holiday. In addition, your old family had a parenting style where Mom did all the disciplining. However, in the new family, the stepfather wants to maintain this role.

This blending of traditions, rituals, and parenting styles can be a very difficult and stressful transition. In turn, this stress will make it more difficult for you to parent. Your teen may resent these changes and act out to strike back.

In addition, stepfamilies often start out with the following unrealistic expectations: (1) that the stepparent and the children will instantly experience a loving relationship; (2) that children do not need to mourn the loss of their former family; (3) that they will not experience loyalty conflicts between their biological parents; (4) that the parent-child relationship needs to take precedence over the new marriage; and (5) that the stepparent can discipline the children without any repercussions or resentment from the children.

If any of these issues is present in your household, it will affect your out-of-control teenager. The following strategies will help you get back on track.

Your Couple Bond Needs Extra Attention

You and your new spouse probably don't realize that your marriage bond is fragile in a stepfamily situation. This is because you probably went straight from marriage into parenthood with no time on your own to be a couple.

Research recommends that you have a minimum of two years together before having children so you can get to know one another and form a strong bond. In stepfamilies you do not have this luxury. You often mistakenly believe that it is the kids who need all your time and attention. They do need time, but so does your marriage. Stepfamilies in general are very chaotic in the beginning.

If you are not a united front, it is highly likely that you will get divorced within the first two years due to all the stress. Therefore, no matter how bad things are, you must set aside at least one date night a week to strengthen your marriage.

You must make a pact with one another that you cannot use that date time to talk about the children. You can only talk about one another. If your marital bond is strengthened, your stepparenting will improve.

The Biological Parent Should Enforce the Consequences

The stepchild often resents the new stepparent for taking the biological parent's time away. The resentment will increase the longer the parent is single and the older the child.

The resentment deepens if the stepparent tries to discipline your teen directly within the first year. If this happens, there is no opportunity for a nurturing bond to develop or to create a "working relationship."

In order for the stepparent and the teen to have a working relationship, it is critical that the biological parent administer the discipline and enforce the consequences whenever possible. Your teen needs time to develop an emotional bond of trust and respect with the stepparent.

Once you agree to let the biological parent discipline, you must clarify the role of the stepparent. For example, if the stepmother is home alone with your teenager and he breaks a rule by not doing his household chores, the stepmother would not get into a confrontation. Instead, she would wait for you to return home.

At that time, both you and your wife will go behind closed doors so that she can debrief you. You would then enforce the consequence, not your wife. You would not undermine your spouse or disagree with her in front of your teen. *You must present a united front.* Remember that your marital bond is already fragile. Taking sides with your teen against your spouse will only make things more fragile.

To maximize your effectiveness, both you and your spouse must agree that consequences do not have to be administered immediately after a rule is broken. They will be just as potent later as long as they are administered by you, the biological parent.

Button-Pushing

If you are a stepparent, you will tend to take your teen's button-pushing personally. The button that gets you the most is "You're not my real parent. I don't have to listen to you." You must understand that *it is a game.* The teen would try to use the same button on anyone who steps in the stepparent role. Your stepchild merely wants to test you to see if you will lose your cool.

You must use the exit-and-wait strategy in Step 4 on button pushing and let the other parent handle it and back you up. You can take a supportive role by establishing secret signals between you and your spouse. For example, in one case, the stepparent agreed to give the biological parent the hand signal of "turning up the heat" whenever she was being too soft with her daughter.

Special Outings with the
Biological and Stepparent

The biological parent and the teen need special outings more than ever before. Otherwise, your teen may resent the stepparent. The shift in roles from co-parent back to teen has to happen, but to cushion the blow, make one day a week your special day with your teen.

This system will yield amazing results and help your teen adjust to the blending of two families. It also will help the teen's grieving process of losing you to another man or woman. The stepparent and your teen also may need to spend time alone together to get to know one another in a nonconfrontational setting.

Teenage Emotional Problems

Teenage emotional problems are a difficult subject area and generate much controversy. Some people may believe that if your teen has a mental illness such as schizophrenia, attention deficit disorder, or depression, the strategies in this book will not work. Other people believe that these strategies are helpful, but only under certain circumstances. I agree with the second point of view for the following reasons.

Structure and Limits

Even teens with the most serious emotional problems still need structure and limits. Have you ever seen children who are hyperactive and who live without structure? They are literally bouncing off the walls. These teens need structure and limits even more than teens without serious emotional problems.

The world is already a scary place to begin with. If you have an emotional problem, you feel powerless and out of control. Structure and limits bring about predictability and consistency. In turn, these decrease your teen's stress and anxiety.

Teens with emotional problems still push buttons just like other out-of-control teens, and they still use the seven aces to get what they want. Therefore, they need ironclad contracts and the strategies in this book.

A major difference is that you may have to customize your contract to fit your teen's severe emotional problems. For example, a teen who is depressed or hearing voices may need medication in addition to structure and limits. An emotionally suicidal teen will need intensive counseling in addition to a twenty-four-hour watch.

In every case, your teen needs to be under the care of an experienced counselor in addition to using the strategies outlined in this book. Ask your counselor for further clarification on the right mixture of love, limits, and therapy for your particular teenager. Each teenager is different, and requires individual treatment.

A Self-Fulfilling Prophecy?

While every troubled teenager needs to be evaluated as an individual, how we define our mentally ill sometimes can have powerful repercussions. This was demonstrated in a recent documentary on HBO. In the 1950s, a small group of parents sent their young children to state mental hospitals if they had physical disabilities, such as blindness or an inability to walk. They defined their children as abnormal. Abnormality meant that they would have to go to a mental hospital with other abnormal children.

The longer these children were treated as abnormal and mentally ill, the more they turned into these labels. Pretty soon they acted and looked like everyone else in the hospital. By the time they were adults, they were completely incapacitated. They had to be hand fed like babies.

This is not to say that mental illness does not exist or that every teen can thrive on structure alone. Every troubled child needs to be evaluated individually by the most expert professional or professionals you can find. In some cases of schizophrenia, deep depression, and extreme hyperactivity, children and teens should be helped with medication. However, medication should only be used if necessary and under the guidance of a competent psychiatrist rather than a family doctor.

Final Thoughts

Thank you very much for taking this journey with me. I hope that this book has been both thought-provoking and helpful. It took two years to write, and I poured my very soul into these pages. I did it for two main reasons: you and your teenager.

I wrote this book for you because you have been through so much as parents. You are tired and burned out. You told me that you wanted something concrete and to the point. You told me that you loved your teen but you no longer liked him or her although you desperately wanted to do so again.

I have not always been politically correct, but I felt that you were tired of the sugar-coating. Desperate times often call for desperate measures. I know that your journey will be difficult. I know that I am asking a lot from you: to take a risk, to take change, and to open up and restore soft love. In return, I have attempted to do everything in my power to help. I hope that the steps in this book will work for you as they have for hundreds of other parents.

I wrote this book for your teenagers because they are the under-dogs of our society. Many people simply do not want to be bothered with them. It is easier to help a screaming child than a large and violent teen. Yet teens are begging for both love and limits. Too often we fail to provide either one. They need direction from you and they need it fast. It is the fourth quarter and we are now at the two-minute warning. If you and I don't take the lead, who will? It will be the gangs, the drug pushers, the violence on the street, and the system. They are waiting for us to fail. Let's not allow that to happen.

Appendix

CHOOSING THE RIGHT COUNSELOR FOR YOU

The following are some suggested guidelines in choosing a counselor who understands out-of-control teenagers and knows how to treat them effectively. More information can be found at *www. difficult.net* under "Help, I Need the Right Counselor Fast!"

Some of the guidelines I cite are basic, core qualities that you should look for in any counselor. Without these qualities, your teen may not get better whether the counselor specializes in teen problems or not. (Some of these guidelines first appeared in Dr. Frank Pittman's excellent article, "A Buyer's Guide to Psychotherapy," in the January 1994 issue of *Psychology Today*. I highly recommend this article.) Other guidelines are based on my work with hundreds of teenagers and their families. Please note that these are just my opinions. You can choose to accept them or not.

Many people spend more time and effort shopping around for a new car than for a new counselor. Ask yourself which is more precious: a new car or the well-being of your teenager? I hope you answered your teenager. If not, things must be pretty bad at home, and you will definitely want to read this section.

Find Out as Much as You Can About the Counselor

Before committing to work with a counselor, you need to know what kind of person he or she is. If possible, hire a counselor who has worked effectively with people you know. You also can learn about a counselor by reading anything he or she has written.

Ask if he or she is a specialist in treating oppositional defiant or conduct disorders in teenagers. If the counselor says "yes," ask how many teens he or she has treated and for an estimate of his or her success rate. If the counselor has seen fewer than fifty difficult children or teens or has had less than a 70 percent success rate, strongly consider moving on. Work with out-of-control teens requires experienced counselors.

You may want to make an initial appointment to meet the counselor without your teen and say something like this:

> "Before I consider treatment for my teen, I want to be the best informed consumer I can be. I would like to give you a brief description of my teen's problem and then get a step-by-step overview of how you would best treat the problem. I realize it will be a general overview until you see my teen face to face, but please do the best you can."

If the counselor cannot give you a good overview of how he or she would treat your teen, find someone else. This counselor may have little theoretical grounding and be unable to see the bigger picture of how everything fits together.

If you wish, visit the website at *www.difficult.net* for a listing of counselors trained in the strategies in this book and a list of parenting classes near you.

Expect Active Responses from Your Counselor

You want a counselor who will talk to you, demonstrate an understanding of your situation, and give good advice. If a counselor passively listens to your story and has nothing enlightening or intelligent to say, don't go back. While you shouldn't demand instant, magical solutions, it's unwise to assume that counselors know what they are doing if they say little after the first or second session. You need concrete, step-by-step tools to stop your teen's misbehavior rather than someone who does little more than reflect your feelings back to you.

Should Your Counselor Agree with You?

On one hand, even if you may risk being labeled as "difficult," you should challenge your counselor when his or her values or opinion on a particular issue seems to conflict with your own. Your counselor may be offering you wisdom that will save your son or daughter, but you still have to examine and understand it thoroughly.

On the other hand, you don't need a counselor who will always agree with you; you can go to your best friend if you need a "yes" person. Your counselor should have the courage to disagree with you and offer at least one concrete alternative suggestion to solve the problem.

If your counselor is too gentle and soothing and makes you feel that you have no part in the problem or solution, run for your life. Instead, choose the counselor who ticks you off occasionally by insisting that you take your share of the responsibility for your life and your relationships.

Be very afraid if your counselor says something like "You really don't need to roll up your sleeves and take charge of your teen's problem. All your teen needs is medication, a group home, detention, or a boot camp." As I emphasized throughout this book, your teen may improve in the short term with one of these approaches, but he or she needs your hands-on assistance to maintain the changes.

Don't Be in Too Much of a Hurry

While brief treatment can bring about great improvements in some situations, work with out-of-control teenagers usually takes time. In my experience, you should see *some* improvement in your teen after approximately four to eight sessions. (If not, you may wish to reevaluate whether this is the right counselor for your family.) To experience deep healing, however, you will likely need more counseling sessions depending on the severity of your teen's problem, your burnout level as a parent, and the severity of other problems in your family (marital problems, alcohol use, depression, etc.). In my work, deep healing can begin to occur after ten to twelve one- to two-hour counseling sessions.

Once the situation improves, it's important to go on seeing the counselor once or twice a month for 3 months or more, depending on your circumstances. These tune-up sessions will help smooth out any rough spots and maintain the changes you have already made.

Consider a Family Therapist or Social Worker as Your First Option

Look for counselors who have the credentials of LMFT (licensed marriage and family therapist) or LCSW (licensed clinical social worker) at the end of their name. Such counselors probably have had some training in what is called a systems theory approach, which is the umbrella model from which the core strategies in this book originated. It is an approach that teaches counselors how to work with your teen as well as with your entire family and outside helpers (friends, neighbors, extended family, probation officers, other counselors, etc.) if the need arises.

Some of the latest research supports this viewpoint. In 1998, leading researchers, Pinsof and Wynn reviewed outcome studies with out-of-control teens and concluded that "the available data suggest that outpatient family therapy is most likely to help moderately conduct-disordered adolescents and their families" (p. 594).

Psychologists and psychiatrists can be helpful as well. Be cautious, however, if they prefer to see your teen only on an individual basis, overuse medication, or rely primarily on outsiders like boot camps, hospitals, or group homes to fix your teen.

In your first session, ask the counselor if he or she uses a systems theory approach. If he or she says "no," ask why, and what approach they take instead. If the counselor says "yes," ask him or her to describe specifically how this approach has been used with other out-of-control teens. You are looking for answers that indicate that the counselor is prepared to involve everyone in your teen's life—from you to the school to friends and family—in solving your teen's problem. If the counselor looks confused or gives you answers that don't make sense, move on.

Work with Your Counselor

I realize that the economics of insurance and managed care as well as your geographic location may limit your choice of counselors. But even if a counselor may not seem ideal from the start, many of them are open to new ideas. For example, ask if he or she would be willing to read this book or my book for professionals, *Treating the Tough Adolescent: A Family-Based, Step-by-Step Approach* (New York: Guilford Press, 1998).

Also be sure to come into the session prepared. For example, if you're working on creating an ironclad contract with your teen, photocopy that chapter in advance and bring it to the session. Don't demand that counselors change their philosophy, but tell them that you need their help using this approach.

Be Creative

Finally, if you have little or no money to pay for counseling and no insurance, you do have one creative option. Look in the phone book and call your local college or university. Ask the main operator to be connected to the family therapy program, counseling psychology, or social work program.

In large cities, the university will likely have family therapy and counseling education clinics right on campus that will see you and your teen for little to no cost. If there are no on-campus clinics, ask the department head for a list of agencies and numbers where graduate students work. Briefly describe your problem and ask for recommendations of intern students or faculty who specialize in teen behavior problems.

Index